St Antony's Series

General Editor: **Jan Zielonka** (2004–), Fellow of St Antony's College, Oxford

Recent titles include:

George Pagoulatos
GREECE'S NEW POLITICAL ECONOMY
State, Finance and Growth from Postwar to EMU

Tiffany A. Troxel
PARLIAMENTARY POWER IN RUSSIA, 1994–2001
A New Era

Elvira María Restrepo
COLOMBIAN CRIMINAL JUSTICE IN CRISIS
Fear and Distrust

Ilaria Favretto
THE LONG SEARCH FOR A THIRD WAY
The British Labour Party and the Italian Left Since 1945

Lawrence Tal
POLITICS, THE MILITARY, AND NATIONAL SECURITY IN JORDAN, 1955–1967

Louise Haagh and Camilla Helgø (editors)
SOCIAL POLICY REFORM AND MARKET GOVERNANCE IN LATIN AMERICA

Gayil Talshir
THE POLITICAL IDEOLOGY OF GREEN PARTIES
From the Politics of Nature to Redefining the Nature of Politics

E.K. Dosmukhamedov
FOREIGN DIRECT INVESTMENT IN KAZAKHSTAN
Politico–Legal Aspects of Post-Communist Transition

Felix Patrikeeff
RUSSIAN POLITICS IN EXILE
The Northeast Asian Balance of Power, 1924–1931

He Ping
CHINA'S SEARCH FOR MODERNITY
Cultural Discourse in the Late 20th Century

Mariana Llanos
PRIVATIZATION AND DEMOCRACY IN ARGENTINA
An Analysis of President–Congress Relations

St Antony's Series
Series Standing Order ISBN 0–333–71109–2
(*outside North America only*)

You can receive future titles in this series as they are published by placing a standing order. Please contact your bookseller or, in case of difficulty, write to us at the address below with your name and address, the title of the series and the ISBN quoted above.

Customer Services Department, Macmillan Distribution Ltd, Houndmills, Basingstoke, Hampshire RG21 6XS, England

Water, Power and Citizenship

Social Struggle in the Basin of Mexico

José Esteban Castro
Senior Lecturer in Sociology
University of Newcastle upon Tyne

in association with
St Antony's College, Oxford

First published 2006 by
PALGRAVE MACMILLAN
Houndmills, Basingstoke, Hampshire RG21 6XS and
175 Fifth Avenue, New York, N.Y. 10010
Companies and representatives throughout the world

PALGRAVE MACMILLAN is the global academic imprint of the Palgrave
Macmillan division of St. Martin's Press, LLC and of Palgrave Macmillan Ltd.
Macmillan® is a registered trademark in the United States, United Kingdom
and other countries. Palgrave is a registered trademark in the European
Union and other countries.

ISBN 978-1-349-52516-4   ISBN 978-0-230-50881-1 (eBook)
DOI 10.1057/9780230508811

This book is printed on paper suitable for recycling and made from fully
managed and sustained forest sources.

A catalogue record for this book is available from the British Library.

Library of Congress Cataloging-in-Publication Data
Castro, José Esteban.
   Water, power, and citizenship : social struggle in the Basin of Mexico /
José Esteban Castro.
      p. cm. – (St. Antony's series)
   Revision of the author's thesis (doctoral)–Oxford, 1998.
   Includes bibliographical references (p.) and index.
   ISBN 978-1-4039-4879-3 (cloth)
      1. Water-supply–Social aspects–Mexico–Mexico, Valley of. 2. Water-
supply–Political aspects–Mexico–Mexico, Valley of. 3. Power (Social
sciences)–Mexico–Mexico, Valley of. 4. Citizenship–Mexico–Mexico, Valley
of. 5. Social conflict–Mexico–Mexico, Valley of. 6. Mexico, Valley of
(Mexico)–Social conditions. 7. Mexico, Valley of (Mexico)–Politics and
government. I. Title. II. St. Antony's series (Palgrave Macmillan (Firm))
HD1696.M64M493 2005
363.6'1'09725–dc22   2005047527

10   9   8   7   6   5   4   3   2   1
15 14 13 12 11 10 09 08 07 06

Transferred to Digital Printing in 2005

To the memory of José Castro and Rosario Muzzupappa

Also by José Esteban Castro

LA SOCIEDAD COMPLEJA: Ensayos en Torno a la Obra de Niklas Luhmann (*co-edited with Antonio Camou*)

Contents

List of Tables

See additional tables in an appendix at:
www.staff.ncl.ac.uk/j.e.castro/WPCAppendix.pdf

List of Figures

Note: Figures 1.1, 1.2 and 2.1 were prepared by David Sansom, Cartographer at the School of Geography and the Environment, University of Oxford.

Conventions of Transcription and Translation

We have used some Spanish and Nahuatl terms which are always written in italics followed by the English translation between square brackets in the first occurrence. A Glossary of non-English terms is added at the back of the book for further consultation. Institutional names are translated but we have retained the acronym of the original Spanish version. A List of Abbreviations is also included on pages xv–xvii. Personal and geographical names are not translated (for example, El Desagüe). Unless otherwise indicated, all translations were done by the author.

List of Abbreviations

ADB	Asian Development Bank
AHA	Archivo Histórico del Agua
AIA	Asociación de Ingenieros y Arquitectos
AMSO	Asociación Mexicana de Salud Ocupacional
ARDF	Asamblea de Representantes del Distrito Federal
BANOBRAS	Banco Nacional de Obras y Servicios Públicos
BNHUOP	Banco Nacional Hipotecario Urbano y de Obras Públicas
CADF	Comisión de Aguas del Distrito Federal
CAVM	Comisión de Aguas del Valle de México
CEAS	Comisión Estatal de Agua y Saneamiento
CEHOPU	Centro de Estudios Históricos de Obras Públicas y Urbanismo
CENCA	Centro de Consulta del Agua
CFE	Compañía Federal de Electricidad
CHCVM	Comisión Hidrológica del Valle de México
CIC	Colegio de Ingenieros Civiles
CIESAS	Centro de Investigaciones y Estudios Superiores en Antropología Social
CNA	Comisión Nacional del Agua
CNC	Confederación Nacional Campesina
CNDH	Comisión Nacional de Derechos Humanos
CNI	Comisión Nacional de Irrigación
CNOP	Confederación Nacional de Organizaciones Populares
CONAMUP	Coordinadora Nacional del Movimiento Urbano Popular
CONAPO	Consejo Nacional de Población
CTM	Confederación de Trabajadores de México
CVCP	Committee of Vice-Chancellors and Principals of the Universities of the United Kingdom
DDF	Departamento del Distrito Federal
DESTIN	Development Studies Institute, London School of Economics and Political Science
DF	Distrito Federal
DGCOH	Dirección General de Construcción y Operación Hidráulica
DGOH	Dirección General de Obras Hidráulicas
DGAS	Dirección de Agua y Saneamiento

DGOVM	Dirección General de Obras del Valle de México
DIS	Dirección de Ingeniería Sanitaria
EC	European Commission
ECLAC	UN Economic Commission for Latin America and the Caribbean
EZLN	Ejército Zapatista de Liberación Nacional
FLACSO	Facultad Latinoamericana de Ciencias Sociales
GDP	Gross Domestic Product
GMP	Gross Manufacturing Product
GWP	Global Water Partnership
IDB	Inter American Development Bank
IEPES	Instituto de Estudios Políticos y Sociales
IIH	Instituto de Investigaciones Históricas
IMTA	Instituto Mexicano de Tecnología del Agua
INAH	Instituto Nacional de Antropología e Historia
INAINE	Instituto Autónomo de Investigaciones Ecológicas
INCO-DEV	International Co-operation for Development, European Commission
INEGI	Instituto Nacional de Estadística, Geografía e Informática
INJM	Instituto Nacional de la Juventud Mexicana
MCMA	Mexico City Metropolitan Area
MRP	Movimiento Revolucionario del Pueblo
MUP	Movimiento Urbano Popular
NAFTA	North American Free Trade Agreement
NAS	National Academy of Sciences
NGO	Non Governmental Organization
OECD	Organisation for Economic Co-operation and Development
PAN	Partido Acción Nacional
PARM	Partido Auténtico de la Revolución Mexicana
PEM	Partido Ecológico Mexicano
PEMEX	Petróleos Mexicanos
PFCRN	Partido del Frente Cardenista de Reconstrucción Nacional
PMS	Partido Mexicano Socialista
PMT	Partido Mexicano de los Trabajadores
PNH	Plan Nacional Hidráulico
POM	Partido Obrero Mexicano
PPS	Partido Popular Socialista
PRD	Partido de la Revolución Democrática

PRI	Partido Revolucionario Institucional
PRM	Presidencia de la República Mexicana
PRONASOL	Programa Nacional de Solidaridad
PS	Partido Socialista
PSIRU	Public Services Internacional Research Unit
PST	Partido Socialista de los Trabajadores
PSUM	Partido Socialista Unificado de México
SAHOP	Secretaría de Asentamientos Humanos y Obras Públicas
SARH	Secretaría de Agricultura y Recursos Hidráulicos
SEDESOL	Secretaría de Desarrollo Social
SEDUE	Secretaría de Desarrollo Urbano y Ecología
SEMARNAP	Secretaría de Medio Ambiente, Recursos Naturales y Pesca
SEP	Secretaría de Educación Pública
SMA	Subsecretaría de Mejoramiento del Ambiente
SOS	Secretaría de Obras y Servicios
SRH	Secretaría de Recursos Hidráulicos
UN	The United Nations
UNAM	Universidad Nacional Autónoma de México
UNCED	The United Nations Conference on Environment and Development
UNDP	United Nations Development Programme
UNECE	United Nations Economic Commission for Europe
UNESCO	United Nations Educational, Scientific, and Cultural Organization
UNRISD	United Nations Research Institute for Social Development
UNWC	The United Nations Water Conference
US	The United States of America
USAID	The United States Agency for International Development
WCED	World Commission on Environment and Development
WHO	World Health Organization

Acknowledgements

The main work that led to this book was completed as part of my doctoral research at Oxford University between 1993 and 1997. I cannot do justice to all the persons and institutions that contributed to make this project possible, but cannot fail to mention Dr María Luisa Torregrosa Armentia and Mr José Luis Barros Horcasitas, at the Latin American Faculty of Social Sciences (FLACSO) in Mexico. María Luisa gave me continued support since I started my studies on water struggles in Mexico back in 1990 and we have developed an enduring academic partnership and personal friendship ever since. José Luis Barros Horcasitas, FLACSO's Director during my time in that institution, also gave me strategic support to complete my research. I am also deeply indebted to my 'old sociology teacher' and friend Juan Carlos Marín, at the University of Buenos Aires. Many thanks Lito for your academic generosity and especially for your continued friendship. In Oxford, I wish to thank especially Herminio Martins for being such a supportive supervisor during my doctoral studies. He gave me invaluable help to develop my interest in water into a subject of sociological inquiry. Also thanks to Erik Swyngedouw, the co-supervisor, who made me aware of crucial debates about water politics taking place outside my field of origin, sociology, and helped me to strengthen the interdisciplinary – he may also say transdisciplinary – approach that I was seeking to achieve in my work. Alan Knight thoroughly commented draft versions of some chapters and strongly supported my work and initiatives in Oxford, not just on water issues. Finally, Laurence Whitehead has been a permanent source of strategic advice and generous support in intellectual and practical matters. I am very grateful to them.

The research work was accomplished with financial support from various sources. I wish to mention in particular the Latin American Faculty of Social Sciences (FLACSO) in Mexico and the Committee of Vice-Chancellors and Principals of the Universities of the United Kingdom (CVCP). In addition I received the generous backing of the Inter-faculty Committee for Latin American Studies, the Committee for Graduate Studies, the Norman Chester Fund, the Oxford Society and St Antony's College, all of these in the University of Oxford. Also, I am very grateful to the Churches Commission on Overseas Students, the Northern Dairies Trust and the Michel Polak Foundation for their kind support in the final stages of the doctoral dissertation. After I finished my doctoral studies, I was able to further expand and deepen my analysis first working as a Lecturer in Development Studies at the Development Studies Institute (DESTIN), London School of Economics and Political Science, and later as a Senior Research Associate at the School of Geography and the Environment, University of Oxford, funded by the International Cooperation for Development (INCO-DEV) Programme of the European Commission to coordinate a research project on water and sanitation in developing countries (PRINWASS, EC Contract PL ICA4-2001-10041), in the course of which I was able to complete the manuscript. Finally, I wish to thank the anonymous reader, whose comments and remarks helped to correct errors, give more precision to the analysis, and improve the overall readability of the text. Of course, I remain solely responsible for the final version.

José Esteban Castro

The author and publishers are grateful to the American Geographical Society for permission to reproduce Figure 2.1 from D. Fox, 'Man–Water Relationships in Metropolitan Mexico', *Geographical Review*, Vol. 55, 1965. Every effort has been made to contact all copyright-holders, but if any have been inadvertently omitted the publishers will be pleased to make the necessary arrangement at the earliest opportunity.

Introduction

This research was triggered by our interest in understanding the meaning and reason of the large number of social confrontations over water recorded in the Basin of Mexico during the 1980s and 1990s. These are conflicts over water resources and services ranging from bureaucratic complaints to mass parades, actions of civil disobedience and even direct violence resulting in the destruction of infrastructure and the loss of human lives. The Mexican authorities recognized that by the early 1980s 'the protests of the majority around water problems were amazing owing both to their depth and breadth' and that 'water had become a strong political concern for society' (Secretaría de Agricultura y Recursos Hidráulicos (SARH), 1988: 175). It seems that water problems attracted even more attention after the urban catastrophes of the mid-1980s, in particular the 1985 earthquakes that seriously damaged the urban infrastructure and further worsened the living conditions in Mexico City.

Despite the political saliency of water conflicts in the Basin of Mexico – and in the country at large – the interrelation between these incidents and broader social and political processes like the struggles for the democratization of the political system or the enhancement and expansion of citizenship rights have received comparatively little attention. This work contributes towards filling this gap by exploring the interconnections between the evolution of the processes and institutions involved in the governance[1] and management of water resources and services[2] and the development of citizenship in Mexico. The confrontations over water, we argue, are part and parcel of a wider social struggle over the conditions that make human life possible and meaningful, and as such, are an expression of the social character of water, as distinct from the biophysical and techno–scientific dimensions.

1

In short, this work investigates the ways in which water, the most essential life-sustaining element, has become interwoven with the socio–economic and political processes structuring Mexican society, like the struggle over what can be termed the territory of citizenship.

Relevance of the topic

Although water and citizenship have risen to prominence since the 1980s, the interplay between the two has been rarely addressed in the literature. On the one hand, social struggles over ethnic, gender, environmental and sexual rights, among other issues, have fuelled changes in the traditional extension, contents and meanings of the concept of citizenship. Moreover, the processes of regional integration and economic globalization have promoted the revision of the notions of citizenship or national sovereignty in the light of the increasing differentiation and complexity of social systems. On the other hand, the rising awareness about the unfairness and ecological unsustainability characterizing the management of water sources and services worldwide has prompted heated debates and radical policy reforms with far-reaching consequences for the consolidation of substantive democracy and citizenship.

In this regard, the notion that water for essential human uses is a common good that cannot be denied to anyone can be traced in most cultures and constitutes a legacy of human civilization that has been inherited by modern societies. This principle has been integrated in some of the traditions of modern citizenship, like in the European notion of social rights that established the universal access to those goods and services deemed essential for sustaining life according to the standards prevailing in society, notoriously public health, education, and safe water and sanitation. Since the late nineteenth century, the provision of safe water supply and sanitation became a social duty, a public sector responsibility, and most developed countries achieved their universalization shortly after World War II. Contrastingly, in most developing countries this process has been much slower, and access to these vital services is still a minority privilege.

In Mexico, as in most developing countries, protracted qualitative and quantitative inequalities have limited the scope of citizenship rights, which finds expression in the large numbers that still lack the most basic conditions of subsistence such as safe drinking water and sanitation. For instance, according to the 1990 census, 30 per cent of the Mexican population lacked access to safe drinking water while

51 per cent had no sewerage. However, the authorities warned that those figures did not reflect the serious defects affecting the services, such as low pipe pressure, intermittency, and lack of control over the 'quality of water, which is normally not disinfected' (Comisión Nacional del Agua (CNA), 1990: 33). Unsurprisingly, preventable water-related diseases continued to cause the 'largest number of deaths in the Mexican population' during the period covered by the research (Kumate Rodríguez, 1991). Ironically, although the Mexican constitution adopted after the 1910–17 Revolution had enshrined the universal right to essential water services, this promise was never achieved. Moreover, the principle of universality itself was erased from the constitution during the neo-liberal reforms introduced in the 1990s.

Although most modern citizenship systems provide for the formal enunciation of the right to essential goods and services such as safe water and sanitation, the real practices have rendered this right meaningless for vast majorities. For instance, despite the important achievements of the international community in improving water and sanitation worldwide since the 1970s, the goals of providing a modicum of 'clean water and sanitation for all by 1990' set by the United Nations Water and Sanitation Decade (United Nations (UN), 1980) were not met. Moreover, there are good reasons to argue that the mainstream water policies[3] implemented since the 1980s may have contributed to the significant worsening of the conditions of social inequality that continue to negate access to essential water and sanitation to millions of human beings.

Acknowledging the difficult challenge ahead the international community has set new targets that can be considered ungenerous when compared with the goals of the 1980s – some would say more realistic instead. Rather than achieving universal coverage the new targets aim at halving the world population with no access to water and sanitation by the year 2015 (UN, 2000, 2002b). In any case, even these objectives might be unfeasible given that the financial arrangements needed to double current investment in the sector as required to meet the targets (Camdessus, 2003) would involve radical transformations in the governance of water resources and related services worldwide, which seem unlikely in the foreseeable future. Furthermore, achieving the goals would require connecting around 200,000–400,000 people per day worldwide respectively for water and sanitation until 2015 (European Commission (EC), 2003), and many water experts believe that the scale of the task renders the proposals technically unachievable. If these critics are right, and considering that more than 5 million people die each year from avoidable water-related infections, of which around 40 per cent are killed by preventable diarrhoeal diseases – mostly children under 5 years old – (EC, 2002b; World Health Organization (WHO), 2003b), there is a bleak future awaiting a large proportion of human beings in forthcoming years. In fact, the situation is even more severe when we consider the diversity of threats and dangers arising from the way in which water resources are governed and managed, which range from the impacts of chemical, physical, and biological agents present in water to the recurrent floods and droughts that regularly affect millions of humans, mainly the most vulnerable (WHO, 2003c; WHO-Europe, 2003; Sims and Butter, 2000).

It is increasingly accepted that crucial changes are needed in the structures and processes intervening in the governance of water resources and services. Unfortunately, mainstream debates tend to obscure the fundamental disagreements existing about what governance means and implies, often neglecting the fact that governance is about exercising power, which in the particular case of water involves decisions about how water resources and services should be governed, by whom, and for whom. This requires, for instance, the development of institutions to ensure that the management of water resources and services is accountable to the people and subject to democratic control. However, the traditional systems of water governance and management have been developed in ways that have precluded, for the most part, the participation and engagement of citizens and have prevented effective democratic monitoring, a situation that has been worsened by the reforms promoted by mainstream water policies since the 1980s.

Water, citizenship and power

In the perspective of this book, the 'conflicts' over water resources and services form part of a much broader confrontation against the prevailing exclusionary – some would say weak-inclusionary – model of social organization characterizing Mexico. Interestingly, despite the centrality of water for human life and social organization, these conflicts have received relatively little attention from the perspective of the social sciences. Perhaps, the overriding dominance of techno-scientific approaches in the sphere of water management and policy, compounded by the slow development of theoretical tools and studies within the social sciences focusing on the interplay between physical-natural and social processes, has contributed to maintain largely unobservable what we call here the social character of water. We believe that bringing into the analysis the interweaving between these processes requires, on the one hand, an inter- and transdisciplinary approach and, on the other, the elaboration of observables[4] on a temporal scale adequate to the processes under attention.

Regarding interdisciplinary co-ordination, although our point of departure is located within the tradition of the social sciences, and particularly sociology, our work also draws on contributions from other fields including economic and social history, history of technology, geography, archaeology, anthropology, and we have also made an effort to establish a dialogue with the traditional bodies of thought engaged with the physical-natural and technological aspects of water. In relation to the time scales, although this research was triggered by events recorded in the late 1980s and early 1990s, we adopted a long-term perspective because the processes under analysis can be better understood through the combination of diachronic and synchronic analysis. Following the model of long-term structural social change offered by Norbert Elias in his study of the Western 'civilizing process' (Elias, 1994), we understand that the normally rationally planned actions directed at the control of water have also had unintended effects both on ecological and social systems. Like in the establishment of human control over fire, which has been examined by the Dutch sociologist Johan Goudsblom in his book *Fire and Civilization* (Goudsblom, 1994), the social apparatuses created for the governance and management of water resources, whether it is for irrigation or flood prevention, for providing regular amounts of safe water or waterborne sewage disposal, or for controlling the pollution and depletion of water resources, impose intergenerational constraints and duties upon human beings with far-reaching economic and political implications.

As shown by Elias, long-term processes of structural social change are the result of the blind dynamics of human beings 'intertwining in their deeds and aims' (Elias, 1994: 445). In this connection, we argue that, independently from the individual deeds and aims of the actors, the confrontations over water in the Basin of Mexico can be understood as forming part of a long-term social struggle over the territory of substantive citizenship. We believe that contributing to a better understanding of the formation of citizenship rights may enhance our capacity to intervene with a higher degree of success in checking undesired outcomes and achieving citizenship's emancipatory potential.

Although there is no scholarly consensus about the contents and extension of the concept of citizenship, it is accepted that T. H.

Marshall's essay on the long-term formation of citizenship rights in Britain has set the standard for addressing the subject (Marshall, 1992). We follow Marshall's analytical breakdown of citizenship into three bundles of rights (civil, political, and social) because it provides a useful criterion for operationalizing the concept, but we are well aware of the controversial character of his analysis and place more emphasis than he did on the internal contradictions of the process.

The links between water and citizenship are multidimensional. One of these facets concerns the interconnections between the social forms of appropriation and allocation of water and the formation of citizenship rights, whereby water (property) rights are related to the civil right to own property. Also, the rights and duties involved in the governance and management of water resources and services, how they are governed and managed, by whom, and for whom, can be examined in relation to the political rights of citizenship. Likewise, the universal right to essential water and sanitation services belongs in the group of social rights, which includes the right to a share in social welfare through the universalization of access to basic services such as public health and education. New rights and duties are recognized over time as a result of ongoing social struggles for the expansion and extension of citizenship, which has also brought about the progressive inclusion of growing numbers of human beings into the territory of citizenship. However, both the boundaries of the territory and the scope for accessing it are also subject to reversion and collapse, whether it happens through the lawful restriction of civil rights during emergency situations, because of the brutal suppression of civil and political rights during authoritarian processes, or as a result of the cancellation of acquired social rights as it has actually happened through the neoliberal reforms implemented since the 1980s.

From the specific angle of the interrelations between water, citizenship and power configurations, the control of water has played a substantive role in shaping human history and has fuelled the development of different institutional arrangements. For instance, while some cultures developed co-operative and decentralized forms of organization to coordinate water use, others ended up with highly centralized and authoritarian systems of water management, especially in irrigation agriculture. However, the extent to which the development of power structures is connected with the activities involved in water operations is still an open question, and the historical evidence shows that there is no one-to-one fixed relationship between technical and environmental forms of water control and the social and political structures developed to ensure their functioning. Nonetheless, there is enough evidence that everywhere the control of water presents certain inescapable requirements and constraints, and that these features have had a strong influence on the forms of socio–political organization.

Classic thinking in this field has considered large-scale water management activities, in particular irrigation works, to be a key explanatory feature of state formation in the case of certain civilizations. For example, drawing on a long tradition of thinking which includes Marx, Engels and Weber's insights about forms of social organization in Eastern societies, Karl Wittfogel argued that Aztec Mexico shared important characteristics with the ancient civilizations that he termed 'hydraulic societies', which developed a high degree of water expertise and despotic and centralized power structures. Wittfogel's theory is highly controversial, but his insights on the interactions between water and power have continued relevance for understanding the social character of large-scale water management, and his work has inspired a rich scholarship, of which perhaps Donald Worster's study of twentieth-century water 'empires' in the United States is the most remarkable (Worster, 1985: 30).

In the case of Mexico, the function played by water control in the formation of political power has received much less attention than other processes such as the appropriation of land. For example, there is well-established knowledge about the role played by mining and *hacienda* [large estate] exploitation since the colonial period and by the combination of railways, agriculture, and industrialization in the pre- and post-revolutionary period.[5] There is also an important tradition in historical, archaeological, and anthropological studies in Mexico addressing the political and economic implications of irrigation agriculture, and water technology and architecture.[6] Nevertheless, as Michael Meyer stated in his social and legal history of water in colonial Mexico, 'although the historiography of Spanish American colonial land tenure is rich, relatively little is known about the historical relationship of land to water anywhere in Spain's huge American empire' (Meyer, 1984: 8). This situation has not changed much since he wrote his book. After all, as Marx mentioned in passing, 'the soil, economically speaking, includes water' (Marx, 1946: 157), a phrase that can perhaps synthesize the rationale behind the dominance of land-centred research.

Focusing now on our main area of interest, the interweaving between water and power in the urban realm has not received much attention. It could be argued that until the late 1970s scholars seem to have assumed that the urban question – paraphrasing Marx – economically speaking, includes water services, and this could explain the rare occurrence of studies in sociology or political science in which water plays a central role. Thus, most of the available references to urban water in Mexico relate to historical studies that have also remarked on the lack of research in this field (Lipsett-Rivera, 1993: 25; Borah, 1984: 552). This situation has been changing in recent years, with a growing number of studies on different aspects of urban water development in the colonial, independent and contemporary periods carried out in Mexican universities.

Still, the links between water and citizenship in Mexico have not received much attention. Some authors have focused on the importance that property rights and their institutions have in the centralized power structures of the Mexican state, and in particular in the extraordinary authority conferred on the President (Elizondo, 1992). Also, there is a large body of literature on citizenship rights in Mexico stressing the case of political rights, and civil rights other than property rights, focusing on issues of political participation and civic liberties in twentieth-century Mexico.[7] In contrast, such issues as the links between citizenship rights and water rights, the development of power configurations, institutions, and practices around the governance and management of water, or the connection between the access to essential water and sanitation services and social rights have been largely neglected and we aim to contribute to filling this gap.

Outline of the book

Chapter 1 introduces the research problem and briefly describes the social impacts of water-related hazards and threats in the Basin of Mexico. It provides clues for understanding why the social character of water activities remains largely unobservable despite the growing social unrest around water and water services. It also advances the theoretical framework structuring the study, and reviews some of the relevant debates that help to place the Mexican case in a wider context. Chapter 2 traces the hydrogeological transformations undergone by the Basin of Mexico during the last five hundred years. It presents the necessary background for understanding why water has played such a crucial role in the basin, and how this development has an impact on the conditions that the present and future generations of Mexicans have to face. The chapter also provides grounds for comprehending the multidimensional character of the social struggles that have punctuated water development in the basin, and how they have become interwoven with the particular formation of citizenship in the country. Chapter 3 examines the process of state formation in Mexico, looking at how human activities aimed at controlling water were inextricably linked to the formation of political power. We explore the balances between coercion and co-operation in the interaction between Spaniards and Indians over the control of water and the changing character of the public–private interface during the colonial and post-independent periods. This section also pays attention to the social and political influence of water experts, especially the role played by specialized water techno-bureaucracies and the crystallization of power structures around the governance and management of water. Chapter 4 examines the empirical evidence of around 2000 events of conflicts over water recorded in the basin during the period 1985–92. We argue that although the immediate reasons moving the protagonists to act are multifarious and that the individual events are discrete and often unconnected, these actions are constitutive of a wider social confrontation over the territory of citizenship, which is largely autonomous from the individual wills and reason of the actors.

However, we do not reduce the concept of struggle to its manifestation in the events analysed in the fourth chapter, as we conceive of the struggle as a multidimensional, multi-level and long-term process. Thus, Chapter 5 examines the specific links between the activities involved in the governance and management of water resources and services and the formation of citizenship rights in Mexico. We discuss first the conceptual links that can be established between citizenship and water, looking at the development of property rights over water – water rights – the governance of water resources and essential water services, and the access to water and sanitation as a social right. Then, we explore the historical processes that by the late nineteenth century had transformed New Spain into an oligarchic capitalist regime that formally granted citizenship rights to all Mexicans but in practice exacerbated the process of social exclusion to unprecedented levels. The chapter shows how water policies, institutions and practices became interwoven with the particular expressions adopted by the development of citizenship, which has been punctuated by protracted social struggles that have not yet been entirely played out. Finally, Chapter 6 explores the changing patterns of governance and citizenship in twentieth-century water policy, shifting between state- and market-led models, as well as the epistemic and political debates informing this process. In particular, attention is paid to the far-reaching neo-liberal reforms implemented worldwide since the 1980s, which have exacerbated the systemic exclusion of large numbers of human beings from accessing the territory of civilized life.

1
The Social Character of Water

'The immanent regularities of social figurations are identical neither with regularities of the "mind", of individual reasoning, nor with regularities of what we call "nature", even though functionally all these different dimensions of reality are indissolubly linked to each other.'—Norbert Elias, *The Civilizing Process*

This chapter introduces our main arguments concerning the interrelation between water conflicts and the social struggle over the territory of citizenship in the Basin of Mexico. This connection has been largely neglected in the literature for a number of reasons, perhaps owing mainly to the overriding weight of physical–natural constraints on the control and management of water resources and services, which may explain the predominance of techno-scientific explanations to problems in this field. However, this prevailing approach tends to neglect the existence of protracted social inequalities in the access to water and safe water services which are the cause of enormous suffering for millions in the basin, and a major factor in precluding them from full membership of their society. This work attempts to make a contribution to better understanding the main factors underlying these unacceptable conditions.

In our perspective, although the physical-natural and technical-managerial problems that are at the base of water-related conflicts in Mexico and elsewhere are well known, key socio-economic and political explanatory factors continue to be underplayed or even neglected. Therefore, our strategy is to explore the interrelations between the establishment of human control over water in the Basin of Mexico, the governance and management of water resources and services, and the formation of power configurations and their crystallization in institutions and practices. We do not assume that there is a necessary relationship between these processes, and therefore we adopted a trans-disciplinary and long-term framework to better understand how physical–natural and social processes coevolve and interweave. However, avoiding environmental and historical determinism and teleological explanations does not prevent us from identifying the discernible direction that the overall process has taken over time, whereby the most essential life-sustaining element for humans has become an unaffordable luxury for large sectors of the population, and has also been transformed into a major threat for human life in the form of devastating water-related diseases and dangers. Understandably, water has also become an object of recurrent social struggles, which have been the main trigger of this research.

We discuss first the main water-related problems affecting the Basin of Mexico, with especial emphasis on the social and political conflicts arising from this situation. Next, we introduce some aspects of the theoretical framework that we develop in the book, whereby the backbone of the analysis is the concept of social struggle, conceptually explored here and further developed and exemplified throughout the book. Finally, we review some of the relevant theoretical and political debates and processes that help to place the Mexican examples explored here in wider perspective.

Physical–natural cycles and social regularities

The Mexico City Metropolitan Area (MCMA)[1] (Figure 1.1) enjoys one of the highest coverage levels of water supply and sewerage in the country. Also, the officially reported average daily distribution of water of about 300 litres per capita is well above the internationally accepted standard of 100 litres to cover essential household needs.[2] However, since the 1980s the MCMA has also been the scenario of recurrent social conflicts flaring up from different problems around water and water services. As discussed later, most of these conflicts result from citizens' reactions to water-related threats and dangers which prevent them from living their lives to the formal standards prevailing in their own society. Indeed, 'the Mexicans who have access to potable water, drainage or irrigation are in a privileged position'.[3]

Water-related hazards in the MCMA range from the dangers posed by recurrent flooding in the rainy season to a whole array of diseases associated with the way in which water and water services are managed. The most threatening aspect is the incidence of water-related

Figure 1.1 The Mexico City Metropolitan Area (circa 1990)

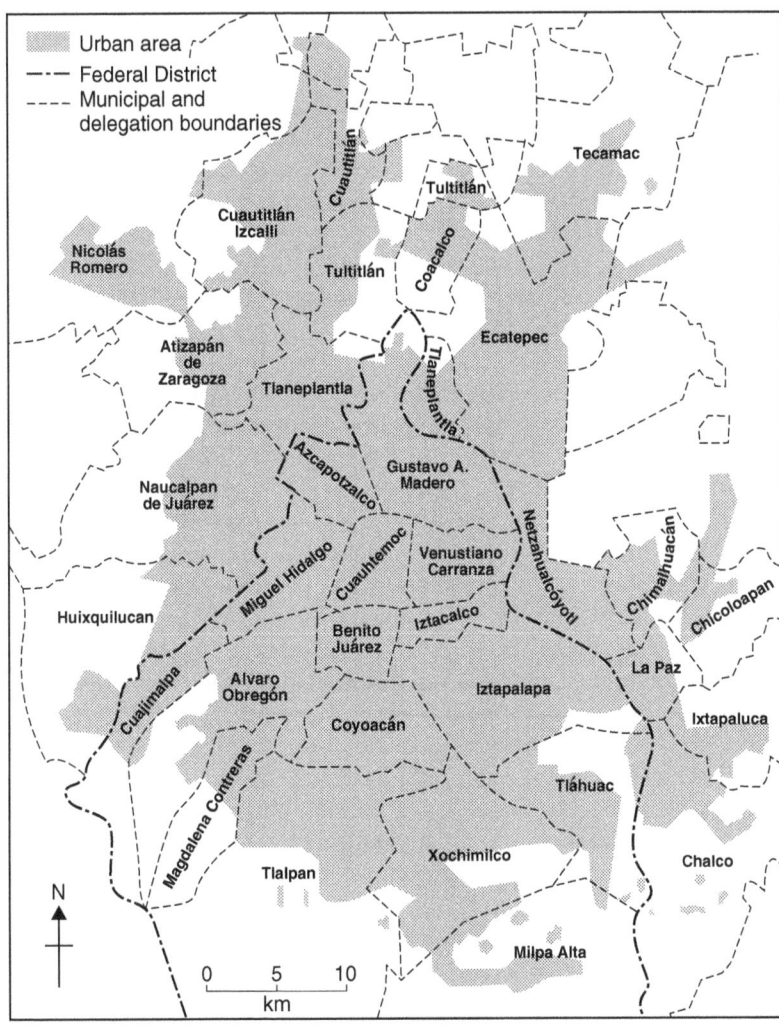

Source: Prepared by David Sansom, Cartographer, University of Oxford.

diseases, including both old diseases associated with poverty such as gastrointestinal and parasitic infections and the new threats derived from modern life, such as water pollution by industrial, agricultural or domestic discharges. As stated in 1991 by the then Federal Health Minister Jesús Kumate Rodríguez, 'the main deficiency in the country's development relates to potable water ... as gastrointestinal diseases cause the largest number of deaths in the Mexican population' (*La Jornada*, 13 August 1991: 44). In the Basin of Mexico, people are exposed to a wide range of water-related infections including amoebiasis, giardiasis, and viral agents which bring respiratory, gastrointestinal, and central nervous system disorders (National Academy of Sciences (NAS), 1995: Ch. 5). In particular, acute diarrhoea is prevalent in the MCMA and according to the 1991 census this was the third leading cause of infant mortality in the State of Mexico and the fourth in the Federal District, with official mortality rates of 450 and 156.7 per hundred thousand respectively. These problems are especially severe in the less urbanized parts of the MCMA, which in general also show the lowest rates of access to water services (Instituto Nacional de Estadística, Geografía e Informática (INEGI), 1991).[4] Although there is a notorious lack of systematic information about the connections between water management and public health, recent research has confirmed that preventable diarrhoeal infections constitute one of the main health hazards in the MCMA. Also, the evidence shows that these infections affect particularly poor children living in the peri-urban areas of the city (Cifuentes García *et al.*, 1999, 2002).

Other important threats come from pollutants leached to the water sources such as nitrates, toxic metals, pesticides and herbicides, which can cause acute disorders or even permanent damage to humans and are extremely difficult to remove in the filtration process. This type of pollution is associated with inadequate disposal of toxic wastes, contaminated rainwater or agricultural runoff, and there is evidence of agrochemical pollution in the Lerma river basin, one of the MCMA's water sources, where studies have found alarming levels of pesticide residues in humans. Also, although domestic water supplies in the MCMA are treated, owing to problems in the distribution system such as leaking pipelines and depressurization that cause the pollution of networked water by raw sewage or other factors there is widespread contamination of the supply at users' taps. These problems are further aggravated by the fact that 90 per cent of the waste water produced in the MCMA is exported from the basin untreated including a vast amount of hazardous industrial effluents. Part of this waste water is used to irrigate around 5,500 hectares in the Chiconautla area and 80,000 hectares in the State of Hidalgo before it is emptied in the Gulf of Mexico (NAS, 1995, Ch. 5; Cifuentes García *et al.*, 1993, 1995).

From the perspective of ecological and economic sustainability, although around 70 per cent of water used in the MCMA is extracted from underground sources the remaining is imported from other basins with high investments in the infrastructure and energy required for pumping and transporting water over long distances. However, piped water in the MCMA is highly subsidized and users pay only a small fraction of the real cost, although most people have to also buy expensive bottled water for drinking owing to the unreliability of the water delivered. Nevertheless, the hazards are significantly greater for the large population settled in shanty towns in the metropolitan periphery who suffer inadequate housing conditions with poor or no urban infrastructure. These sectors are afflicted by chronic water shortages, poor quality water and higher water prices that compromise a large share of their household income and accentuate their vulnerability to health threats.[5]

Finally, the control and allocation of water resources in the basin is subject to acute conflicts between competing users, political entities and involved agencies, which has led to a very complex structure of water governance. The increasing exacerbation of these conflicts over time has prompted several institutional reforms since the 1980s, which have formally sought to promote active citizen participation and the democratization of the structures of water governance in the metropolis. However, in practice water policy continues to be largely unaccountable to the citizens and despite the formal recognition that the water problems are interwoven with socio–economic and political processes, the prevailing explanations and the actual solutions adopted continue to underplay the relevance of the social dimension.

The techno-scientific approach to water conflicts

Although from a certain perspective a large share of the population in the MCMA is defenceless against these water threats and dangers, the widespread conflicts flaring up around a whole range of water problems recorded since the 1980s suggest that people have been active in seeking solutions or, at least, voicing their grievances. These actions range from the presentation of peaceful demands to the authorities to violent events, which in the extreme include the destruction of property and the loss of human life. We also found that the annual cycle of these conflicts follows closely the rhythm of physical-natural processes such as the seasonal distribution of rainfall, and the patterns of evaporation and temperature. During the period 1985–92 the number of events increased sharply in November–December with the arrival of the dry season, reached a peak between January and February, and began to decline slowly from March onwards, remaining more or less stable during the rainy season between June and October (see Figure 4.1). Notably, this pattern differs from that of the urban conflicts over land tenure, housing problems or environmental degradation which do not have such a strong correlation with physical–natural cycles (Bolos and Perdomo, 1990: 10).

Understandably, physical–natural and technical factors are often presented as the key explaining factors of the MCMA's water problems and conflicts, while the crucial socio-economic and political aspects continue to be largely neglected. Unfortunately, the most influential social science contributors to this debate have also limited their scope to technical considerations, such as designing mechanisms for creating private water markets or accelerating the conversion of water services into private goods. Nevertheless, these 'technical' contributions by social scientists have paramount social and political significance, as in fact they have informed far-reaching institutional transformations in the water sector worldwide since the 1980s. Public policy reforms such as water sector liberalization, de- and re-regulation, and privatization, have often provoked widespread citizen reactions ranging from public demonstrations to open violence even leading to the collapse of national governments as happened in Bolivia in 2000, 2003 and 2004.[6] However, contemporary mainstream social scientists continue to neglect fundamental socio-political considerations, such as the inequalities of power arising from the governance, management, and distribution of water resources and services, which are the main focus of this work.

In contrast with the low importance given in mainstream social science to what we call here the social character of water, the subject has been a prime concern for the Mexican authorities for decades. This, perhaps, was helped by the high levels of social mobilization that has marked urban life in Mexico, in which water played a significant role. For instance, since publishing the 1975 National Hydraulic Plan (Plan Nacional Hidráulico (PNH)) the water authorities have increasingly recognized the conflict-ridden nature of water management in Mexico. Thus, the 1981 re-edition of the PNH introduced the notion of 'conflicts over water', and even attempted to predict sequences and levels of water conflict in the main ninety-three urban centres of the country between 1980 and 2000 (see Figure 1.2).

Undoubtedly, acknowledging the paramount importance of water conflicts for policy and planning was a big step forward towards incorporating the social dimension vis-á-vis physical-natural and technical processes. Nevertheless, in practice the notion of conflict laid out in

Figure 1.2   Map of conflicts over water supply services in the main Mexican urban centres (1980–2000)

∇ With current and future   ◇ Currently with conflict but with alternative   ● Without conflicts until the year 2000
   conflicts   supplies   ▼ With current conflicts about water quality
○ With future conflicts   ◆ With evidence of underground water reserves

1. Tijuana	25. Guadalajara	48. Leon	71. Iguala
2. Mexicali	26. Guasave	49. Lagos de Moreno	72. Uruapan
3. Ensenada	27. Los Mochas	50. Aguascalientes	73. Lázaro Cárdenas
4. San Luis Rio Colorado	28. La Paz	51. Tepic	74. Colima
5. Nogales	29. Culiacán	52. Puerto Vallarta	75. Manzanillo
6. Cd. Juárez	30. Mazatlán	53. Ocotlán	76. Zihuatanejo
7. Hermosillo	31. Durango	54. Zamora	77. Acapulco
8. Guaymas	32. Fresnillo	55. Irapuato	78. Chilpancingo
9. Empalme	33. Zacatecas	56. Morelia	79. Tehuacán
10. Cd. Obregon	34. Matehuala	57. Zitácuaro	80. Oaxaca
11. Navojoe	35. San Luis Potosi	58. Toluca	81. Coatzacoalcos-Minatitlán
12. Cuauhtémoc	36. Cd. Victoria	59. México	82. Salina Cruz
13. Chihuahua	37. Cd. Mante	60. Cd. Sahagun	83. Juchitán
14. Delicias	38. Cd. Valles	61. Apizaco	84. Tuxtla Gutiérrez
15. Hidalgo del Parral	39. Tuxpan	62. Jalapa	85. Cárdenas
16. Piedras Negras	40. Poza Rica	63. Veracruz	86. Villa Hermosa
17. Nva. Rosita	41. Tulancingo	64. Córdoba	87. Campeche
18. Nvo. Laredo	42. Pachuca	65. Orizaba	88. Chetumal
19. Monclova	43. San Juan del Rio	66. Tlaxcala	89. Mérida
20. Matamoros	44. Querétaro	67. Puebla	90. Tampico-Cd. Madero
21. Reynosa	45. Celaya	68. Izucar de Matamoros	91. Tapachula
22. Monterrey	46. Salamanca	69. Cuautla	92. Cancun
23. Saltillo	47. Guanajuato	70. Cuernavaca	93. Ciudad del Carmen
24. Torreon-Gómez Palacio Lerdo			

Source: Adapted from Secretaría de Agricultura y Recursos Hidráulicos (SARH), 1981: 50. Prepared by David Sansom, Cartographer, University of Oxford.

the PNH was limited to hydrogeological and techno-administrative features, whereby conflicts over water would be the outcome of a negative correspondence between volumes of 'naturally available water supply', 'expected water extraction', and 'expected water consumption'. For instance, the results mapped in Figure 1.2 were obtained by classifying cities according to the correlation between the volumes of water extracted and consumed[7] and the volume of water naturally available, where it was assumed that the latter would remain constant between 1980 and 2000 (SARH, 1981: 66). The model predicted that cities with a favourable correlation would be free of conflicts over water because the available water volumes would be adequate to meet the demand, while cities where water volumes were very limited to meet demand were very likely to experience water conflicts. On this basis, the PNH offered a classification of cities ranging from those already affected by water conflicts to others where 'no conflicts were expected until the year 2000' (ibid.: 50).

In fact, the PNH forecasts seem to have been largely accurate, as the empirical indicators effectively confirmed the expected trends in the cases studied. For instance, in Ciudad Juárez, Chihuahua, a city classified as subject to ongoing and future water conflicts, the correlation between water availability and consumption significantly worsened between 1980 and 2000. By contrast, in Tuxtla Gutiérrez, the capital of Chiapas, the state with the largest freshwater reserves, the correlation remained highly favourable as predicted and no water conflicts were expected. However, despite its accuracy in predicting the overall trend in the water balance,[8] the model was not effective in forecasting water conflicts as in fact events of social unrest around water problems mushroomed in both cities during this period (Castro, 1992). In fact, water problems became the leading issue in the 1988 electoral campaign for the governorship in Chiapas, and shortly afterwards the federal government launched a vigorous investment programme to improve the state's water infrastructure. Moreover, the uprising launched in Chiapas by the Zapatista Army for National Liberation (Ejército Zapatista de Liberación Nacional (EZLN)) on 1 January 1994 helped to expose the calamitous situation affecting the local indigenous population, not least regarding the control of water resources and the access to essential water services (EZLN, 1994: 33–5; see also Montemayor, 1997).

More examples can be added, but what we want to emphasize here is that water conflicts cannot be explained solely by their hydrogeological or techno-administrative aspects and that there is need for a closer examination of the interrelations between the physical–natural and social processes involved. After all, water 'scarcity' and conflict often happen where there is abundance of water resources, as illustrated by Guayaquil, the largest city in Ecuador. Although Guayaquil is crossed by the fresh waters of the river Guayas, over one third of the population has no access to safe water supply while those connected to the network are subject to chronic water shortages. A protracted structure of social inequality, clientelistic politics, and collusion between the authorities and private water entrepreneurs are among the main factors that explain the deficiencies of the city's water systems which underpin much social and political unrest (Swyngedouw, 1997). The description can be easily generalized to many cities in developing countries. In fact, although water volumes are certainly a crucial and legitimate consideration, a closer examination shows that the availability of water for essential needs or the technical capacity to make these volumes available for human use, are not the main problem.

And yet, in the current scenario of the MCMA the socio-political roots of the reigning water stress may be much less obvious for the contemporary observer. As shown in Chapter 2, physical–natural constraints undoubtedly reduce the room for manoeuvre for water management, and their saliency tends to overshadow the social character of the process. However, we shall challenge this reduction of the water conflicts to their physical–natural and techno-administrative aspects by exploring the interdependence of hydrogeological, technical, and socio-political processes.

Water conflict as an object of knowledge

Although there is growing evidence showing that water conflicts are largely autonomous from physical–natural and technological conditions, achieving truly interdisciplinary explanations of the problem that account for the intertwining of natural and social processes remains an elusive target. In water research, it can be argued that knowledge of the social dimension is almost negligible compared to the accumulation achieved in other areas such as hydrology or water engineering. One reason for this is that the conditions for scientific observation of the interdependencies between physical–natural and social processes have developed in a very slow and fragmentary fashion, and they have suffered from stagnancy, inertia and even erasure. In particular, the traditions of social science more concerned with the study of social inequality and conflict have made slow progress in integrating the ecological and environmental dimensions in the analysis, although this situation has been rapidly changing in recent years (Redclift and Benton, 1994; Benton, 1996; Harvey, 1996; Foster, 2000; Martínez Alier, 2002). Still, progress is punctuated by a high fragmentation of efforts and mutual distrust between what in many respects constitute mutually complementary disciplinary fields.

In this connection, the fragmentation of accumulated knowledge that is reproduced along the lines of 'epistemic cultures' some of which have developed largely unconnected remains a crucial obstacle for understanding the processes underpinning water conflicts. Thus, bodies of knowledge that might one day be catalysers of higher levels of cognitive restructuration in the field, remain today alien and oblivious to each other, entrenched in their self-perpetuating 'knowledge machineries' and power structures (Knorr Cetina, 1999: 1–11). However, our task here is not to analyse the relative importance or political weight of different disciplines and professions involved in water research, as this would be beyond the scope of this work. Instead, our goal is to highlight some of the epistemological obstacles that continue to impede the understanding of those interrelations between the physical–natural, technical and socio-political processes expressed in the water conflicts.

Epistemic subjects

In this regard, an initial task involves examining – borrowing from Jean Piaget – the *epistemic subjects*, that is, the holders and producers of distinctive bodies of knowledge in relation to water an as object of scientific inquiry or techno-scientific endeavours, which may be embodied in institutions, in working teams as well as in individuals. Our focus here is on the interactions between distinct cognitive structures organized around 'artificially circumscribed domains' and the possibilities for inter- and transdisciplinary coordinations between them (Piaget, 1971: 137–9). As this is a limited exercise we have restricted our consideration to three of the subjects that have prominent roles in the processes examined here, which we have termed the *water expert*, the *water functionary*, and the *social scientist*.

Water engineers and water scientists are perhaps the principal examples of the water expert, and they represent a highly sophisticated accumulation of knowledge about the physical–natural and technical aspects of water management. In Mexico, as shown later, they have a long-standing history that can be traced back well beyond colonial times, and in the modern period they have been key actors in the consolidation of the Mexican nation state. In turn, the water functionary plays a different role and deals with those aspects of water management that fall outside the techno-scientific domain of the expert. We think here of political functionaries who handle such issues as 'popular discontent' in relation to the provision of water services, 'the social and economic characteristics of the population' that may affect their access to the water services, or 'the economic, social, psychological and environmental values of water' (SARH, 1981: 14). While these aspects are external to the physical–natural and techno-scientific processes that compose the domain of the water expert, for the water functionary they become crucial factors that may rank very high in the political agenda, for instance becoming key elements in electoral programmes and development projects.

The fact that many water functionaries in office are water experts by training must not blur the point under discussion: while the water expert represents the technical rationality that has historically characterized water management activities, the water functionary embodies the political rationality informing decision-making and implementation processes. Actually, some authors have argued that in Mexico these two subjects have often been embodied in different agencies of the state apparatus that compete with each other over the control of the water sector (Ward, 1986: 39, 40, 89–93). Although tensions between the technical and political systems of reference can be traced back at least to the beginning of colonial water management in the basin, in the late twentieth century their main features appear somewhat exacerbated. We come back to this later.

The third subject, the social scientist, is far from been a newcomer in the field but in our perspective it has had a limited degree of influence in both the production of scientific knowledge and in the exercise of social and political power in relation to water. Let us note that in this conceptualization of the social scientist we refer mainly to those bodies of thought that have been directly concerned with, broadly speaking, the interdependence between social regularities and physical–natural processes, traditions that include nineteenth-century figures prior to the professionalization of the social sciences.[9] This work has been written from within the perspective of this epistemic subject and attempts to make a contribution towards further developing inter- and transdisciplinary coordinations in the field.

The meanings of conflict

A clearer understanding of the different intellectual trajectories represented by our epistemic subjects can be achieved by examining the meanings associated with the notion of water conflicts. For instance, when the water expert refers to conflicts over water, as in the forecasts presented in the 1981 National Hydraulic Plan, the observables are mainly quantities. The key concepts (in that case, water demand, supply, consumption, cost) point to water volumes per time units, to numerical series correlating expected population growth with water volumes, metres of pipes, kilowatt hours, and so on, within a certain time period. For instance, in addition to the water balances used to predict water conflicts, the official diagnosis offered by the 1981 PNH listed as key factors explaining the conflicts the

> deficient conservation and maintenance of networks and electromechanical installations; low efficiency in the uses of water due to leaks in the networks and wastage by the users; lack of financial sufficiency in the municipalities; low income in the water operational agencies due to underpricing, and social and political problems due to water transfers between regions and states, and to changing patterns in the use of the resource. (SARH, 1981: 49)

Despite this explicit reference to 'social and political problems', conflict in the perspective of the water expert is mainly the result of the lack of expected correspondence between quantitative variables, which was the criterion employed to develop the map of water conflicts discussed earlier. However, for the water functionaries the notion of conflict derives from a very different set of observables. Thus, they may be referring to the recurrent events of social protest happening in the city owing to the poor quality of the water services, to the civil disobedience of water consumers who are unwilling to pay their bills or to the more aggressive action of those who have decided to take over the offices of the water utility or to destroy water meters in protest against a new policy aimed at improving cost recovery in the water services. As shown in closer detail in Chapter 4, these actions constitute an intricate web when observed at the scale of the daily interaction between *demandantes* (claimants) or *usuarios*[10] (users) and the water utilities.

In addition to these differences in the understanding of what water conflict means, these subjects have historically resorted to physical–natural and techno-administrative factors for predicting and explaining these conflicts, thus overlooking the social character of the process. Unfortunately, the most influential incursions of social science in this sector have not contributed to reverse this trend, and have rather exacerbated the reduction of the process to its physical–natural and techno-administrative dimensions.

Making social regularities observable

If we remain within the techno-scientific and administrative framework crucial factors underpinning the emergence of water conflicts are overlooked or underplayed. Let us consider the legal and technical requirements normally laid down by the water utilities in Mexico to deliver networked water services: legal land tenure and technical feasibility.[11] Although these two requirements look straightforward on paper, when observed in more detail they have actually multidimensional ramifications. At least formally, to gain access to networked water services the claimants must have a legal title to their land, to be 'regularized'. However, regularization also refers to the technical feasibility of bringing the services to the neighbourhood, which is often hampered by the difficult geographical locations of the most disadvantaged human settlements or by the overlapping of legal and political jurisdictions. The fact is that claimants are categorized into two main groups according to these characteristics: regularized and non-regularized.

The number of non-regularized claimants is huge. Just taking into account the requirement of technical feasibility, about ten million people in the MCMA, especially in the State of Mexico, live in urban areas considered unsuitable for the provision of public services, such as the rocky slopes to the south-west of the city, or the now desiccated lake beds to the east, which are exposed both to flooding during the rainy season and to dust storms in the dry period. Moreover, many of these settlements have been developed illegally and, therefore, they are also non-compliant with the legal requirement of having a land title (Rowland and Gordon, 1996: 191). These irregularities continue to be the main formal impediment for the introduction of networked water and sanitation services. As stated by a former director of the State Commission for Water and Sanitation (Comisión Estatal de Agua y Saneamiento (CEAS)) of the State of Mexico when addressing the situation of around half a million people lacking networked water supply in the Valley Cuautitlán-Texcoco:

Most of these people are located in 120 colonias that are in the process of regularizing their land titles. Because of their situation, they are not creditworthy and do not pay any taxes ... these people have settled in invaded ejidal[12] and communal lands in the municipalities of Tultitlán, Ecatepec, Ixtapaluca, Chimalhuacán, Chicoloapan, Los Reyes-La Paz and Valley of Chalco where, unfortunately, the largest irregular human settlements are located. (*El Sol de México*, 11 March 1987)

We cannot discuss here the intricate processes involved in the land invasions in Mexico and their eventual regularization, a topic addressed by many authors,[13] and will focus rather on the particular problem of the water services. In the last analysis, as illustrated in Chapter 4, to be regularized is just a necessary but by no means sufficient condition to gain access to these services. In fact, there are cases of non-regularized *colonias* [urban quarters] that have been able to circumvent the formal requirement of regularization to obtain public services.[14] However, this does not change the prevailing pattern of individuals and families being categorized as irregular or regularized, unworthy or worthy of accessing essential water services. Thus, what initially appears to be an abstract and universal identity, the claimant interpellated by the water authorities, acquires a richer texture when we explore the multidimensional facets of the problem, such as the qualitative and quantitative inequalities determining people's conditions as regular or irregular in legal or geographical terms. In the last analysis, the process that determines the inclusion or exclusion of individuals and families from accessing water services is composed by a dense web of social interactions.

In this connection, as social scientists we are sceptical of the undifferentiated treatment of the population as claimants or users, which overlooks those processes that create and reproduce the structural socio-economic inequalities and injustices determining the lack of access to essential water services affecting millions in Mexico and elsewhere. In this perspective, water conflicts cannot be reduced to physical–natural and techno-administrative considerations, but rather they should be analysed in their interconnections with wider socio-economic and political processes. Unfortunately, although water inequality and the constellation of social blots associated with it have become the object of laudable programmes and declarations of policy worldwide, the underlying processes remain unobservable as an object of knowledge and, consequently, largely overlooked in the formulation and implementation of policy.

In this regard, we argue that water conflicts such as those identified in Mexico are part and parcel of the social struggle for widening and securing a fairer access to the conditions that are essential for human survival and for the enjoyment of basic living standards. Therefore, the significance of the actions carried out by the population in relation to water problems cannot be reduced to their techno-bureaucratic aspects, because what is at stake is the conquest and defence of the conditions that make human survival and social life possible. Unsurprisingly, water is a recurrent object in the social struggles over the access to such basic conditions, but they constitute a territory often demarcated by rigid legal and social barriers and fiercely defended from intrusion. For this and other reasons explained below, we have chosen to approach this topic from the perspective of the social struggle over the territory of citizenship.

Social struggle, water and citizenship

Our work is a study of long-term structural social change, taking the processes of control, management and distribution of water resources and services in Mexico as our empirical reference. In particular, we focus on how these processes have been intertwined with the forma-tion of citizenship rights in Mexico, a development that has been punctuated by protracted social struggles. We draw inspiration from the model suggested by Norbert Elias for studying the interweaving of ecological, sociological, and psychological aspects of long-term devel-opment processes. He put forward the notion of a 'triad of basic con-trols' characterizing human interactions that can be identified in processes of social change in all stages of development: controls over 'non-human' or 'natural' events, controls over 'interpersonal' or 'social' (inter-human) relationships, and controls over our own individual selves (intra-human) (Elias, 1978: 156–7; see also Goudsblom, 1977: 137–8 and 1994: 10–11). Our work concerns mainly the first two aspects, as we explore the interlink between human endeavours to establish and sustain control over water and the concomitant social and political processes.

Conflict and social struggle

We need to specify and differentiate the concept of social struggle from the concept of conflict used by water planners and authorities in Mexico, whose observables are mainly in the physical–natural, legal, and techno-administrative fields. We found inspiration for a theoreti-cal approach to the concept of social struggle in the theory of war put forward by Carl von Clausewitz, whose insights are still influential in this field of study (Roxborough, 1994: 621).[15] In particular, his analysis of war as composed by many individual duels, and his incorporation of the different scales and dimensions that intervene in war activities, afford powerful insights for the elaboration of a sociological concept of social struggle. In this regard, he argued that

> War is nothing but a duel on a larger scale. Countless duels go to make up war, but a picture of it as a whole can be formed by imagining a pair of wrestlers. Each tries through physical force to compel the other to do his will; his immediate aim is to throw his opponent in order to make him incapable of further resistance. *War is thus an act of force to compel our enemy to do our will.* (Clausewitz, 1989: 75)

We wish to stress this analysis of war as composed by 'a large number of engagements, great and small, simultaneous and consecutive', a very complex fragmentation of activity into many separate actions that nevertheless belong to the war as a whole (ibid: 227). From another angle, Clausewitz also pointed out that war was bound up with chance to the extent that it resembles a gamble rather than a perfectly planned activity whose outcomes can be known in advance. Therefore, 'absolute, so-called mathematical, factors never find a firm basis in military calculations. From the very start there is an interplay of possibilities, probabilities, good luck and bad that weaves its way throughout the length and breadth of the tapestry' (ibid: 85–6). This image is particularly useful to elaborate the links between the multifarious and apparently unconnected water conflicts described in more detail in Chapter 4 with the wider development involving the struggles for the democratization of socio-economic and political processes in Mexico. As discussed later, beyond the individual reasoning and will of the actors participating in both sides of the water conflicts, the overall process can be understood as forming part of the wider struggle for substantive citizenship rights. This conceptualization, as demonstrated in forthcoming chapters, is not just a metaphorical resource, as the actual confrontations examined in our study also result in real material losses, human casualties, and territorial conquest.

However, this image of the struggle also allows us to transcend the limits of the contemporary events of water conflict explored in Chapter 4 by examining them in the context of long-term historical processes, in particular the development of citizenship. Citizenship, for the moment defined in the broad sense of full membership of a community as suggested by T. H. Marshall (Marshall, 1992: 18), demarcates a social spatiality that has become a crucial territory under dispute in the social struggles characterizing modern Western society. As discussed in more detail in Chapters 5 and 6, the evolution of citizenship over time has been both instrumental to and 'at war' with the expansion and consolidation of capitalism. Formally, citizenship entails bundles of rights and duties determining the character of the relationships within a political community, but these relationships are evolving and in permanent transformation. Ongoing confrontations for the extension of the contents of citizenship rights and for the inclusion of ever greater numbers of human beings have come to define – to use a psychoanalytical metaphor – a 'space that encompasses the gratifying objects and can be termed "territory"' (Laborit, 1986: 68). We discuss later the concept of citizenship, its controversial implications and how it can be related to water, but let us point out here that, from this perspective, citizenship has become the territory of desires and expectations and, unsurprisingly, a prime object of social struggle.

Going back to the notion of war, the establishment and defence of the basic conditions needed for the survival and reproduction of human beings has been perhaps the single most important factor determining its social character. In this connection, Marx, who stated that war is 'one of the earliest tasks of every primitive community', pointed out the intimate interaction between war and the very foundations of social life in human society (Marx, 1978: 89). He argued that war is at the very origin of social existence as the 'all-embracing task, the great communal labour' required for the occupation by human groups of the objective conditions for existence and for their protection and perpetuation (ibid: 71). Clearly, the notion of territory is central for the analogy between the model of war and a sociological concept of social struggle, whereby territory refers to the objective conditions of existence of human beings organized in social groups: to demarcate a territory means to constitute the social conditions of existence, which entails its defence from rival groups. War, therefore, has been historically the social form of establishing and defending territories (survival units) among human groups, which in modern times have taken the form of territorial nation states increasingly integrated in a worldwide capitalist system (Weber, 1995: 77–8, 222).

In this connection, drawing on Marx's and Weber's classic insights on this topic, Norbert Elias proposed a sociological model of long-term structural change, which gives the social struggle over territorial domination a central role as the driving force that shaped the modern system of nation states (Elias, 1994). He distinguished three main elements in this long-term historical process, which he termed 'the monopoly mechanism', 'the royal mechanism', and 'the transformation of "private" into "public" monopolies', all of which were at work simultaneously and in close interaction with each other during the formation of modern nation states in Europe (Mennell, 1992: 66–79). In Elias' sense, monopolization refers to an incremental, though not linear or necessary, process of concentration of control over available sources of social power by a decreasing number of social units. The backbone of the process was the gradual concentration of the means of violence and taxation in the hands of territorial rulers, while the constant struggle among rival 'monopolists' who were compelled to enlarge their own territories in a sequence of 'elimination contests' in the long run led to the consolidation of the modern system of states (Elias, 1994: 338–55; see also Weber, 1978: 909, and Tilly, 1975). In this perspective, the state has historically emerged as the embodiment of the domination that a given social fraction established within a certain territory by creating 'conditions of increasing pacification' (Weber, 1978: 908). This, in turn, was reflected in the formation of markets, regarding the economic sphere, and in the emergence of citizenship systems demarcating and regulating the conditions of governance prevailing in these territories.

Water, the state and the territory of citizenship

As argued by Jean-Pierre Goubert, in addition to its ancient role in basic human survival, water acquired renewed centrality since the late eighteenth century with the increasingly water-devouring uses adopted by modern society. Not only did water attain even greater importance as the main instrument of hygiene and health, but also became the vehicle for the ever more sophisticated attention paid to the human body characterizing the process of individualization in the Western world. At the same time, water altered the urban landscape both above and below ground, and penetrated all spheres of public and private activity, while retaining its ageless importance in sustaining life (Goubert, 1986: 22–6). More importantly, perhaps, water was increasingly transformed into a commodity and became the object of a rapidly expanding industry, though this particular development has been punctuated by permanent social and political confrontations that continue to hold down the pervasive expansion of capitalist forms in the field of water resources and water services.

Unsurprisingly, water has continued to be a recurrent object of social conflict, a characteristic that has been enhanced by the growing demand for and competition over water resources. Over the last few decades, international security experts have warned that water was becoming more important than oil as a potential source of conflicts (Gleick, 1993). And there are good reasons for this, given that freshwater resources are unevenly and irregularly distributed, that some regions of the world are extremely water-short, and that these resources are often shared by two or more countries. It is estimated that fewer than 10 countries control about 60 per cent of the world's freshwater resources, while about 300 river and lake basins and a large number of groundwater aquifers are shared by two or more countries (Ohlsson, 1992; Samson and Charrier, 1997). Understandably, there is a growing body of literature on water conflicts, which emphasizes the so-called non-military aspects of international security (for example, elements which can become a target for military action), among which water and water systems rank very high.

Most of this scholarship focuses on international confrontations around water, but there is also a growing awareness about the intranational dimension of the problem. Given that water is an essential factor in ensuring the universal human right to 'a standard of living adequate for ... health and well-being' (Article 25, Universal Declaration of Human Rights), it is evident that governments increasingly face the threat of social and political conflicts triggered by citizen demands for adequate and regular amounts of safe water and related services. Although intra-national water conflicts have received comparatively less attention, there are important contributions to the topic, ranging from Donald Worster's provocative study on water 'empire' building in the US (Worster, 1985) to the literature on water security and the growing body of work that can be broadly termed as 'the political ecology of water' dealing with socio-ecological distribution conflicts (Swyngedouw *et al.*, 2002).

Within this broad thematic field, this book addresses the interlinks between the social struggle over the control, governance, and management of water and the development of citizenship rights from a long-term perspective. The reason for this is that to capture the multidimensional dynamics of the social struggle we need to elicit observables adequate to its different scales and spatial-temporal features. Struggles over water have been a central factor shaping Mexican history and, among other issues, they long ago influenced the formation of institutions and customs that have persisted until today. The universal importance that water has for human life was enhanced in the Basin of Mexico owing to the convergence of natural constraints and human intervention. Over the long term, the establishment of human control over water in the basin has been intimately interwoven with inter-human struggles in the socio-economic and political spheres. In our perspective, these struggles have determined the distinctive social character of water-related activities in the basin and, particularly in recent times, they have taken the form of a struggle over the territory of citizenship.

Temporal scales

This research was triggered by events that occurred during the 1980s and 1990s in the MCMA. However, this timespan provides the synchronic element for the observation of processes that require the introduction of a broader temporal scale to be fully understood. Our dynamic world is driven simultaneously by long-term cumulative processes and unique events of sudden change, and we aim to link our observations of contemporary water conflicts with the long-term struggle over the territory of citizenship, which necessarily requires the incorporation of the diachronic dimension as an effort towards the elaboration of holochronic explanations.[16]

It was already argued that understanding the development of citizenship requires a theoretical perspective of the long-term process of state formation, which we further develop in Chapter 3. From this standpoint, to the process of state formation there corresponds a twin process concerning the formation of the citizen as a particular social category and of citizenship as a set of institutions governing the interactions between the state and its individual members. Thus, citizenship demarcates a social spatiality, a territory where the social conditions of existence are regulated in the form of a system of rights and duties. This territory has been and remains under permanent dispute in contemporary society.

As discussed in Chapter 5, many problems arise from the use of the concept of citizenship. Strictly speaking, citizenship is bound up with the modern state, and particularly with the state in the 'western cultural circle since the Renaissance' (Heller, 1942: 43, 78). However, some of the processual components of the formation of citizenship rights can also be found in other historical experiences such as in the Mexican case. There are many ways available to approach the study of citizenship over time, and we chose to examine it in relation to water due to its centrality in the Basin of Mexico. Following Norbert Elias' insights, we aim to stress that water control played a key part in the process of social organization and state formation in Mexico, and the model put forward by Elias provides clues for the explanation of how this process happened, and what the consequences have been for the development of citizenship rights.

The long-term 'conquest of water' in Mexico

In his study of Western European water history, Jean-Pierre Goubert coined the term 'the conquest of water' to refer to the double-edged process by which humans domesticated water and at the same time became conquered by it. He argued that since the late eighteenth century water had become a subject of interest for scientists, monarchs, aristocrats and the middle classes. Slowly, water was besieged by science and technology and during the nineteenth century it became an industrial and commercial product. However, in the process the conquered came to be the conqueror as water finally transformed our world by slowly penetrating and 'subjugating' our daily lives (Goubert, 1986: 24–5).

We found this historical metaphor useful in addressing the development of water governance and management in the Basin of Mexico, which has certainly had the characteristics of a mutually binding venture between humans and nature. However, our main interest concerns how the processes involved in establishing human control over water became inextricably linked with the consolidation of inter-human control through the formation of specific configurations of social power. For the sake of clarity, we have divided this long-term process into three stages: first, the pre-Columbian period characterized by the water-oriented indigenous civilization that thrived in the basin; second, the four centuries from the Spanish conquest (1521) to the Mexican Revolution (1910–17), that could be characterized as the long process of consolidation of Western-style social relations and institutions; and, third, the 'short twentieth century', to borrow Eric Hobsbawm's phrase (Hobsbawm, 1994), which started with the Revolution and, like in Hobsbawm's example, in many respects came to an end before its chronological time expired.[17]

The pre-Columbian period, which has already been explored from the perspective of the 'hydraulic hypothesis' put forward by Karl Wittfogel (Wittfogel, 1956, 1959; Palerm, 1990), is worth examining because water played a central role in the social organization of the Indians. Not only some of the socio-ecological transformations undergone by the basin were set in motion during this early stage, but also some of the principles and practices developed at the time have survived until today owing to the syncretistic character of the colonial process. Among other issues, community-oriented water uses and rights, sophisticated water expertise, and an incipient process of monopolization of land and water by the warrior elite were characteristic of the Basin of Mexico's human settlements before the Conquest. Moreover, water resources, infrastructure, and services were instrumental in determining the socio-spatial organization of the pre-Columbian metropolis, which strongly shaped the posterior colonial development in important ways.

In this regard, the colonial process brought about a radical socio-ecological transformation, introducing irreversible changes in the basin's hydrogeology and leading to the formation of an oligarchic social order where land and water became concentrated in the hands of a small elite. Nevertheless, the emerging social configuration had also a strongly syncretistic character, whereby Western European traditions, social relations (common, public, and private property forms), institutions (property rights, courts of justice) and identities (ciudadanos)[18] became interwoven with the indigenous ones. This development was not reversed after Independence from Spain (1821), and was rather intensified by the nineteenth-century process of state formation characterized by the superimposition of liberal institutions upon the Ibero–Indian legacy. This period was marked by renewed confrontations between the communitarian and individualistic models of social organization that had been at work throughout the colonial process. The nineteenth century, through the liberal-led attack on the community and corporate forms of land and water ownership prevailing in the Indian villages and the Church possessions, deepened the process of social exclusion. As discussed in Chapter 5, the liberal reforms formally sanctioned universal civil and political rights drawing on the US and French models, but the actual process deepened the alienation of the indigenous and peasant majorities and eventually led to the Mexican Revolution (1910–17). Precisely, one of the most significant consequences of the Revolution was the formal decision to reverse the process of exclusion by formalizing the universalization of citizenship rights on a much broader basis, whereby the indigenous and Hispanic traditions of collective land and water ownership became legalized along with the more individualistic forms of liberal democracy in the epoch-making Article 27 of the revolutionary Constitution (Tannenbaum, 1965: 103–16), which sanctioned that:

> The property of land and water within the boundaries of the national territory belong originally to the Nation, which has had

and still has the right to grant control over them to individuals thus constituting the private property ... The nation will permanently retain the right of imposing on private property the requirements dictated by the public interest, as well as regulating, for the social well being, the development of natural resources.

However, although the Revolution was a big step forward in the struggle for the expansion of substantive citizenship in Mexico, in the long run the revolutionary process did not live up to the promises and a large proportion of the Mexican population continues to be excluded from full access to this territory until today. From another angle, the rapid expansion of capitalist relations that literally boomed in Mexico since the Porfiriato (1884–1911) was part and parcel of the swift incorporation of the country into the world market, and the control and management of the access, distribution and consumption of water for different uses played a key role in this development. In the late Porfiriato, after the railways proved to have only a limited impact on the country's modernization, water became a central concern for the state, in particular for agriculture and hydroenergy. In this regard, the emergence at this stage of modern water experts was not an experience exclusive to Mexico, but was rather the local expression of a worldwide development (Goubert, 1986: 23–5; Worster, 1985: 143–6). Late nineteenth-century water scientists and engineers participated in intense and passionate confrontations over the strategies that the country required for the exploitation of its water resources. Among other issues, they debated a variety of contrasting models of land and water rights, and indeed of citizenship, as they had a clear understanding of the interconnections between the water policy models they discussed and the rival models of citizenship that informed the social and political process of the time. As shown later, although as individuals they had little control over the overall process that was taking an increasingly revolutionary shape around them, as collective actors they played a crucial role in the construction of the highly centralized Mexican State and in the particular power configurations that would characterize twentieth-century Mexico.

Finally, during the short twentieth century that started with the Revolution the growing importance of water control and management proceeded at a faster pace than ever before and became crystallized in powerful state structures, especially regarding irrigation and the production of hydroenergy. However, the expansion of safe water and sanitation systems so much needed to reverse the extremely unsanitary conditions affecting the majority of the population was postponed for many decades, which from the perspective of this study contributes to make observable the slow development and segregating dynamics of citizenship in Mexico. In this later stage, we focus especially on the last two decades of the twentieth century.

Dismantling the 'benefactor' state?

The last two decades of the twentieth century brought about a significant break with the past in important respects. In particular, we explore the introduction since the early 1980s of policy reforms aimed at dismantling the paternalistic state system developed since the Revolution. According to the reformers, the post-revolutionary Mexican state had become 'a supplier, donor, benefactor State' (CNA, 1990: 13), but this state model was no longer sustainable and had to be reformulated. Consequently, during the 1980s and early 1990s radical changes were attempted in the institutional structure of the water sector aiming at reducing the role of the state and re-centering the governance of water resources and services around free-market principles. These reforms were certainly part of a qualitative change in the formal roles of the Mexican state that had been sanctioned in the 1917 revolutionary constitution.

In particular, the administration of President Carlos Salinas de Gortari (1988–94) introduced a series of juridical changes in 1992 which helped to consolidate the process: a) reforms to Article 27 of the Constitution with the objective, on the one hand of creating land markets through giving *ejidal* and communal land the status of private property, while on the other hand stopping the *reparto agrario* [land distribution] and effectively cancelling the principles of Article 27; b) a new Land Law to implement these changes to Article 27; c) a new Water Law to give water 'the same tradability as agricultural land to allow the introduction of market mechanisms for transferring water rights' (Presidencia de la República Mexicana (PRM), 1992b). President Salinas de Gortari's policies also deepened the process of decentralization and promotion of private sector participation in the water sector that had been started in the early 1980s, while simultaneously attempting to concentrate control over water resources in the hands of the state.

These policies were in line with a worldwide wave of water sector reforms promoted by the international financial institutions, inspired by the neoliberal policies of deregulation, liberalization and privatization that became mainstream since the early 1980s.[19] In a nutshell, the neoliberal model of water reform was aimed at transforming water resources from public or common good into a private good that can be traded in the market, and converting public services such as water and sanitation into commodities delivered by private, profit-oriented, operators. In the official words of the Mexican reformers, the aim was 'to eradicate the notion valid in other epochs that air and water are free because today, neither air nor water can be considered free'.[20] Therefore, in addition to the ambitious changes in the role of the state, these policies also envisaged the transformation of water users into customers. The official discourse assumed that Mexicans were receiving water for free from a benevolent state which no longer had the capability to deliver the goods. However, as shown later, these policies were based on a double fallacy: firstly, the assumption that water was being delivered as a free good and, secondly, the assumption that the solution to the problems affecting water and sanitation services, in particular the need for huge investments in the rehabilitation and expansion of the systems, could be solved by transforming water and water services into marketable commodities and transferring responsibility for the funding and management of these services to private companies. We come back to this debate and its implications in greater detail in later chapters.

Going back to the policies of reform, although decentralization policies had already been introduced in the 1981 National Hydraulic Plan (PNH), little progress was actually made in carrying them out. In the case of urban water and sewerage systems, the authorities had started a programme to transfer the public utilities to local levels of administration during the early 1980s. Previously, these systems had been administered by the Ministry of Agriculture and Hydraulic Resources (SARH) and the Ministry of Human Settlements and Public Works (Secretaría de Asentamientos Humanos y Obras Públicas (SAHOP)). Under the new programme, the water utilities were gradually transferred to state and municipal administrative agencies known as Operating Bodies, a project that was complemented with financial decentralization. However, the reforms were far from successful and caused the stagnation and even deterioration of the services, especially in intermediate urban centers (Torregrosa Armentia, 1990: 50–6), which constituted the background of the conflicts over water that we identified between 1985 and 1992.

In this connection, the policies of reform formally recognized the existence of protracted conflicts in the water sector and that any solutions must take into account the participation of the users in solving the problems. Thus, in 1989 the government of President Salinas de Gortari created the National Water Commission (Comisión Nacional del Agua (CNA)), a state body with the status of quasi federal ministry, 'to channel and solve without bureaucratism the different conflicts being generated with relation to the distribution, use and exploitation of water' and to concentrate control over water resources at the federal level (PRM, 1992a: ii). The involvement of water users in the resolution of conflicts had already been envisaged by the 1981 PNH, which had proposed the creation of integrated systems for water management, mainly in the Basin of Mexico and in the Lerma river basin, to promote 'a wider participation by the users in solving common problems' (SARH, 1981: 117). Thus, the notion of participation, which is a central dimension of citizenship, had become formally incorporated in water planning activities at least since the early 1980s. Now, it became institutionalized with the creation of the Co-ordination of Participation in the CNA, and the Under-co-ordination of Social Participation in the Mexican Institute of Water Technology (Instituto Mexicano de Tecnología del Agua (IMTA)). Furthermore, the National Solidarity Programme (Programa Nacional de Solidaridad (PRONASOL)) of President Salinas de Gortari gave paramount importance to people's participation in the introduction of public services, especially in the poorest neighbourhoods. However, in many ways PRONASOL was a top-down strategy deeply rooted in the Mexican political tradition, to the extent that even the government claimed that inspiration for the policy could be traced back to pre-Columbian times (Knight, 1994).

Indeed, both the reforms inspired in the neoliberal model and the promotion of water users' participation have to be examined cautiously. Regarding the first, and with hindsight, it is clear that the Mexican style of liberalization and privatization was far removed, at least in the water sector, from the experiences of other developing countries such as Argentina or Bolivia, where the reforms involved an almost complete withdrawal of the public sector. This was not the case in Mexico, where for different reasons the public utilities were not simply replaced by private agents operating in a market environment under minimal state regulation as foreseen in the mainstream literature that inspired the reforms. On the contrary, the Mexican state sought to reassert its hold over the water sector promoting different forms of private sector participation but exercising a qualitatively incremental degree of control over the system. In fact, this was the explicit policy of the Mexican government:

> Today the Mexican water sector faces challenges of the highest political relevance, to the extent that the President himself has set

as a top priority the search for solutions to attend the problems affecting the sector's development. With the recent creation of the Ministry of Social Development (Secretaría de Desarrollo Social (SEDESOL)) and the modifications to the Internal Regulations of the Ministry of Agriculture and Hydraulic Resources (SARH), the National Water Commission has been confirmed as the sole water authority in the country, thus revitalizing the leading role of the state and widening the active participation of the population in solving the problems of the sector. (CNA, 1992: 24)

Summing up, it could be argued that the transformations in the role of the state introduced in the water sector during the 1980s and early 1990s constituted a project of social engineering aimed at reformulating the historical power configurations developed in the post-revolutionary period. In relation to our specific topic, the official diagnosis asserted that the failure of the state to provide safe and universal water and sanitation services was the result of a paternalistic culture, whereby a donor, benevolent state had been unsustainably delivering water for free. Understandably, the water authorities called the process of reform 'the birth of a new culture of water in Mexico' (PRM, 1992a: ii). Taking advantage of this literary image, it could be said that the process examined in the following chapters reflects the intensity of the labour pains.

Concluding remarks

In our perspective, the agonistic social landscape characterizing the Mexican water sector since the 1980s offers an insight into wider processes of socio-political change which are the main focus of our work. In particular, we are interested in exploring how these 'water conflicts' are actually part and parcel of the social struggle for the expansion and consolidation of the territory of citizenship. In this regard, it is increasingly recognized that solving the crucial problems affecting the water sector worldwide, in particular protecting people from the continuing and worsening dangers and threats associated with the way water ecosystems and services are governed and managed, requires the active and meaningful participation of the population. However, this important aspect, which is a central component of the rights and duties of citizenship, in practice continues to be overlooked or even neglected by mainstream water policies. The events of water conflict that we examine are, in our perspective, an expression of this situation, whereby different actors – often in mutual contradiction

– have been challenging the prevailing forms of water governance and management.

However, our exploration has also led us to look into the interwoven dynamics of physical–natural and social processes, as we consider that in order to elucidate what is broadly termed here the social character of water we need to adopt a cross-disciplinary approach. As shown in the following chapter, the Basin of Mexico provides an excellent opportunity to explore the interconnections between those activities directed at establishing human control over 'non-human' and 'inter-human' processes. In this regard, the present situation in the Basin of Mexico could not be understood without a reference to the radical transformations brought about by human actions directed at the control of water, while looking into the social history of water governance and management helps us to better understand the forms of social and political organization characteristic of contemporary Mexican society.

2
The Sociogenesis of Water Stress

'There is where water is dammed and stored by order of Hutzilopochtli ... who then told the Mexicans: "water has been dammed; sow willow, ahuehuete, reed, tulle, flower of atlacuezonalli, and let the fish, frogs, ajolotes, shrimps, and ducks breed there". Then, the god sang and danced.'—**Crónica Mexicáyotl** [1609] (1975)

'In all [colonial] water works in the Valley of Mexico water has been considered as an enemy which it is necessary to defend against.' —**Alexander von Humboldt**, *Essai Politique sur le Royaume de la Nouvelle-Espagne (1811)*

This chapter examines the intertwining between environmental and social processes in the transformation of the Basin of Mexico's hydrogeology and in shaping socio-economic, cultural, and political structures and patterns. It shows how human intervention in the aquatic ecosystems, punctuated by protracted social confrontations, has burdened successive generations of Mexicans with an ever-spiralling mortgage to repay in relation to the material and social investments needed to sustain human control over water and make life possible in the basin. From pre-Columbian times, access to water became a key factor of social differentiation and segregation, establishing patterns of social inequality that were deepened and exacerbated by colonial water policies and, particularly, by the modern urbanization process since the late nineteenth century. Also, although the encounter between Indians and Spaniards took largely the form of a syncretistic process, it happened in the context of a colonial system of domination, which was not substantially transformed by the Mexican Independence or even by the Mexican Revolution. Drastic transformations took place not only in the forms of human control over the physical environment but also, and more importantly, in the economic, socio-political and cultural aspects of the relation between humans and water, thus also transforming the forms of social control over inter-human processes. In this regard, the chapter also provides evidence about the interconnections between human activities directed at harnessing water resources in the basin and some aspects of the process of state formation analysed in more detail in Chapter 3. From another angle, the chapter analyses the multi-dimensionality of the social struggles that have marked the development of the basin's waterscape during the last five centuries, which have also become interwoven with the particular configurations characterizing what we called the territory of citizenship, as discussed in Chapters 4 to 6.

The body of this chapter has been organized chronologically, and covers the pre-Columbian antecedents, the colonial and independent periods, and the post-revolution development.

Hydrogeological profile

The physical characteristics of large stretches of Mexico gave water a central place in societal development. The country clusters together with other areas of the world where water management has required a great deal of sophisticated and sustained human effort. Most of Mexican territory is located within the latitudes 19 degrees and 31 degrees, a range which both in the northern and the southern hemispheres is characterized by a scarcity of rains and concentrates the biggest deserts and arid zones of the world. Around 56 per cent of the Mexican territory is arid or semi-arid, 67 per cent of the total annual rainfall (772mm) is concentrated between June and September, and some areas, such as the northwest, record an interannual variability in the rainfall average of more than 40 per cent, similar to sub-Saharan and south-western Africa, Saudi Arabia, and western India (CNA, 2001: 26).

However, on top of these natural constraints, the accumulated and largely unplanned effects of human activity have made much more critical the already difficult conditions. As a result, by the 1990s, population, industrial activities and irrigation agriculture tended to concentrate where water resources are least abundant to the extent that two-thirds of the population, 70 per cent of industrial activity, and irrigation agriculture were located in the northern and central areas, where only 19 per cent of the country's total annual rainfall occurs. By contrast the water rich south-east that receives 67 per cent of the total annual rainfall housed only 12.5 per cent of the population and has a very incipient industrial development. Viewed from another angle, more than a quarter of the national population was settled in areas over 2000 metres above sea level, where only 4 per cent of total rainfall occurs, while a similar amount of people was located in areas under 500 metres above sea level, where about 50 per cent of total rainfall takes place (PRM, 1992a: v).[1]

This uneven distribution of water resources also takes place intraregionally, as is the case in the Basin of Mexico, which houses the Mexico City Metropolitan Area. This region, that represents only 1 per cent of the country's territory, concentrates about 19 million people (20 per cent of the country's population), and accounts for 31.3 per cent of national Gross Domestic Product (GDP), but has only 0.8 per cent of the country's estimated average water availability. Moreover, while in the south of the country estimated water withdrawals range from 1 to 5 per cent of total water availability, the Basin of Mexico is a net importer of water.[2]

Although these indicators hide the wide range of intraregional variability, they provide a glimpse of the current hydrogeological conditions affecting water management in Mexico, which are largely the result of long-term environmental and anthropogenic transformations. In particular, this statement is valid for the Basin of Mexico, where the sociogenesis of the local waterscape can be traced back at least to 700 BC (Díaz-Marta and García Diego, 1991: 148–50; Palerm, 1990: 56–68). Let us now focus on this region and its history.

The Basin of Mexico

The Basin of Mexico occupies the centre of a volcanic area and forms a closed system that was artificially opened in the seventeenth century to protect Mexico City from recurrent flooding.[3] In pre-Columbian times the basin worked as a radial system of rivers and minor streams draining into a central lake chain that runs in a north–south direction. Today the basin has a surface of 9600 square kilometres with an average altitude of 2240 metres above sea level in the south, and 2390 metres above sea level in the north with mountains reaching elevations of more than 5000 metres (National Academy of Sciences (NAS), 1995: Ch. 2). In jurisdictional terms, the basin occupies territories controlled by four different political units – the Federal District, and the states of Mexico, Puebla and Hidalgo.

Since the 1950s, because of rapid urban expansion, Mexico City became one of the largest and fastest growing cities in the world. By 1980, it became a large metropolitan area containing the 16 delegaciones of the Federal District and seventeen conurbated municipalities of the State of Mexico,[4] and by 1990 it had reached an extension close to 4000 square kilometres and an estimated population of 15.1 million. Although the rate of population growth slowed since the 1980s, by the 1990s the MCMA had developed complex regional articulations with other metropolitan areas such as Toluca (Mexico) and Cuernavaca (Morelos) to constitute the Mexico City Megalopolis (Garza and Damián, 1991: 27).

The basin enjoys a highland subtropical environment, temperate, half-dry, with an average temperature between 15 and 16 degrees centigrade. However, it is affected by a very uneven rainfall regime, from an annual average of 750 millimetres in the south to a notorious scarcity of rain in most of the northern region. Moreover, rains are seasonal, concentrating between June and September when up to 90 per cent of the total annual precipitation occurs. In the rainy season, the basin receives some 6000 million cubic metres, with an annual average of about 700 millimetres. More than 80 per cent of rainwater is lost through evaporation and transpiration, while an average of 13 per cent percolates into the subsoil. From the rest, 4 per cent is consumed, and a similar amount is drained out of the basin in the form of natural discharges and wastewater (Llerena V. *et al.*, 1989: 7–32; Mora, 1989: 8–35).

Although this area of the basin is located over an aquifer system and has access to natural springs produced by snow melting and rainfall percolation, the physical characteristics of the terrain present a major challenge for delivering water services. On the one hand, there is a scarcity of large, free flowing, surface water sources and the basin's altitude constitutes a formidable obstacle to water import ventures. On the other hand, the absence of natural drainage from the basin and the intense seasonal rainfall pattern has made the management of wastewater and storm runoff extremely difficult. However, what a few centuries ago were natural hydrogeological constraints have been largely worsened by human intervention.

The pattern of socio-ecological change

The current hydrogeological conditions in the Basin of Mexico are largely the result of a very long-term socio-historic development.

However, the rapid expansion of human settlements in the basin during the last 500 years irreversibly transformed the local and regional ecosystems on an unprecedented scale. In our perspective, the crucial driving force behind these transformations has been the social struggle underpinning the conquest, control and social organization of the use of water resources.

Archaeological studies have reconstructed the pre-Conquest hydrological cycle of the basin: rainfall and snow melting percolated into the soil replenishing the aquifers and natural springs, or flowed into the lakes in the central plateau, where most of it evaporated. The urbanization process, which had begun well before Aztec rule was imposed in the fifteenth century, transformed this cycle and exacerbated the impact of drought and flood events. Urban expansion, the erection of dams and drainage works to control floods – that in the long run led to the desiccation of the lakes, the construction of aqueducts and urban networks to conduct fresh water and drain wastewater, the deforestation of the surrounding heights, overexploitation and pollution of the aquifers, and high levels of demographic and industrial concentration have been the hallmark of the basin's history (Mora, 1989: 9–24; Musset, 1991: 89–107; Sahab Haddad, 1991: 153–61; Fox, 1965: 523–9; Ezcurra *et al.*, 1999). Today, 99 per cent of the pre-Columbian lacustrine system has disappeared, and the same has occurred to the original 2000 square kilometres of forests, while 85 per cent of the basin has been urbanized, and two thirds of the non-urban areas have undergone an irreversible process of erosion. In addition, overpumping of the aquifers has depleted the water tables and transformed subsurface water flows, which has affected the soil structure and provoked the subsidence of large parts of the city. As a result, over the last century the central area of the MCMA has sunk on average seven and half metres, causing deterioration in the urban infrastructure (NAS, 1995: Ch. 3; Llerena V. *et al.*, 1989: 33–5; Fox, 1965: 532–40). Some of these processes have been in progress for centuries, and a general overview of the transformations operated over the long term will be helpful to understand the forces at work.

The pre-Columbian scene

The water expertise achieved by the pre-Columbian inhabitants of the basin is widely documented. Notably, the Indians discovered that the basin was a closed system whereby the lakes composed a multilevel chain of connecting vessels, so flood protection waterworks or dams to prevent saline intrusion from Lake Texcoco into the freshwater western lakes had effect on other parts of the system. In addition, control and regulation of storm runoff required sophisticated techniques and considerable human and material resources given the intense seasonal rainfall regime, which still constitutes a major challenge for sustaining human settlements in the basin.

Also, provision of fresh drinking water and wastewater disposal, irrigation, and conservation of navigable ways, were main concerns for the indigenous water experts (Centro de Estudios Históricos de Obras Públicas y Urbanismo (CEHOPU), 1991: 9–106; Musset, 1991; Palerm, 1990; Gibson, 1964: 1–6; Fox, 1965: 523–7; Brundage, 1972: 34). Archaeological research suggests that the characteristic agricultural systems known as *chinampas*[5] and irrigation were introduced in the basin as early as in the late Formative or Pre-Classic period, before the Christian Era (León-Portilla, 1984: 29; Gibson, 1964: 5 ff.; Brundage, 1972: 51–2), while dam building in the region goes as far back as the seventh century BC (Díaz-Marta and García Diego, 1991: 148–50). However, the greatest development occurred in the span of 600 years preceding the arrival of the Spanish *conquistadores*, known as the Post-Classic period, when a wide range of waterworks were built, including dams, causeways, aqueducts, canals, irrigation systems, terraces, and island cities such as Tenochtitlan-Tlatelolco, which became the Aztec capital. In the early sixteenth century, according to Gibson, 'it was one of the great cities of the world' (Gibson, 1964: 5).

Before the conquest, the hydrology of the basin had already been subject to important transformations. For instance, in the fifteenth century King Netzahualcóyotl built a dyke to protect the capital from floods and preserve the freshwater lakes from saline intrusion, which introduced substantive changes to the lacustrine system. The 16 kilometres-long structure, built with stone and soil, helped to boost the process of sedimentation and hence the food-producing capacity of the southern and western shores, which became more populated than the eastern parts (Fox, 1965: 524). As shown later, this segregation caused by the division between fresh and saline waters underpinned the already emerging patterns of social inequality and largely determined much of the subsequent spatial organization of the basin.

Regarding drinking water, the Aztecs built at least two aqueducts. The *Caño Viejo de los Indios* (Old Indian's Pipe) as the Spaniards called the main water conduit of the Aztec capital, was built by King Netzahualcóyotl by the mid-fifteenth century to replace an already existing 12 kilometre-long system destroyed by a big flood in 1449.

The water circulated through underground pipelines to palaces and temples, while vendors in canoes distributed the public supply. A second aqueduct was built in the late fifteenth century by King Ahuitzotl, who resorted to military action to take the waters which were controlled by King Tzotzoma of Coyoacán. The new watercourse collapsed in 1499, bringing disaster to the capital by destroying dwellings, palaces, orchards, and the aqueduct itself was never rebuilt. The water systems in the Aztec capital supplied an estimated population of between 200,000 and 300,000 people, and the daily flow of water has been calculated at 20 million litres (Fritz de la Orta, 1991: 386). Understandably, the Caño Viejo and the sewer systems raised the admiration of the Spanish *conquistadores*, of which Cortés gave testimony in his Letters from Mexico (Cortés, 1986). Concerning sewage disposal, the city had a system of gutters that ran in a west–east direction and emptied into Lake Texcoco, and the effluents were used in leather tannery, salt production, and crop-fertilization, which helped to reduce the contaminating effect of wastewater discharges (Sahab Haddad, 1991: 155, 161; Musset, 1991: 112–6).

As shown in more detail in the following chapter, water control was also a prime military concern and it helped to consolidate Aztec territorial and political domination over rival ethnic groups (Musset, 1991: 112–14). In turn, Hernán Cortés conquered Tenochtitlan-Tlatelolco in the early sixteenth century by fighting an odd naval war at about 2000 metres above sea level, and his success relied largely on the water expertise of the city's Indian enemies. According to the records, once the attackers cut the city off from its fresh water supply by destroying tracts of the Caño Viejo the defence collapsed and the city dwellers suffered the ravages of water-related diseases such as smallpox, which might have been a crucial factor in the Aztec defeat (Díaz del Castillo, 1963: 359; Cortés, 1986; McNeill, 1977: 75, 76, 199–234; Crosby, 1994: 200–1; Musset, 1991: 115).

The colonial transformation

An important feature of the colonial period was the endurance shown by pre-Hispanic socio-technical water systems[6] in a context of relentless monopolization of power and resources by the colonists. In this regard, pre-Columbian water technologies and practices have survived until today, for instance in the *chinampas* that are still in use in the canals of Xochimilco[7] and Tláhuac in southern Mexico City or in the wetland agriculture practiced in the lowlands of Veracruz (Siemens, 1998). This may well be a particular case of water technology lock-in, which like in the example of ancient Chinese water management studied by the historian Mark Elvin, would have resulted in a highly resilient traditional technology being preserved because the social and economic costs of innovation were unacceptable or unfeasible (Elvin and Ninghu, 1995: 44–8). However, the endurance of the indigenous hydro cosmos in the Basin of Mexico can also be understood as the outcome of protracted and multidimensional social struggles, which also took place in the technical sphere, in the context of a colonial process of state formation driven by largely syncretistic forces. In this perspective, when observed as discrete events, the social contests – borrowing from Norbert Elias – involving the control of water resources in the basin throughout the colonial period were multifarious, multi-actor, and multidimensional. However, they formed part of the wider social struggle for the demarcation and defence of social territories that in the long run shaped New Spain into an oligarchic social configuration where land and water became an elite monopoly, a situation that even the Mexican Revolution in the early twentieth century could not entirely reverse.

In this connection, we look in more detail at the particular ecological distribution conflicts that fuelled the struggle over water in the basin in forthcoming chapters. Following Elias' notion of 'monopoly mechanism', we argue that the long-term development which led to the concentration of land and water in the basin in the hands of a small elite had already started in the late pre-Cortesian period, was taken over and boosted by the colonial development, and was exacerbated by the nineteenth-century liberal reforms that introduced the large-scale privatization of land and water in the country. However, in this section we will concentrate on the interrelation between socio-technical and hydrogeological processes in the struggles over water. Although it is difficult to draw a clear division within the relevant scholarship on this topic, for analytical reasons we have singled out two main arguments, which we called the 'technological deadlock' hypothesis, and the 'water technology innovation' hypothesis.

The 'technological deadlock' hypothesis

It has been argued that the Spaniards did not introduce important technological innovations in the basin's water systems during the colonial period (1521–1821). For instance, some authors have argued that flood control under Spanish rule relied almost entirely on ancient indigenous techniques while the pre-Columbian aqueducts – repaired and extended – continued to be the main sources of fresh water for the city until the mid-nineteenth century (Musset, 1991: 116; Levi Lattes, 1991: 128). Again, at first glance this could be explained as examples of technological lock-ins, whereby the cost of innovation would have been unacceptable (or unaffordable) for the colonial authorities. However, the historical evidence also suggests that the endurance of the indigenous technology was not just the result of purely technical or economic considerations but it was also the outcome of an intricate web of social, cultural and political factors. In particular, the Indians engaged in persistent and never ending low-intensity struggles to retain control over their water resources and infrastructure or, when control was lost, to make water management activities in the basin difficult for the Spaniards. These struggles certainly involved the defence of indigenous water rights – which we address in more detail in Chapter 5 – but also included confrontations over the technical and managerial aspects of water management.

In this connection, shortly after the conquest the Indians began to reorganize and repair their water networks, which had been damaged during the battles. This led to a series of revolts concerning the control of the city's water systems:

> In the year 1542 ... a 'great fear' arose among the Spaniards of Mexico City. They were afraid of an indigenous rebellion ... and these fears awakened the memories of the conquistadores about the role played by water and by the Indians' water expertise during the siege of Tenochtitlan. With renewed vigor, the Indians started to rebuild their destroyed water system, which prompted a strong opposition from the Spaniards. (Palerm, 1990: 349–50)

When the Indians lost control of the urban water infrastructure, they resorted to sabotage of the system by dumping waste into the water conduits to poison the Spaniards' water supplies. In response, as early as in 1524 the viceregal authorities appointed water guards to protect the water supply from indigenous attacks (Llamas Fernández, 1991: 190).

Interestingly, in the early colonial period an important share of the confrontations to establish control over water in the basin was played out in the technical dimension. Thus, the construction of flood defences to protect Mexico City, which became the object of endless confrontations in the intersection of the conflicting interests of the Crown, the colonial authorities, *gente de bien* (respectable families), religious orders, and indigenous communities, often took the form of a technical contest between indigenous and Spanish water expertise. Often too, the indigenous technologies were preferred, as it happened in the seventeenth century when Viceroy Velasco had to repair the destroyed flood control barriers. After comparing the indigenous methods recorded in ancient paintings with the proposals of the colonial experts, the Viceroy decided that the Indians' technology was quicker and more effective (Gibson, 1964: 27). In a similar episode, the Indians questioned the Viceroy's plans for the building of flood protection works in the Cuautitlán River. They argued that the project was technically unsuitable, offered alternative solutions to the problem, and described the advantages of their system over the Viceroy's project. After consulting his own experts, the Viceroy finally passed the Indians' project (Rojas, 1974: 93). In many respects, these confrontations reflected the dissimilar – often opposite – approaches to nature held by Indians and Spaniards, as expressed in the diversity of meanings, uses, values and technologies connected with water (Musset, 1991: 17–35).

The historical evidence briefly summarized here seems to lend support to what we termed here the 'technological deadlock' hypothesis, which argues that the Spanish brought little technological innovation to the basin's water sector. Let us examine next an alternative argument.

The 'water technology innovation' hypothesis

Alternative descriptions of early colonial water technology depict a different scenario. Thus, some authors have argued that it is the lack of research and information on the early colonial period that led some scholars to make a negative evaluation of colonial water policies, and of colonial technology at large, in the Basin of Mexico (Hoberman, 1980: 386–7). In fact, recent research on the history of water technology suggests that there was an important degree of technological transfer, which took place through the activities of a wide range of actors including official water experts sent by the Crown and private entrepreneurs who introduced new irrigation systems, water-driven mills, and more sophisticated urban water networks (Díaz-Marta and García Diego, 1991: 133–52; Llamas Fernández, 1991: 193 ff.). Water technology innovations also contributed to the development of a 'mestizo architecture' through the combination of completely new elements such as the *norias* [waterwheels] and the renaming and refashioning of already existing water devices such as wells, *aljibes* [cisterns], *jagüeyes* [receptacles for rainwater storage termed *tlaquilacaxitl* in Nahuatl] and aqueducts built in the characteristic styles of the Iberian Peninsula. Similarly, bath- and wash-houses, troughs of stone and fountains, new materials such as lead and glass, and new methods for water purification formed part of a water universe that was completely new to the Indians (Icaza Lomelí, 1991: 221–49).

Regarding urban water supply, it has been argued that taking into consideration the difficult natural conditions of the basin's subsoil, early colonial water technology would have been highly sophisticated. Thus, Mexico City would have been one of the most advanced urban centres of the time, enjoying underground systems and flow controls of water supply long before many other cities. The water supply network was inaugurated as early as in 1535, and was built on the basis of the existing system developed by the Indians. However, the colonial water experts tested old and new materials including clay, glass, stone and metals, and designed a pioneering system of flexible pipelines aimed at overcoming the unstable conditions of the subsoil. In this, though, they did not succeed, as underground pipelines were permanently affected by pollution owing to the poor impermeability of the materials used to build the pipes (Llamas Fernández, 1991: 189).

Irrigation systems and water-driven mills were also crucial in this development, and the introduction of waterpower in the production process started the pre-industrial age in New Spain. The first water-driven mills were inaugurated shortly after the Conquest, and in 1525 Hernán Cortés was the first entrepreneur authorized to build one. A few years later, the western and southern parts of the city had become the chosen placements for water mills and grinders, most of them located alongside the Santa Fé aqueduct, and the Tacubaya River became the main source of energy for most early colonial industries in Mexico City (Musset, 1991: 299–302).

These examples suggest that the overall effect of colonial water policy in New Spain can neither be reduced to its negative effects nor to the inadequacy of early peninsular techniques to deal with the peculiar hydrogeology of the basin, as suggested by the 'technological deadlock' line of thinking. From another angle, the technological innovations brought about by the Spanish colonizers in the water sector played a crucial role in the basin's development, introducing radical transformations both in the hydrogeological and social dimensions.

Colonial water development

The construction of new aqueducts and the introduction of a wide array of elements of water architecture transformed completely the urban landscape in the basin. Likewise, European water-based technologies helped to develop key productive ventures such as the *haciendas* and mines and the early manufacturing industries. On the one hand, the building of new waterworks influenced the spatial reorganization of the metropolis and the subordination of the indigenous social structure to the colonial order. On the other hand, the introduction of new water uses and values, new names and meanings for water-related objects and activities, new water measures, new forms of water rights, higher water consumption for urban and industrial uses, and the slow but irreversible introduction of scientific elements for the control and manipulation of water, shaped the development of a syncretistic and internally contradictory water universe. Also, as discussed in Chapter 5, the new disease regime established after the Conquest, which involved water-related infections unknown in America, was a significant factor in the huge collapse of the indigenous population in the basin, which according to recent estimations may have fallen by as much as 73 per cent between 1519 and 1597 (Whitmore, 1992: 119). The ensuing radical transformation of the basin's hydrogeological and social configurations was, however, neither a peaceful and consensual development nor the result of rational decision-making, but rather the largely unplanned outcome of multidimensional and multi-actor social contests driven by the goals of territorial and social control over both natural and social systems.

Water supply and social structure

Colonial water policy, especially in the areas of water supply and distribution, had also a significant influence in the socio-spatial reconfiguration of the urban space.[8] In this connection, the French geographer Alain Musset has pointed out that the colonial aqueducts were key 'instruments of power' in the policies of relocalization of Indian communities, and their presence encouraged the settlement of towns, *ranchos* [small farms] and haciendas. The waterworks became also a factor of urban discrimination owing to the fracture in the spatial organization between the well-serviced western quarters and the declining eastern neighbourhoods, a process that had been related to the existing division between saline and freshwater lakes since pre-Columbian times. However, the social and spatial segregation was deepened and extended by colonial water policy from the seventeenth century onwards, and the urban structure became increasingly shaped by the new conditions of access to fresh water introduced by the aqueducts (Musset, 1991: 111–43).

During almost three centuries, the colonial city relied mainly on two sources of fresh water, the old Chapultepec stream, and the Santa Fe conduit. The Caño Viejo, later known as the Chapultepec aqueduct, was rebuilt shortly after the conquest using indigenous techniques and was later modernized and extended in the 1570s (Musset, 1991: 117–21). The second was the result of a 1536 project to bring water from Cuajimalpa and Santa Fe. The influence of the main aqueducts on the social and spatial reorganization of the city was determinant, as the well-off families of Spanish origin abandoned the ill-serviced eastern quarters and resettled in the western area. There, the provision of drinking fountains made the access to fresh water easier, while the rich were also entitled to apply for private water rights – *mercedes de agua* – symbol and privilege associated with a high social status. The religious orders, a key actor in colonial Mexico, also built their residences in water-rich quarters such as Tacubaya and Tacuba. Other important aqueducts were built during the colonial period, such as the sixteenth-century conduit built by the friar Francisco de Tembleque to the north-east of the city and the Tenango aqueduct in the south-east, which were built in response to the demands of the indigenous communities.

In addition to the spatial segregation brought about by the municipal water supply networks, the low-standard services provided further reinforced the existing inequalities. Although the authorities established formal controls to avoid abuse and to grant access to water to all sectors of the population (Llamas Fernández, 1991: 190–3), in practice, the shortcomings fuelled the emergence of illegal practices and of parallel systems of supply. On the one hand, poor quality building materials and lack of skilled labour, compounded by a cumbersome water bureaucracy, caused severe delays in the regular repairs needed for maintaining the systems. On the other hand, indifference, pillage, and clandestine connections also played an important part in preventing the efficient functioning of the water services (Musset, 1991: 150–2). Small private entrepreneurs took advantage of the rising needs for water stemming from increased domestic use and the poor conditions of the public supply. When the indigenous practice of water vending in canoes was abandoned with the closure and desiccation of canals, street water vendors known as *aguadores* took over. These colonial pre-decessors of today's *piperos* and *burreros*[9] became increasingly important and their number grew rapidly, to the extent that *aguador* was still a very valued occupation in the late nineteenth century, when they had their own corporation and a large membership (Musset, 1991: 155–8).

Productive waters

As already mentioned, European irrigation systems and water-driven mills were among the main water innovations introduced in New Spain. Spanish agricultural techniques and water-intensive crops such as sugar cane spread throughout the land. Rich entrepreneurs monopo-lized sugar cane and the production of sugar crystals, as it required heavy investment in land, irrigation systems, and infrastructure, which led to the development of the first colonial agro-industry. Also, the production of wheaten bread, exclusively for Spanish consumption, became a strategic security concern for the Spaniards, who denied ownership of water-driven grinders to Indians and blacks (Musset, 1991: 300–1).

The replacement of the *encomienda*[10] by *hacienda* exploitation from the early seventeenth century onwards also boosted the monopoliza-tion of land and water. In order to counteract the negative effects of the frequent climatic variations on agricultural production, the *hacien-das* resorted to extensive farming, which led the landowners to monop-olize 'the greatest possible variety of land (irrigated or seasonal arable land and pastures) and of natural resources (rivers, springs, woodlands, and quarries)' (Florescano, 1984: 175). This expansionist strategy led to permanent confrontations with the indigenous communities and other actors. By the eighteenth century, when most land suitable for farming had been appropriated, the struggles for territorial expansion in the basin shifted to the reclamation of the lakeside (later also the lakebed) with the object of transforming it into farmlands. According to the official records, the authorities blamed both Spanish ranch owners and Indian communities for the desiccation of the lakes, and for creating wealthy country estates at the expense of the Crown (Rojas, 1974: 56).

Another significant example of the expansion of productive water use was in silver production, as the most efficient ore refineries (*hacien-das de minas*) used water-powered mill systems. Waterpower was a vital technological advantage as it allowed duplicating the volume of pro-duction and increasing the productivity of labour as much as five times in comparison with animal-powered systems. However, as water was a scarce resource in much of New Spain, only one third of the about 370 ore refineries that existed by the early seventeenth century were water driven mills, while horses or mules drove the rest (Bakewell, 1984: 114–15).

Underpinning much of these innovations in the water sector was the influence of the military engineers appointed by the Crown to help in the territorial conquest through the design and building of public works (Moncada Maya, 1991: 337–49). In particular, they would play a crucial role in the construction of *El Desagüe* (The Drain), the master colonial water work that became the hallmark of post-Aztec water technology.

The drain of the Basin

The design and excavation of a master canal for draining the closed basin and protecting the city from flooding is considered to have been the 'biggest scientific-technological challenge' faced by the viceregal authorities (Moncada Maya, 1991: 341). This project led, in the long run, to the desiccation of the lake system and, consequently, to the drastic transformation of the basin's environment and hydrologic cycle, with far-reaching ecological and social impacts. Figure 2.1 shows different stages of the desiccation process from the sixteenth to the twentieth century.

In many aspects, El Desagüe constitutes a sound example of technological innovation in the colonial period. Although drainage canals were not new either for Spaniards or Indians, the about six and half kilometre-long tunnel that formed part of the project had no immediate precedents in the pre-Columbian or European water traditions either (Hoberman, 1980: 393). Works began in 1607 under the direction of the German cosmographer and water expert Heinrich Martin, known in Mexico as Enrico Martínez, with the excavation of a 15 kilometre-long canal connecting the Cuautitlán River in the Basin of Mexico with the Tula River. This first stage was completed in eleven months using an estimated workforce of 4700 Indians, about 15 per cent of the adult male population of the basin (ibid: 392). In the first four years, about 130,000 men and over 3000 women from the indigenous population had been allocated to the excavation works (Gurría Lacroix, 1978: 95). This venture is perhaps the clearest expression of the antithetic approaches to nature, and water in particular, characterizing Indians and Spaniards. Moreover, the building of El Desagüe was marred by confrontations at different levels, not only between water

54

Figure 2.1   The process of desiccation in the Basin of Mexico (1500–1990)

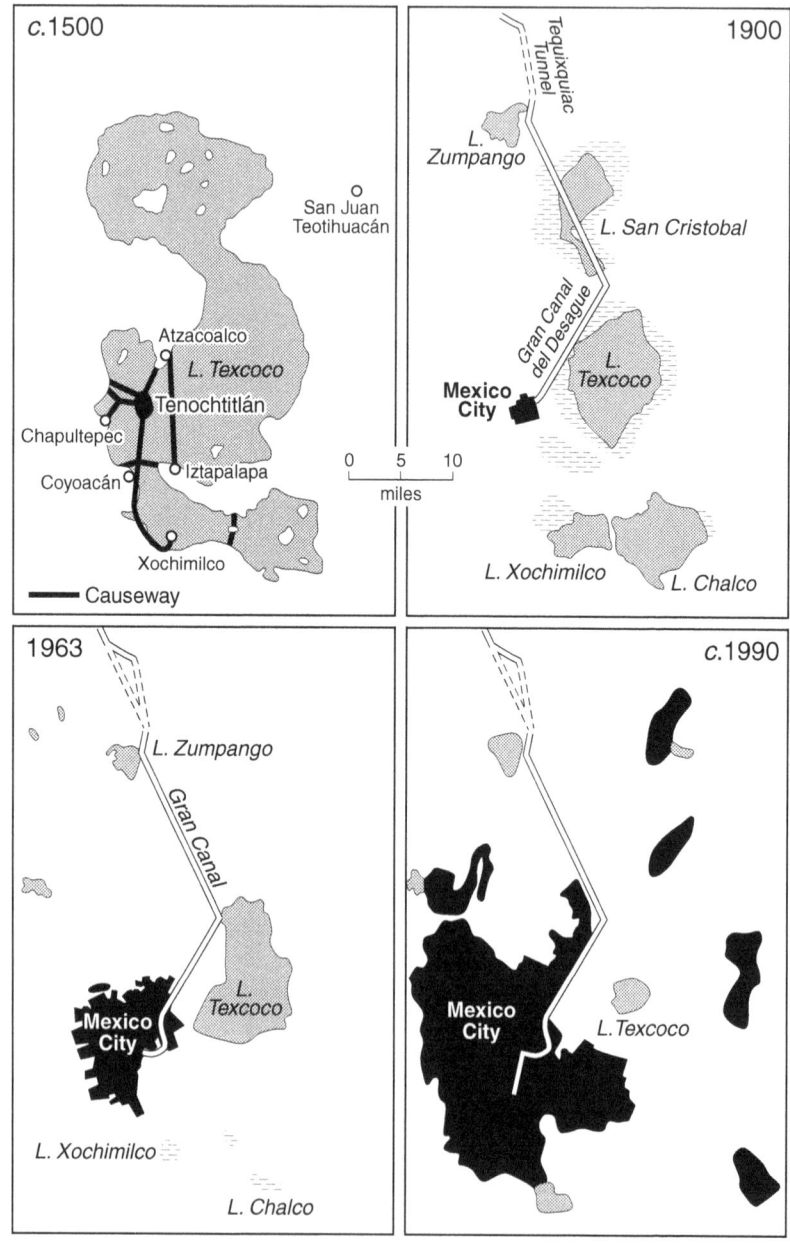

Source: Fox (1965: 524), with permission of the American Geographical Society from its *Geographical Review*. Prepared by David Sansom, University of Oxford.

experts competing with alternative projects, but also between experts and functionaries, between the Crown and the colonial authorities, and of course between whites and Indians.[11]

More than anything else, El Desagüe irreversibly shifted the uneven balance between the indigenous and colonial socio-ecological regimes in favour of the latter. As observed by Alexander von Humboldt, 'in all [colonial] waterworks in the Basin of Mexico water has been considered as an enemy which it is necessary to defend against' (Humboldt, 1811: 230). This statement was later restated by Gibson, who argued that the Spaniards never adapted to the lacustrine environment and all their efforts were directed at replacing canals by roads, canoes by vehicular traffic and mule trains, and draining away the annoying lake system (Gibson, 1964: 8; Simpson, 1963: 324–6). However, although Gibson's judgement might seem valid in the light of the outcome, it must be pointed out that the desiccation plan was not supported unanimously by the Spanish authorities and experts, and in fact there were alternative projects envisaging a different outcome.

For instance, after the 1555 flooding of Mexico City, the Spaniard Francisco Gudiel advanced a project for diverting some rivers and partially draining the lakes, but also considering the conservation of the lakes and canals for transportation and irrigation. Likewise, a 1616 Royal Decree stated that to protect the city from floods it was not necessary to drain the lakes completely and provided for conservation measures to ensure adequate water levels in the lakes for navigation and other uses (Gurría Lacroix, 1978: 48–56, 100–1). This royal project was probably influenced by the Dutch engineer Adrian Boot, who arrived in New Spain in 1614. He discounted the utility of Martínez's tunnel and proposed instead a system inspired by the inland dykes used in The Netherlands. In his view, water levels in the lake system could be controlled by sluices and wind-driven drainage pumps, complemented by a crane mechanism to lift the canoes when the rainy season made it impossible to open the floodgates, and the use of scoop dredges for controlling the sedimentation at the foot of the dykes. In addition, Boot anticipated the problem of subsidence that would affect the city's foundations in the case of a complete drainage of the lakes (Hoberman, 1980: 400–3). Although Boot's model had its own drawbacks, his project illustrates the sophistication of the technical debates of the time and the antithetic positions in the technological drama over the control of water in the basin, which could not by any means be reduced to a mere confrontation between Indians and Spaniards. In the long term, however, those struggling for the preservation of the lake system were defeated.

Nevertheless, the radical transformation of the basin's waterscape brought about by El Desagüe was not just the outcome of a technical debate between European water experts, but it also involved protracted confrontations in the socio-economic, legal, political and cultural dimensions. Let us consider, for instance, the transformations in the socio-spatial organization of the basin. The Spaniards carried out a reconfiguration of the urban space but kept in place the basic elements of the lake-centred urbanization characteristic of the Indian settlement. Thus, the *cabeceras* [head towns], which were the main colonial instrument for the political and economic reorganization of the city, were concentrated in the lakeside according to the indigenous tradition. This determined not only 'the distribution and density of populations, but [also] the administrative networks and local economies of capital and subordinate towns'. The impact of the desiccation process on the indigenous population was irreversible, leading to the decline and even abandonment of important towns and destroying the environmental, socio-economic, political, and cultural foundations of the indigenous society (Gibson, 1964: 45, 366–7; Horn, 1997: Ch. 1). However, as shown in later chapters, this process was permanently contested through long-lasting struggles, as the Indians tried to defend and even recover their lost territories to the extent that an important share of the indigenous population was still 'living from the lakes' in the late nineteenth century when the last traces of the lake system were finally drained away (Rojas, 1974: 54; Musset, 1991: 369; Tortolero, 1994: 385–429).

Water syncretism and colonial domination

With hindsight, the confrontation between the antithetical approaches of Spaniards and Indians to nature, and to water in particular, underpinned a complex and dynamic process of socio-technological synthesis that could be termed the *water syncretism*[12] of the colonial period. This was a long-term process in which the indigenous values, meanings, uses, techniques, knowledge, and artefacts related to water, together with the social practices and institutions formed around its control and management, intertwined with the Spanish water universe in a process that can be termed syncretistic, and whose largely unplanned outcomes can be called syncretic. However, the process took the form of a 'technological drama' – to borrow Pfaffenberger's expression – as the syncretistic forces operated within a politicized framework of contested technological domination (Pfaffenberger, 1992: 505).

Summing up, in the long period from the Conquest to the late oligarchic colonial order, the Basin of Mexico underwent critical transformations in which the social struggle for the control and management of water was a crucial factor. The environmental and ecological processes that resulted in the complete alteration of the basin's waterscape during this period were interwoven with socio-economic, political, and cultural transformations. As shown in later chapters, this meant the break-up of the ancient Indian relations of property and production, beliefs, institutions and the whole indigenous cultural framework, but also their transformation and incorporation into the colonial world of social relations and institutions. In spite of the Indians' resistance, radical transformations took place not only in the forms of human control over the physical environment but also, and more importantly, in the forms of social control over inter-human processes.

After Independence

Although most of the nineteenth century after Independence (1821) is widely considered a stagnant period in the basin's development, in particular concerning urban infrastructure, the water sector was to some extent an exception. An important reason for this was that water became a crucial factor of production in the industrial development of the time, and the increased demand prompted the development of the basin's aquifers and an increasing dependence of the city on underground water which also accelerated the process of environmental transformation. Moreover, the ever-present need for flood protection continued to be a major challenge for the metropolitan authorities and a source of grievance and social conflict.

Regarding urban water supply, the colonial systems remained the sole sources until the late 1840s when the first wells were drilled, and by the late 1880s underground water became the most important source. However, the impact of the proliferation of artesian wells on the basin's hydrogeology was dramatic, dewatering and depressuring subsurface water systems, and contributing to the process of soil subsidence. As a result, by the mid-1890s Mexico City was sinking at an average speed of five centimetres per year (NAS, 1995: Ch. 3).

In connection with flood control, shortly after independence El Desagüe regained the status of top priority. In a report presented to the National Congress in 1823, Lucas Alamán, the Minister of Home Affairs and Foreign Relations also responsible for public works, addressed the state of abandonment of the water work and pointed out the need for 'scientific knowledge, constant vigilance, continuous application, and incessant work' to protect the city from its everlasting hydrogeological fate (Lemoine Villicaña, 1978: 26–7). Simultaneously, José María Luis Mora, who would later play a crucial political role in the liberal reforms and in the institutionalization of citizenship rights, was ordered by the Provincial Council to prepare a report on the hydrological situation. The concern of the leading political figures of the time was not only rhetorical, and in 1831 Alamán became personally engaged in the restart of the drainage works. However, overall, the development of waterworks – and of public infrastructure at large – was weak and discontinuous during much of the nineteenth century, largely as a result of the turbulent episodes affecting Mexico, including the 1832 Civil War, the 1847–53 wars with the United States, and the French occupation of 1862–6. Unsurprisingly, the state of abandonment of El Desagüe and the advanced ecological depletion of the basin caused by deforestation and desiccation of the lakes were the recurring themes of European travellers of the period (ibid: 26–39).

Nevertheless, El Desagüe and the need for an integrated approach to the basin's hydrological problems did receive attention from the authorities even during the military conflicts. For instance, during the 1847 US invasion of Mexico City, the Federal District commissioned two water experts, the US military engineer Lieutenant M. L. Smith, and the Mexican engineer Francisco de Garay, to elaborate a water plan for the basin. Later on, as a result of the 1856 flooding, Smith and Garay's work inspired a new project that was never implemented owing to the unstable political situation. The 1865 flooding during the French occupation reawakened the debate, and Emperor Maximilian took some actions like naming Garay General Director of El Desagüe and sending Engineer Miguel Iglesias on a mission to bring modern machinery from Europe (diggers, traction engines and dredges). The works started in 1866 and continued well into the Restored Republic (1867–76), but were suspended again in 1873 (ibid: 51–61). It was not until the Porfiriato (1884–1911), when foreign capital began to participate on a scale never seen before in the country, that the project was completed.

The Porfirian modernization

The ongoing transformation in the interrelations between humans and the aquatic environment of the basin reached a new peak during the

Porfiriato. In this regard, the impact of the Porfirian modernization on the basin's hydrogeology was intimately bound up with the social processes that eventually led to the Mexican Revolution (1910–17). In the 1880s, the government laid the basis for the promotion of private, in particular foreign, investment, in different sectors of the economy. The Congress passed a Federal Water Law in 1888, which complemented a legislation package on transport, mining, agriculture and external trade. As a result, foreign investors were attracted by the prospects of the water industry, which led to a substantial technological innovation in the production of energy, with the development of the Mexican hydroelectric sector and the early twentieth-century mining boom. In addition, irrigation agriculture became an obsession in this period, leading to the proliferation of private companies specializing in irrigation and colonization, which many in the Porfirian elite believed would be the drivers of progress, liberal democracy and citizenship.

Nevertheless, the single main transformation of the basin during the Porfiriato was undoubtedly linked to the completion of El Desagüe, which became the symbol par excellence of the regime's modernizing philosophy. In 1881, the Congress authorized the concession of El Desagüe to a private company, including the completion of the work, the canalization of navigable rivers, and the building of sanitation works, in exchange for property rights over the land to be reclaimed from the lakes. Although the venture collapsed, it set an important precedent for more successful attempts such as the desiccation of Lake Chalco by the hacendado Iñigo Noriega in the 1890s (Lemoine Villicaña, 1978: 92).

The successful completion of El Desagüe was based on Smith and Garay's project, modified and implemented by Garay's rival, Engineer Luis Espinosa. Provided with steam-powered dredges, this time the colossal waterwork was completed and finally inaugurated in March 1900 by the British contractor Weetman Dickinson Pearson (Lord Cowdray).[13] However, despite this technological achievement, the protection of Mexico City against floods was not assured. More importantly, the technological modernization had also a dark side, as the transformations operated by the regime's water policies were inextricably linked with the ensuing process of violent social change.

The construction of large-scale waterworks during the Porfiriato triggered numerous conflicts, and the region of Chalco became one of the most important battlefields. Chalco was dominated by the economic activity of about 30 haciendas and 15 ranches, which were characterized by their innovative practices and modern agroproduction techniques (Tortolero, 1994: 389–410; Tutino, 1988). The indigenous population, however reduced in number and subordinated to the global dynamic, was still living from the lakes, some of them as hunters and fishers, but also practising chinampa agriculture and other activities of the lacustrine economy (Tortolero, 1994: 387–95; Musset, 1991: 261–3; Gibson, 1964: 340–3; Payno, 1983). In this context, in 1894 Iñigo Noriega, a leading Chalco hacendado, applied for permission to drain completely Lake Chalco and reclaim the fertile lakebed. Owner of the Xico hacienda, which had rights over Lake Chalco, and close friend of Porfirio Díaz, Noriega achieved his purpose in 1895 despite the opposition of leading water experts to the desiccation project. The issue divided water experts and other professionals. The group favouring the desiccation argued that the water body was not a lake but a fetid marsh, a notion dating back to colonial times and revived time after time by the Noriegas, government officers, health experts, and influential engineers such as Roberto Gayol. Those opposing the project, such as Engineer Luis Espinosa, defended 'the lake', warned against the venture's environmental dangers, and blamed the hacendados for subordinating the public good to their own private interests (Tortolero, 1994: 414; 1996: 4, 5).

With hindsight, these events were deeply rooted in the old confrontation between the lake-based civilization and its provisional defenders, the Francisco Gudiels, Adrian Boots, or Francisco Espinosas of each period, and the rival model embodied first in the hacienda system and in the colonial urban and industrial development, and later in the fast modernization process of the late nineteenth century. The political arbitrariness of the Porfiriato, backed by the opinion of water experts in favour of the desiccation, decided the fate of Lake Chalco and thus the result of the last battle for the lakes.

The process of ecological transformation could not have been faster and more dramatic, and at the turn of the century the lake had disappeared together with the last traces of the ancient lacustrine civilization. It was replaced by a new space delineated by railways, irrigation works, agro-industries, and water-consuming paper and textile factories (Tortolero, 1994: 410–25). Notoriously, the Chalco indigenous peasants were among the most active Zapatista revolutionaries, who played a central part in bringing the Porfirian regime to an end in 1911 (Knight, 1990: 104, 338; Tutino, 1988).

Post-Revolution trends

The drastic transformation of the basin's hydrogeology did not stop with the Mexican Revolution (1910–17), but rather was accelerated by the main driving forces of post-Revolution development: urbanization and industrialization. Emerging forms of water consumption contributed to diversify the structure of the water services, while the growing water demand for domestic and industrial uses, for irrigation, and for recreational purposes also led to increasing amounts of wastewater for disposal. Furthermore, despite the completion of El Desagüe, the threat of flooding continued, ant it actually worsened with the progress of soil subsidence and the urbanization of the dried lakebeds.

The spatial segregation that had characterized the city since pre-Columbian times was deepened by the early twentieth-century urbanization process, which has been described as a two-sided development. On the one hand, urban growth to the north and to the east of the city, first through the chaotic creation of the 'invasion colonies' by marginal sectors under the control of urban speculators and, since the late 1930s, through the proliferation of the 'proletarian colonies'. On the other hand, there was a resettlement of high and middle sectors organized by specialist private companies. The overall result was the spatial expansion of the city, which grew from some 30 square kilometres in 1926 to about 140 square kilometres by 1939, and the consolidation of structural patterns of differential access and consumption of water services. In the process, the metropolitan population increased by 36.6 per cent from 1900 to 1910, then 30.6 per cent by 1921, and a staggering 67.2 per cent by 1930, which had a dramatic impact on the distribution of available water (Instituto Nacional de Estadística, Geografía e Informática (INEGI), 1990; Fernández, 1990: 54–6; Torregrosa Armentia, 1990). Although from 1910 to 1930 the city's water supply increased from 1700 litres up to 3100 litres per second, average daily per capita distribution fell from 309 litres to 260 litres. Also, during the 1910s and 1920s the city was affected by shortages and regular interruptions of the service, which included the virtual collapse of the water supply in 1922 triggering public discontent in a context of mounting social and political conflicts (Fernández, 1990: 7–16). The process of industrialization became a main driver of this metropolitan expansion. While in 1930 Mexico City housed fewer than 5 per cent of the country's industrial plants and accounted for 28.5 per cent of the country's Gross Manufacturing Product (GMP), by 1950 the city had concentrated almost 20 per cent of the industrial units and 40 per cent of the national GMP (Torregrosa Armentia, 1990: 7b). These trends would have a significant impact on water resources and services accelerating the ongoing environmental transformations.

In this connection, in a 1925 report to the Mexican Society of Engineers and Architects, Roberto Gayol presented the results of surveys showing that the city was sinking, and that this phenomenon was probably linked to the desiccation of the lake system. Also, the related hypothesis linking land subsidence and aquifer exploitation received further support from evidence that water tables were being depleted to the extent that the natural springs that had provided drinking water for centuries had dried up in the 1930s. The response was the intensification in the exploitation of the aquifer with the use of deeper wells of 100 to 200 metre depths, which is blamed for the acceleration of soil subsidence that between 1948 and 1953 reached a speed of 46 centimetres per year in the most affected areas. Over time, the awareness of these critical changes in the face of increasing water demand prompted the decision to import water resources from outside the basin, and use injection wells for the artificial recharge of ground water reservoirs with storm water runoff (NAS, 1995: Ch. 3).

As shown in later chapters, the drive to secure water sources from outside the basin considerably increased the pace of environmental change, extending the impact of metropolitan water use well beyond its borders (Ezcurra *et al.*, 1999: 143–9). Within the basin, perhaps the most dramatic expression of the environmental crisis was the change in the relative position of Lake Texcoco, which in the past had been the lower point within the lake system. The bed of the lake that in 1900 was about three metres below the average level of the city reached a height of two metres above the city's level by 1974 (NAS, 1995: Ch. 3). These transformations affected the urban infrastructure and posed enormous problems for the functioning of the city's drainage. When El Desagüe was inaugurated in 1900 the water flowed by gravity out of the basin, but owing to the subsidence process by 1950 it was needed to build dykes for controlling storm water flows and a pumping system to raise water from the city up to the level of the canal (Fox, 1965: 532–40).

The current context

Since the 1950s the MCMA became one of the biggest and fastest growing cities in the world, although this trend has slowed down since the 1980s. In the early 1990s, water consumption in the MCMA was estimated at about 65 cubic metres per second, 72 per cent of which consisted of groundwater pumped from the aquifer through more than 1000 wells. In this regard, systematic controls on ground water tables since the early 1980s have shown that the annual rate of depletion reaches one and a half metres in some areas, while between 1986 and

1992 the total decline of water tables in the most affected areas reached between six and ten metres (NAS, 1995: Ch. 3). Surface waters from the basin account only for two per cent of the total supply, while another 26 per cent is imported from the Cutzamala and Lerma basins. The Cutzamala system alone provides 22 per cent of the water supply, which requires the use of a highly sophisticated and energy-intensive pumping system to cover a distance of over 160 kilometres and a total elevation of 1366 metres (CNA, 1997).

Water imports have always been a bone of contention between the metropolis and the surrounding areas and they continue to fuel social and political struggles. These contests reflect not only the conflict of interests between the metropolis and affected users in the water-exporting regions, but also entail a confrontation between different models of water management. In particular, projects like Cutzamala have historically faced the opposition of water experts who have argued against further trans-basin water transfers and rather favour the implementation of demand management policies to reduce wastage, rationalize consumption, and implement water reuse and conservation. For instance, one of the key arguments put forward by the critics is that the amount of water lost in the MCMA by leakage and other deficiencies is estimated at 18 cubic metres per second,[14] offsetting the volumes imported from outside the basin, and suggesting the urgent need for the implementation of a leakage and losses reduction programme rather than further water imports. Nevertheless, the debate continues and supply-side solutions, including plans for additional inter-basin transfers, continue to rank high in the agenda of the water authorities. Among other projects under consideration are increasing the volume imported from Cutzamala and tapping additional water resources from the Temascaltepec, Amacuzac, Tecolutla, Tula, Oriental and Libres river basins (Ezcurra *et al.*, 1999: 145).

The other side of the coin is the control and disposal of wastewater and stormwater. Currently, the MCMA produces over 44 cubic metres of wastewater per second in the dry season, most of it untreated municipal wastewater. In the rainy season, however, the area is affected by many intense storms of short duration, which can produce up to 70 millimetres in a few hours. The drainage system, which has been designed to carry 200 cubic metres per second, collects both wastewater and stormwater for the whole MCMA, and empties out of the basin to the north. The network is over 10,000 kilometres long, and is served by 68 pumping stations, dams, lagoons, and regulatory tanks for flow control, 111 kilometres of open canals, 42 kilometres of rivers, and 118 kilometres of underground collectors and tunnels (NAS, 1995: Ch. 4).

Around 10 per cent of wastewater is treated and reused for groundwater recharge, agricultural irrigation and urban-landscape irrigation, while the sludge produced is redirected untreated to the sewer system. The bulk of the wastewater flow is drained away from the basin and used for irrigation in the Mezquital area, state of Hidalgo, and then drained into the Panuco River that empties in the Gulf of Mexico. Although important projects have been implemented, like the construction of a lagoon wastewater treatment system, the reclamation of stormwater using the dry bed of former Lake Texcoco, and the use of reclaimed municipal wastewater to improve the ecosystem of Xochimilco, wastewater treatment is still one of the most important problems to be addressed owing to the negative public health impact of untreated effluents. As already discussed, water-related diseases continue to be one of the main factors of morbi-mortality in the MCMA, especially among children. Moreover, another significant environmental impact produced by the basin's water inflows and outflows is the energy cost. It has been estimated that water imports consume about 70 per cent of the energy used to run the MCMA's water systems, which in the 1990s had an approximate cost of US$ 900,000 per day. The total daily energy input, estimated at around 370 MW, is equivalent to over 50 per cent of the total energy output of the thermoelectric generator that supplies energy to the MCMA (Ezcurra *et al.*, 1999: 146–7).

Concerning the delivery of domestic water services, during the period covered by this study 94 per cent of dwellings in the MCMA had some kind of access to water services. These official figures, however, hide two crucial facts: first, they include every kind of access to water, not only in-house piped water; and, second, the level of coverage is very uneven between municipalities, *delegaciones*, and colonias. Thus, the proportion of households enjoying in-house piped water was 74 per cent in the Federal District and 52 per cent in the metropolitan jurisdiction of the State of Mexico, while the percentage of houses with no access to water was 3 per cent in the Federal District and about 9 per cent in the conurbated municipalities considered in the study. In addition, the average per capita water consumption in the Federal District was 58.6 per cent higher than in the State of Mexico, though this figure does not take into account the fact that in the State of Mexico there exist an important number of uncontrolled private wells (NAS, 1995: Ch. 4).[15]

The level of coverage varies greatly between jurisdictions. In the Federal District, the southern area composed by the *delegaciones* of Tláhuac, Tlalpan, Xochimilco, and Milpa Alta is the most negatively affected. Similarly, in the adjacent municipalities, the eastern area encompassing Chimalhuacán, Ixtapaluca, and Chalco is the worst serviced. In Chalco, about 70 per cent of housing units were reported without any access to drinking water in the 1990 Census. However, it is worth highlighting that while in the Federal District the rate of improvement in the delivery of water supply and sewer systems has been relatively constant, in the State of Mexico there was stagnation and even decline during the period of the study and the percentage of houses connected to the piped networks fell sharply between 1980 and 1990 (NAS, 1995: Ch. 4). These differential levels of coverage and quality of service have prompted different solutions, including public delivery of water supplied by water tanks or private water vending, the latter being much more expensive than the networked supply and largely uncontrolled.

In this connection, during the whole post-Revolution period population growth has run ahead of the expansion of water services delivery. However, population increase has not been a homogeneous process and, for instance, in the north central areas of the Federal District the rate has slowed down and even declined since the 1970s. In contrast, some *delegaciones* in the Federal District and part of the conurbated municipalities have experienced rapid population growth and urban expansion. Much of this is the result of immigration flows that have taken the form of illegal settlements, *ciudades perdidas*[16] in the local jargon, where provision of urban services has been long delayed and considered extremely difficult and expensive. Although the absolute number of houses with access to water services has been steadily increased in the MCMA since the 1970s, population growth and urban expansion are still ahead in the race. Last but not least, despite the enormous and recurrent efforts, large areas of the MCMA suffer either from regular flooding during the rainy season or from *tolvaneras* [dust storms] in the dry season. This is particularly acute in the settlements located in the former lakebeds and riversides, where people are more exposed to the effect of these extreme events.

Needless to say, the high uncertainty facing millions of human beings in relation to water management in the MCMA, whether in connection with disputes over water rights, with problems of access and poor quality of water and sanitation services, or with the vulnerability of the population vis-á-vis recurring extreme climatic events, have been at the centre of the contemporary social conflicts recorded in the basin.

Concluding remarks

The environmental and ecological changes that have turned the Basin of Mexico from the water-rich landscape celebrated by Huitzilopochtli into the current water-stressed socio-territorial configuration have been largely driven by and closely interwoven with processes of socio-economic, political, and cultural change. As shown here and further illustrated in forthcoming chapters, these processes have been punctuated by multidimensional social struggles over the control and management of water resources and derived public services. Despite the impressive advances in scientific knowledge in the fields of water science, technology, and management achieved since the nineteenth century, despite the accurate diagnoses made by water experts over the years about the causes underpinning the MCMA's environmental crises, and despite the increasing ascendancy and influence of water experts in the power structures (as described in later chapters), the threat of different forms of water uncertainty and water-related hazards and dangers continues to haunt the basin's human settlements.

Undeniably, hydrogeological constraints have continuously posed a formidable obstacle to water control in the Basin of Mexico. However, the exploration of the socio-historical processes that led to the current situation helps to understand that we are not confronted here with the workings of physical–natural forces alone but rather with a particular configuration in which human-driven processes have been largely responsible for irreversible environmental, ecological, and social transformations.

In this chapter, we have explored some aspects of the first dimension suggested by Norbert Elias' 'triad of controls', processes leading to the establishment of human control over non-human processes. However, our central interest in this study concerns mainly the second dimension suggested by Elias, that is, processes leading to the establishment of human control over inter-human processes. In the next chapter we explore how these two dimensions have been interwoven in the Basin of Mexico.

3
Water and Power in the Basin of Mexico

'[The] basic tissue resulting from many single plans and actions of men can give rise to changes and patterns that no individual person has planned or created. From this interdependence of people arises an order *sui generis*, an order more compelling than the will and reason of the individual people composing it. It is this order of interweaving human impulses and strivings, this social order, which determines the course of historical change; it underlies the civilizing process.'—**Norbert Elias**, *The Civilizing Process*

We have just explored the long-term processes that irreversibly changed the Basin of Mexico's hydrogeology and waterscape. In this chapter we examine this transformation from a different angle, elaborating on Norbert Elias' suggestion that processes of human control over the non-human world are inextricably interwoven with processes leading to the formation and reproduction of forms of social control at the inter-human level (Elias, 1978: 156–7; 1994: 443–56). We pay particular attention here to the process of state formation in Mexico, looking at how human activities aimed at controlling and managing water were inextricably linked to processes of social and political control. This chapter is also organized chronologically and considers (a) the evolution of power configurations in relation to water control (for example, the balance between coercion and cooperation in the interaction between Spaniards and Indians during the colonial period or the changing character of the public–private interface), (b) the social and political influence of water experts (for instance, the role played by specialized water techno-bureaucracies), (c) the crystallization of power structures related to water control (such as in the state apparatus, in the legal system, and so on), and (d) the links between water policy and the development of modern citizenship rights, although we address citizenship in more detail later. In the following discussion 'state' refers sometimes to the state apparatus, in particular to the agencies concerned with the administration of water resources and services. In other places it will direct attention to the power configurations emerging from the activities of water control in Mexico. This approach will help to better understand the interrelations between water struggles and the development of citizenship examined in forthcoming chapters.

Water control and state formation

A widely variegated scholarship has corroborated the thesis that large-scale water management activities such as irrigation and flood control have been a crucial factor in the process of state formation in different civilizations. Thus, in his controversial work on the interrelationship between water control and 'total power', Karl Wittfogel argued that the constellation of water expertise, mass labour control, centralized administration, and despotic rule had been the hallmark of state formation in ancient 'hydraulic societies'. He identified Aztec water politics as a 'semi-complex' case, because the role of water works in keeping territorial and social control had not been as 'compact' in pre-Columbian Mexico as it was, for example, in Sumer (Wittfogel, 1959: 258–9). In turn, Wittfogel joined a long-standing debate on the concept of Asiatic Mode of Production put forward by Marx and Engels,[1] which in turn had been referred to the question of 'Oriental despotism' raised by many previous scholars.[2] In a remarkable passage, Wittfogel stated that:

> Even in its simplest form, agrohydraulic operations necessitate substantial integrative action. In their more elaborate variations, they involve extensive and complex organizational planning. The effective management of these works involves an organizational web which covers either the whole, or at least the dynamic core, of the country's population. In consequence, those who control this network are uniquely prepared to wield supreme political power. No matter whether traditionally nonhydraulic leaders initiated or seized the incipient hydraulic 'apparatus', or whether the masters of this apparatus became the motive force behind all important public functions, there can be no doubt that in all these cases the resulting regime was decisively shaped by the leadership and social control

required by hydraulic agriculture. (Wittfogel, 1959: 26–7; 1956: 152–4)

Wittfogel's theory generated widespread debate and his work is still a landmark for the study of water politics. His generalization of Max Weber's proposition that large-scale water works led to the 'despotic' monopolization of political power in China, India, and Egypt has been disputed both on theoretical and empirical grounds.[3] However, other authors have been persuaded by Wittfogel's argument and developed an ecologically based anthropology – some would say environmentally deterministic – since the early 1950s, mainly in the United States (Worster, 1985: 29–30). In this connection, scholars of ancient Mesoamerican civilizations have also followed Wittfogel's insights, remarkably the Spanish–Mexican anthropologist Angel Palerm (Palerm, 1990; Martínez Saldaña and Palerm Viqueira, 1997).

Although the debate about what type of water problems were more decisive in moulding power relations in pre-colonial times continues, there is little doubt that water control has been one of the most important, if not the most significant, public endeavour in the Basin of Mexico since pre-Columbian times. And there are important reasons why, in certain circumstances, the establishment of human control over water has also been a major factor in shaping the configurations of social and political power. As pointed out by Mark Elvin in relation to water control in China:

The most important of [the requirements posed by water control] is the sustained, or regularly recurring, cooperation of numbers of human beings on a scale that varies greatly, but which at the upper end exceeds that required by any other activity, apart from major warfare. This means that a social and cultural capacity must exist, or be created, and then be sustained, for organizing this cooperation, and also for levying the usually quite considerable resources – financial, material, and administrative – that are needed for water control. A water system, once created, however, constitutes a mortgage on the future use of these resources, since it has to be maintained to preserve the investments, and lives, that depend on it. (Elvin, 1994: 4)[4]

This description captures important elements which can be observed in the Mexican case. In this connection, I have adopted here Norbert Elias' suggestion that the establishment of human control over the physical–natural domain can be analysed as a double-sided process: increases in control, largely intended, have led to increases in dependency, normally unintended (Elias, 1978: 156–7). Of course, this is not an exclusive characteristic of the interactions between humans and water. As pointed out by Johan Goudsblom, the domestication of fire also entailed a tighter regulation of social relations and individual impulses, the establishment of a 'fire regime' involving the development of new social codes and practices, which in turn have been in constant evolution over time (Goudsblom, 1994: 41). As suggested by the evidence examined in the previous chapter, we can also argue that the extension of human control over water in the Basin of Mexico brought about unintended increases in dependency for people upon the need for the regular attention of the water systems, especially for flood control, water supply and the disposal of rain and wastewater. As a result, the ever greater mortgage that Mexicans have to repay collectively in order to maintain life-supporting conditions in the basin is not only economic but also, ecological, social, and political. However, though water control is a source of social and political power, the specific power configurations resulting from the process can take different forms.

In this connection, rather than discussing the degree of coercion or voluntary co-operation involved in water control we rather focus on the formation of new restraints and interdependencies between human beings fostered by the actions directed at the control and management of water. For instance, the approaches and mechanisms of water control change over time owing, among other issues, to the evolving understanding of the functioning of ecosystems or of the interrelations between water management and human health, to the development of new technologies, or to the increasing recognition that essential water services must be universalized as a human right. For instance, when a given society accepts that essential water and sanitation services must be universalized and not treated as a commodity, they have taken a political decision with crucial intra- and intergenerational consequences some of which are certainly unplanned. Not only must these water systems be maintained indefinitely, but they must also be continuously expanded and improved to cover ever growing numbers of users and enhance service quality as required by increasingly stricter standards. In turn, the ensuing transformations are often punctuated by multidimensional social and political struggles, ranging from ecological distribution conflicts over water resources to confrontations over the values and principles that must orient the provision of water and sanitation services.

In this regard, Norbert Elias studied how processes of human control over the non-human domain are enmeshed in the larger macro societal evolution that in the Western world led to the formation of territorial states. He suggested the notion of 'monopoly mechanism' to explain how the process of state formation in Western Europe was driven by the increasing concentration of control over natural resources and human populations through the centralization of the means of violence and taxation by a decreasing number of single rulers. In the earlier phases there was an emergence of 'private monopolies' that over time were gradually transformed into 'public' when the monopoly powers of the feudal monarchs came under the control of a wider spectrum of social classes. These processes were interwoven with the depersonalization and institutionalization of the exercise of power that informed the development of centralized state apparatuses and their consolidation since the eighteenth century (Elias, 1994: 390; Mennell, 1992: 78). Although the Mexican case differs substantially from the European cases studied by Elias, his analytical model is useful for exploring the long-term co-evolution of human control over water and power configurations in Mexico.

Pre-Conquest water politics

As anticipated in Chapter 2, water control was central in the social and political organization of the pre-Columbian settlements. By the late-fifteenth century, the Mexicas controlled a large political and socio-economic conglomerate described in the literature as an empire, a kingdom, a confederation of chiefdoms or tribes, and a state (León-Portilla, 1984: 33; Lameiras, 1986; Burkholder and Johnson, 1994; Conrad and Demarest, 1990). They settled their capital in the twin island cities of Tenochtitlan-Tlatelolco, on land reclaimed from the lakes, and set in motion a fast process of monopolization of land and water (Chevalier, 1963: 185–6).

Although there is no firm consensus about the relative importance of water control for Aztec political and social organization, the evidence suggests that they were closely interrelated. The dominion established by the Tenochtitlan-Tlatelolco elite was largely based on the control of water resources, which they achieved by applying a wide range of tactics including war, despotic imposition, and matrimonial and ethnic alliances (Musset, 1991: 112–16; Durán, 1967: 67–71; Brundage, 1972: 56–70; Palerm, 1990: 256–82, 302–18; Torquemada, 1964: 192–3; Gibson, 1964: 20–1; León-Portilla, 1984: 33; Lameiras, 1986: 265–6,

291–2; Burkholder and Johnson, 1994: 11). Nevertheless, as Musset put it:

> If Mexico was successful in dominating the Valley as a whole, it was because of a war that started around the problem of water control. Therefore, since the earliest stages of the city's urban expansion water has been the paramount expression of its dominion over the neighboring cities. (Musset, 1991: 112–14)

In effect, tensions between the city and its neighbours regarding water resources have been recurrent ever since and today they are still an important source of social and political struggles.

Regarding the link between water control and political power, Wittfogel suggested that the permanent threat of floods could have played a more important role than agro-managerial achievements in the pre-Hispanic urban settlement (Wittfogel, 1959: 18, 27, 165). This hypothesis receives some support from recent historical and archaeological research, which highlighted the importance of large-scale flood-prevention water works in the Aztec capital (León-Portilla, 1984: 16–25). Notwithstanding this, several authors have argued that there were also significant agro-hydraulic achievements that led towards higher levels of political integration and also to important population increases (Katz, 1972: 152–5). Some believe that the need for well-coordinated bureaucratic-administrative institutions for managing irrigation systems must have been a key factor in the formation of Aztec state power. Thus, archaeological evidence prompted Angel Palerm to suggest that on the eve of the Conquest there were four different types of agro-hydraulic organization simultaneously at work in the basin, while most surface waters had already been harnessed. Palerm identified small and large irrigation systems adapted to the different terrains and water sources available, and also two versions of the *chinampa* system: in-land *chinampas* and in-lake *chinampas*, encompassing dams, causeways, freshwater conduits, pools, and artificial swamplands. He argued that these different systems were the object of coordinated management, first in Texcoco, Chalco and Coyoacán, and later in the whole basin, and that the level of co-ordination required for the simultaneous functioning of such systems suggests that there was a strong link between the technical and administrative organization of water control and political integration (Palerm, 1990: 192–5; Levi Lattes, 1991: 126–7; Lameiras, 1986: 358–9).

Water and the 'obedient citizen'

From another angle, the historical evidence shows that the level of coordination required for successful water control in the basin also had strong implications for the intra-human dimension of the process. According to Wittfogel, in despotic 'hydraulic' societies the 'basis of good citizenship' rested on absolute obedience, while state power was based on the reproduction of 'obedient subjects' (Wittfogel, 1959: 149). In this connection, descriptions of the Aztec education system support the view that individuals were trained to become obedient subjects subordinated to the needs of the State. Youngsters were trained to work in teams in the building and maintenance of public works such as digging canals and cleaning the aqueducts through the institution of *telpochcalli*, which was a training ground for commoners and the lower nobility alike. There they were taught the need for virtue and obedience to the State and were cruelly punished in case of infractions (Brundage, 1972: 164–5).

Nevertheless, the evidence suggests that most public works were more likely carried out under coercion, as the Mexica had a well-organized labour system based on the compulsory recruitment of workers known as *coatequitl*. This was the method used by King Ahuitzotl in 1499 to build the Acuecuexco aqueduct, which required a war to expropriate the water resources from the vassal kingdom of Coyoacán (Gibson, 1964: 22; Brundage, 1972: 86, 127). Other public services like urban cleansing or the maintenance of roads, drains, and aqueducts were also organized under strict state control (Ruiz, 1973: 196–8).

Historians like Charles Gibson have perhaps romanticized unpaid compulsory labour among the Aztecs as a social, moral, and spiritual concern, although Gibson has a point when he blamed the Spaniards for manipulating masses of Indian workers by transposing the indigenous labour traditions 'into the economic and physical categories of Europe' (Gibson, 1964: 221). However, most authors adopt a position closer to Wittfogel's and accept that pre-Conquest compulsory forms of labour such as the *coatequitl* were based on military might and political subordination subject to severe control. In fact, Aztecs developed different forms of slavery and forced labour and it has been estimated that about 30 per cent of the population of central Mexico had been reduced to the status of forced labourers by the early sixteenth century, whereas slaves numbered perhaps 5 per cent (León-Portilla, 1984: 17–27; Burkholder and Johnson, 1994: 8–11; Brundage, 1972: 219–20).

From another perspective, although subordination and obedience played an important part in maintaining Aztec power configurations, this same structure of domination simultaneously elicited centrifugal forces. Thus, the achievement of the 'Pax Azteca', to borrow Katz's words, and the development of a great metropolis such as Mexico-Tenochtitlan, were obtained at the expense of fiercely subjugating powerful rival chiefdoms whose alienation finally became a key factor in the fall of the Aztec regime (Katz, 1972: 194).

The colonial development

The Spanish colonization substantially increased the competition for water resources with the introduction of water-consuming industries, rising stock, and new irrigation practices, which fuelled significant alterations in the power configurations that evolved around water control in the basin. The pervasive intrusion of Spaniards into Indian territories caused innumerable legal disputes over the definition of land and water rights, which in the long run led to the legalization of private and corporate monopolies over these resources. Also, the flood-prone conditions of Mexico City demanded permanent attention from the colonial authorities, prompting the creation of a state bureaucracy specialized in flood control works which required huge financial investments and had a colossal human and ecological cost.

It is worth recalling that shortly before the Conquest Spain had experienced a process of centralization of political power in the hands of the Crown in which the struggle for water control was paramount. In fact, public control over water in Spain would not be formally established until 1866, when the first national water law came into force (Pérez Picazo and Lemeunier, 1990: 35). Contrarily, in Spanish America Crown property over water, land, pastures, wood, and mineral wealth was enforced from the outset. Therefore, in the colonial possessions the Crown started as the single monopolist of a huge empire, whose territorial control was permanently challenged by competitors, either private such as the encomenderos and later the hacendados, or corporate, such as the native indigenous communities and the religious orders. In a development not dissimilar to the Iberian experience, the control of water became a crucial battlefield in the struggle between private and public monopolists, which has not yet been entirely played out.

However, Crown policy often contradicted the formal model of royal monopoly and favoured the process of private monopolization by granting land and water rights to foster the colonization of poorly controlled territories. Also, often the construction and maintenance of infrastructure works in urban centres was entrusted to private parties and religious orders in order to avoid the financial and bureaucratic burdens involved. This was the case in the city of Puebla, where the municipal authorities relied on private initiatives to build conduits, gutters and other installations, to open the service later to the population in the name of public interest (Lipsett-Rivera, 1993: 28–9). Contrastingly, in other colonial cities such as Santiago de Guatemala, known today as Antigua, the provision of water services was a state undertaking. The Audiencia assumed responsibility for the works, and the municipal authorities were entrusted with the ownership and control of the water system (Webre, 1990: 67–74). In Mexico City, the viceregal capital, water operations and control became a major state concern and an object of struggle between the concerned actors, the Crown, the local government, private entrepreneurs, the religious orders, and the indigenous communities.

The politics of flood control

As described earlier, the disposal of stormwater during the rainy season has posed a substantial technological and economic challenge to the basin's settlements. Flood control became often an overriding consideration during the colonial period because large-scale floods devastated the city on a regular basis, like in 1629 when most Spanish families abandoned Mexico City and resettled in safer places like Puebla (Departamento del Distrito Federal-Secretaría de Obras y Servicias (DDF-SOS), 1975, Vol. 1: 219). Unsurprisingly, the construction of El Desagüe became a top security matter in Mexico City and the total cost of this work during the colonial period (1607–1789) almost doubled the amount spent between 1536 and 1813 in building the city's cathedral (Hoberman, 1980: 392).

The political centrality of El Desagüe was expressed in the changing alliances and recurring conflicts between the Crown, the Viceroy, the city authorities, the merchant guild, the monastic orders, and influential citizens. A major bone of contention was that the costs of this water work had to be met with local funding from taxes and other levies because all colonial revenues were sent to the metropolis with the exception of funds destined for local defence and administration, which may help to explain why the construction of El Desagüe lasted almost three centuries. Creoles opposed the project because it meant higher taxes and the mobilization of their black slaves and Indian workers, while the non-whites were also against working in El Desagüe because of the mortal risks involved. Colonial water works were built with compulsory labour recruited mainly among the Indians, and according to some estimates in the early seventeenth century at least 15 per cent of the Basin's Indian male population was destined to work in El Desagüe (Hoberman, 1980: 392). The Spaniards had adopted the *coatequitl* system and given it legal sanction through the institution of *repartimiento*, which consisted of forced, though paid, labour. *Repartimiento* became widespread in the second half of the sixteenth century when it replaced the *encomienda* system of unpaid labour, and was the main recruitment source for public works like El Desagüe (DDF-SOS, 1975, Vol. 1: 220). According to different testimonies, from 1628 to 1634 between 3000 and 7000 Indians were working simultaneously in the construction of El Desagüe at any given moment, subject to inhuman working conditions from which many died (Gibson, 1964; Hoberman, 1980: 392).

Unsurprisingly, according to von Humboldt the Indians developed a profound hatred for El Desagüe and regarded water works in general as a public calamity. It has also been argued that forced labour for this water work may have played a role in the decrease of the basin's population, as suggested by the fact that over time the Spaniards had to recruit Indian workers from ever more distant communities (Connolly, 1991, Vol. 1: 27). According to the traveller Thomas Gage, from about 100 indigenous towns located in the lakeside at the time of the Conquest, by 1635 there were only about 30 left and none of them had more than 500 families (Thompson, 1958: 62). Many Indians died in the works and many others fled in order to avoid being recruited, while others organized recurrent insurrections against the colonists (Boyer, 1975: 33–44). Although *repartimiento* was abolished for agricultural labour in 1663, it was still being used in El Desagüe during the late eighteenth century. However, by the early nineteenth century the authorities were replacing Indian workers with prisoners due to, in the words of the Superintendent, 'the growing horror that the works had caused in the Indians and had been transmitted from their ancestors' (Connolly, 1991, Vol. 1: 30).

The other significant opposition to El Desagüe came from members of the Creole elite, who opposed tax-based funding of the works and the recruitment of their free workers and slaves, which ruined their economic activities. For example, early sixteenth-century reports showed that in Cuautitlán alone there were about 150 abandoned haciendas because their workers had been recruited for El Desagüe (Boyer, 1975: 46). Creoles also responded with civil disobedience to the taxes imposed from the very start of the works in 1607 by creating black markets and deploying similar actions of resistance (Musset, 1991: 353–5; Gurría Lacroix, 1978: 159–60).

Finally, there was much infighting within the colonial elite owing to contradictions between the Crown that, formally at least, tried to protect the Indians and the lacustrine ecosystem, and the colonial authorities, which in turn were themselves divided in many respects such as in the selection of flood control technologies. In the end, the long-term process leading to the completion of El Desagüe brought about not only a radical transformation of the basin's ecosystems, but also erased the last traces of the indigenous socio-ecological regime.

Water expertise, institutions and political power

Although the fragmented structure of colonial rule slowed down the centralizing trends in water legislation, policy and management, over time the strategic activities of maintaining water infrastructure and security became institutionalized. The technical and organizational requirements of these activities prompted the development of specialized water experts, functionaries, and skilled and semi-skilled workers. In turn, these processes were intertwined with the changing configurations of power that by the late colonial period had transformed the basin into an oligarchic social order controlled by the religious and secular factions of the small elite of Creole citizens.

As discussed in Chapter 5, from the beginning water legislation in New Spain asserted the public monopoly over water and other natural resources. This principle was incorporated in a 1541 ruling by King Charles V and later included in the recompilation of Spanish-American Law completed in 1681, commonly known as *Leyes de Indias* (Cano, 1991: 372–3). The first body of law that attempted to comprehensively regulate water uses in New Spain was the 1761 General Regulation of Water Measures, which was a synthesis of existing dispositions both from Spanish Water Law and from the Leyes de Indias, and restated the character of Crown property for 'waters, lands, and mines' (Lanz Cárdenas, 1982, Vol. 1: 19–29). Although in practice the public monopoly over water was contested by the actual formation of private monopolies, the principle subsisted, became a central component of Mexican water law, and was instrumental in the consolidation of the state's territorial control in the late nineteenth century.

On another count, the provision of water supply was traditionally a municipal responsibility. This principle was formalized in the Water Ordinances passed by Viceroy Duque de Albuquerque in 1710 and later reinforced by an 1813 decree of the Spanish Cortes concerning the 'health and comfort of the population' (Talavera Ibarra, 1997: 341–55). At the consumer end, water was distributed by *aguadores* [water vendors], who carried it from the aqueducts and fountains for selling in the streets following the indigenous tradition. Although *aguadores* belonged to the lower strata, over time they acquired a comparatively respectable social standing and developed a well-established reputation of guild organization, which according to some authors had its fore-runners in pre-Columbian times and endured until the late nineteenth century (Musset, 1991: 155–8; Talavera Ibarra, 1997: 334–59). However, although water supply was formally entrusted to the city's govern-ment, in practice control over these activities was subject to recurrent power struggles between the viceregal and municipal authorities (Musset, 1991: 167–73).

Nevertheless, the connection between water activities and political power was more evident in the areas of flood control, water infrastruc-ture, and water security. Flood control policies, as already discussed, occupied a central stage in the colonial period. As shown in Chapter 2, during the first stage of El Desagüe between 1607 and the disastrous flood of 1629 there were two leading international water experts involved in its design and construction, the German Enrico Martínez, and the Dutchman Adrian Boot, each backed by powerful political groups. According to Musset, less famous than Martínez and Boot but equally important in this period were Jesuits such as Juan Sánchez Vaquero, who made important intellectual and practical contributions to the project. In fact, in 1627 the Viceroy entrusted the Jesuits with the post of Judge-Overseer of El Desagüe, appointed directly by the Crown and with responsibility for the works and for the flood defences, which gave the order a significant degree of authority and command over a large body of functionaries, construction experts, and security personnel. The Judge was closely supported by the Senior Guard of El Desagüe in charge of an army of accountants, treasurers, notaries, and rank and file administrative clerks, while construction activities were in the hands of foremen, supervisors, and guards. Fate turned against the Jesuits with the flooding of 1629, when the popula-tion blamed them for the disaster, and control of the work was handed over to the Franciscans for most of the remaining colonial period. In the long run, the Franciscans also failed to complete El Desagüe and in

1767 the works were entrusted to the Consulado de México, the merchant guild of the city, which reflected the significant alterations that were affecting the power configurations between religious and civil actors in the late eighteenth century (Musset, 1991: 335–42).

Concerning water infrastructure and security, in the early days the colonial authorities organized squads of water guards recruited mainly among the Indians and led by a Spanish officer to protect the aqueducts. Although these squads were formally accountable to the municipality, the highly sensitive character of water control in the city often merited the personal intervention of high-ranking officials or even the Viceroy in the nomination of water guards and officers. Infrastructure control became more specialized towards the end of the sixteenth century with the creation of new posts like Project Manager or Water Master, which were filled by Spanish water experts and technicians. In the late seventeenth century, the increasing specialization and redistribution of functions led to the appointment of a Head Water Officer in charge of the direction of all waterworks in the city, a post reserved for political functionaries. The nomination of this officer frequently expressed the intrusion of royal authority in the municipal jurisdiction that became more severe over time as viceroys started to appoint other high-ranking officers such as the Water Judge and the Overseer of Water Mains and Arches, who were imposed on the city authorities (ibid: 335–42).

Summing up, the strategic importance of water-sector activities in the basin fuelled the development of technical and administrative expertise and the consolidation of legal practices, principles and institutions. However, the configurations of political power that evolved with the monopolization of land and water in the hands of a reduced elite was not crystallized in centralized state apparatuses during the colonial period. This development would have to wait until the late nineteenth century.

Independent Mexico

During most of the nineteenth century after Independence (1821), water policies in the basin were affected by the dramatic political and military events that dominated the period: the Civil War (1832), the Mexico–US wars (1847–53), and the French occupation (1863–6). The resulting political instability meant that public works were almost limited to the conservation and repair of the existing infrastructure. Also, until the Disentailment Law enacted in 1856 by the Minister of

Finance Lerdo de Tejada, which led to the transformation of the structure of property, the spatial organization of the city remained almost unchanged. However, there were important institutional developments in the water sector, including some unintended outcomes of the political-military events that would greatly influence the consolidation of national water policies, institutions and practices by the end of the century. These transformations would also have an impact on the power configurations within Mexican society, exacerbating the oligarchic trends inherited from the colony. These trends would eventually lead simultaneously to the further concentration of water and land ownership and to the consolidation of national water policies and institutions, in a radical reconfiguration of the power balance between religious and civil actors, between whites and non-whites, and between the public and private sectors.

One of these emerging trends was the overall centralization of political power in the hands of the executive and, ultimately, of the President. For instance, after the creation of the Federal District in 1824 a process was set in motion that shifted the power balance against the municipality vis-à-vis the other levels of government. Thus, a set of Ordinances passed in 1840 simultaneously allocated responsibility for delivering urban public services to the *Ayuntamiento* [Municipality] and also reordered the power hierarchy by subordinating the Ayuntamiento to the Governor of the Department of Mexico. This decision would set the pattern for the forthcoming years: all important decisions at the municipal level had to be approved by the Governor, who in most cases needed the authorization of a state minister and even of the President (Rodríguez Kuri, 1996: 18–28). Still, formally the 1840 ordinances established that the *ayuntamientos* were responsible among other issues for urban cleansing, water supply, drainage, rivers, and sanitation, following the colonial tradition. Accordingly, in 1846 the Ayuntamiento enforced new regulations concerning the duties and responsibilities of water officers, re-enforced regulations about the concession of *mercedes* [royal water rights], and promoted the introduction of water-saving technologies in public and private fountains and the regulation of the activity of *aguadores*, in particular regarding hygienic standards (Talavera Ibarra, 1997: 341–55). Despite the shift in the power balance, tensions between the municipal and other levels of government regarding public services, and water services in particular, would never cease in the years to come.

Other important steps in the centralizing trends were the creation in 1853 of the Ministry of Public Works, the development of comprehensive water management plans for the basin during the US and French invasions, and the creation of new taxation to fund water works. Regarding the Ministry's main activities, the growing importance of steam power inspired plans for developing a fluvial transportation system in the basin's remaining lakes and canals, although the many ventures that were set up finally collapsed one after the other (Lemoine Villicaña, 1978: 46). These projects might have been the last opportunity to preserve the lacustrine ecosystem that would later succumb to the desiccation process fuelled by the Porfirian modernization. On another note the US and French invasions of the 1840s and 1860s had also unintended outcomes for water policy. As noted before, the water management plans elaborated during the US invasion would later form the basis of late nineteenth-century water policy, while during the French invasion the municipality carried out an assessment of water sources, water quality, distribution systems, and of the financial situation of the water services. Finally, during the Restored Republic (1867–76) the government imposed new taxes to complete El Desagüe, and although the works were permanently suspended in 1873 the 'provisional' taxes remained in place (Calderón, 1955: 534–43). These trends towards the centralization and consolidation of state water control would be greatly reinforced in the following phase.

Water politics under Porfirio Díaz

Water became a significant component of Porfirian public policy (1876–1911) in the Basin of Mexico. This period saw not only the start of a new technological stage in the development of the country's water sector, but also the insertion of Mexico in the international community. In addition to completing El Desagüe after almost three centuries, the regime introduced major technological innovations in the urban systems of water supply, drainage, and sewerage. It also fostered the development of a powerful water bureaucracy, which contributed to the regime's success in modernizing the Mexican state and reinforcing its territorial control. This period also brought about the consolidation of Mexican water law and the development of powerful public institutions related to water management. This was a doubled-edged process whereby the monopolization of water control by the state was interwoven with the large-scale privatization of water and land that exacerbated existing social inequalities and would, eventually, lead to the Mexican Revolution (1910–17).

Table 3.1   Expenditure on public works during the Porfiriato. Mexico City and El Desagüe 1880–1910

Works	Total cost (million pesos)	Percentage
Public services (lighting, telephones, pavement, and other works)	23,000	18.7 %
Medical care, and public health	10,600	8.6 %
Education	2,500	2.0 %
Transportation	10,000	8.0 %
Urban modernization (public buildings, monuments)	33,100	26.8 %
Water works	44,100	35.8 %
Total	123,300	100 %
Breakdown of water works		
El Desagüe	18,400	14.9 %
Sewerage	8,200	6.7 %
Water supply	17,500	14.2 %

Source: Mansilla (1994: 98).

The relative weight of the water sector during the Porfirian period can be illustrated by the fact that it accounted for about 36 per cent of the total expenditure in public works between 1880 and 1910 (see Table 3.1). However, these figures would be much higher if we included the expenditure in hydroelectric activities and the budget of the growing water bureaucracy.

The completion of El Desagüe in 1900 became the symbol of the Porfirian regime. However, there were also significant advances in hydroenergy, irrigation, and in the expansion and modernization of the urban systems of water supply, drainage, and wastewater collection. Engineer Roberto Gayol designed a modern drainage system for the metropolis that was completed by 1903, and in 1899 Porfirio Díaz appointed Engineer Manuel Marroquín y Rivera as Technical Director of the newly created Managing Board of the Mexico City Water Supply Works. Marroquín y Rivera modernized the water supply network and introduced demand management measures like compulsory water metering and a differential tariff structure penalizing large consumers and favouring low-income sectors (Perló Cohen, 1989: 4–10). He firmly believed that essential water services required a special organization different from other municipal departments given their strategic importance for the well being of the population, and designed a plan to provide 24-hour attention by well-trained water officers and to keep detailed records of users' complaints for monitoring service quality (Marroquín y Rivera, 1914: 549–66). Marroquín y Rivera's project was finally inaugurated during the Revolution, in October 1913.

Despite these advances, the significant scientific and technical modernization of water management in the Porfirian period did not result in a widespread improvement in people's lives in terms of health and well being. Rather the exclusionary trends would be reinforced and for decades to come access to clean water and sanitation would remain the preserve of a privileged sector of the population.

Water expertise and state power

The Porfirian modernization took place in the cultural and ideological atmosphere dominated by the intellectual elite known as the *científicos*.[5] The emergence and consolidation in this period of a modern version of the water expert, however, exceeded both the científicos phenomenon and the Mexican scene and was rather the local expression of a worldwide development. The newly trained squads of Mexican water experts and functionaries were part of what Worster termed the 'international fraternity of experts', a real 'brigade' of water engineers, scientists and bureaucrats taking shape in the late nineteenth century (Worster, 1985: 143–6; see also Goubert, 1986).

In Mexico, expert knowledge about the country's water resources was deemed essential for the consolidation of the state's territorial control, and this fuelled the demand for water experts. There were no precise records of the water rights granted during the colonial period, and there was little control over the amounts of water actually used. For instance, a far-reaching conflict over water rights in the Laguna region during the 1890s, which had international repercussions because of the involvement of US and British interests, had required the active participation of the State in solving the problem.[6] The recommendations made by the federal water experts, who asserted that the Republic was the legal owner of the water and that it alone could bestow the right to take it, reflected the growing consensus within the ruling elite about the need for a more assertive role of the State in water management (Kroeber, 1994: 122). The water experts involved in this decision, which was replicated in a large number of similar cases, were making history and foreshadowed post-revolutionary water policy.

The increasing political relevance of water underpinned the rising of water experts within the state apparatus, especially in the Ministry of Public Works. On the eve of the twentieth century they were already playing a key role in designing and implementing federal policies, and carrying out hydrological and legal studies on the most important river basins and water sources throughout the country. In turn, these water experts became fervent supporters of the expansion of the state's role in producing scientific knowledge about water, promoting innovation in water management practices, and providing incentives for private investors (Kroeber, 1994: 104–5, 162–89, 251–2).

It must be emphasized that although the immediate concerns of these experts were largely influenced by the local political and social conditions, their overall approach to water management and policy was also shaped by their close interaction with the international epistemic community. They had close links with their colleagues in Europe and the United States, where many received training and were exposed to the development of new water technologies and institutions. Leading figures among them like Engineer Roberto Gayol became highly influential among the political, intellectual, and technical elites of pre- and post-revolutionary Mexico (see Gayol, 1994; Herrera y Lasso, 1994; Palacios, 1994).

On the one hand, this marriage between scientific and technological water expertise and the consolidation of state power contributed to reinforcing the state's territorial control. On the other hand, in the process the pre-existing power configurations developed around water control in the basin experienced a significant shift. In particular, Porfirian water policies like the extensive land reclamation from lake beds, implemented through harshly repressive policies against indigenous peasant resistance, completed the expulsion of the Indian communities from their territories and further relegated them to smaller territorial units, such as Xochimilco and Tláhuac.[7]

Changes in the legal sphere

The trend towards increasing state monopolization of water control also contributed to consolidate Mexican water law, although this process was marred by conflict, contradiction, and ambiguity (Aboites Aguilar, 1998: 81–9). The 1813 Act of Independence had established that all properties of the Spanish State and the Crown, including water resources, became the property of the Mexican State. Also, the 1814 Apatzingán constitution[8] stated that colonial legislation had to remain in force until the Mexican State elaborated its own. In fact, many of the colonial principles and regulations were incorporated into the 1888 Federal Water Law and survived well into the twentieth century (Lanz

Cárdenas, 1982, Vol. 1: 19–29). An important consequence of this process was that although by the late nineteenth century most water resources were privately controlled and free from public scrutiny, the overall trend was towards increasing monopolization of water control in state hands.

While the nineteenth century was characterized by dramatic changes in the structure of land property resulting in an extraordinary concentration of land through the expropriation of the Indian and religious corporate holdings, water followed a somewhat different pattern. Although the appropriation of land entailed the de facto appropriation of any water resources included in it, towards the end of the nineteenth century water became differentiated from land as a *sui generis* resource that progressively came under state control. Interestingly, privatization of land and state water control were complementary as shown by the fact that the state monopolization of water was supported by large landowners and leading members of the Mexican oligarchy before the Revolution. This was not, however, a straightforward process, and the ambiguities in the water law were such that well into the 1890s lawyers defending the water rights of private companies were able to argue that water use was in the private domain and therefore ruled by civil law, thus contesting the trend towards securing public control over water (Aboites Aguilar, 1998: 82–5).

Nevertheless, Porfirian water policies contributed to the redefinition of the private and public spheres in water law. For instance, faced with the need to meet the expanding water demand of Mexico City, Porfirio Díaz authorized the Ayuntamiento to expropriate water from the Desierto de los Leones in 1878. The private owners of the water rights opposed his policy, but the National Congress authorized the expropriation on the grounds of public interest in 1882 (DDF-SOS, 1975, Vol. 1: 253). This case illustrates the direction of the process towards increasing water control in state hands, which was sanctioned soon after – though imperfectly and ambiguously – in the 1888 Federal Water Law. This strengthening of state control was challenged by many critics who believed that water legislation was contributing to 'the centralizing trends' that were already curtailing the sovereignty of provincial governments. Subsequent developments would prove the critics right, and the social forces supporting state monopolization of water control would eventually obtain a sound victory over their opponents. The principle of state water monopoly was reinforced by successive laws enacted in 1894, 1902 and 1910, and became a crucial element in the 1917 revolutionary constitution (Kroeber, 1994: 192).

Modernization, social change and citizenship

The achievements of Porfirian water policy were an expression of the socio-economic and political transformations leading to the centralization of power in the Mexican State, although the process was punctuated by persistent and worsening quantitative and qualitative social inequalities. The country remained largely, in Simpson's words, 'many Mexicos' in terms of cultural and regional identities (Simpson, 1963), while economic and political power became further concentrated in the national oligarchy surrounding Porfirio Díaz (Knight, 1990, Vol. 1: 15–23). Water policy in this period was often conceived as a vehicle for social change, especially irrigation agriculture, which many believed, 'would provide the social basis for democracy that Indians and Spaniards', they asserted, 'had not been able to deliver'. For instance, Engineer Francisco Bulnes, a leading *científico* and a member of the Liberal Party, believed that 'the Mexican Indians [were] not able to progress because they belong, according to natural history, ethnology, general history and sociology to an inferior race which has proved itself to be slow to develop and progress through civilization' (Sáez, 1980: 315, 271). Actually, Bulnes foresaw with a pessimistic and insightful perspective that the future of democracy in Mexico was compromised by the ingrained structures of traditional power relations, although the reasons that he offered to substantiate his views were deeply racist and biologistic:

> In Mexico, he argued, 'there will only be political rights when another race will occupy our country by conquest or by immigration, and will impose itself in an aristocratic way as master or by crossbreeding with Mexican blood. In Mexico, the incapacity for democracy is not only a matter of illiteracy because even the most enlightened Mexicans are insensitive to democracy in the same way as Indians are. The Spaniards have always been and can only be autocrats or slaves. Therefore, we cannot inherit a democratic character'. (Ibid: 316)

Bulnes believed that this incapacity for democracy was inherited from the Spanish domination that had taught Mexicans to be docile and obedient, and therefore the country needed to wipe away the hindrance derived from three centuries of colonial subservience. According to him, democracy would only come with industrialization, and this would only proceed after solving the agricultural problems of the country, which required that state investment should be concentrated on irrigation. He, like many others, believed that massive irrigation works built by the State would contribute to the emergence of a class of small landowners, thus expanding and safeguarding private property and preventing the possibility of a social revolution. Although there was no monolithic position within the Porfirian elite, these arguments were broadly shared by many other influential figures (ibid: 269 ff; Kroeber, 1994).

However, alternative positions advocated the need to foster the urban 'domestication' of water, which in the industrial democracies had become a quintessential element of the processes of urbanization and improvement of the health and well-being of the population. The leading voice arguing for the massive expansion of urban water services through public investment was Andrés Molina Enríquez, later co-author of the key Article 27 of the 1917 revolutionary charter. For Molina Enríquez urban water services and the production of hydropower had to be the top priorities for state investment (Molina Enríquez, 1964).

The case of Molina Enríquez, a state functionary, shows that the emerging movement promoting more efficient water management, state water control, and the universalization of the access to essential water services was not confined to the water experts. He was a member of an international intellectual and scientific community that, borrowing from Goubert, were joining forces to promote water use and hygiene among the population by transforming the status of essential water supply and sanitation into universally available services (Goubert, 1986: 23–5). In Mexico, however, this process was very slow and inconsistent. Already in 1911, leading water experts were acknowledging the failure of Porfirian water policies and betrayed serious doubts about their efficacy (Kroeber, 1994: 261). Before 1920, the provision of water services was limited to the central areas of the city while the surrounding quarters and towns had to meet their needs without state support (Bribiesca Castrejón, 1975b: 314–15). Writing in the middle of the Revolution, Engineer Alberto J. Pani lamented 'the backwardness in civilization – concomitant with the situation of public health – of the Federal District', despite the fact that this was 'the most advanced part of the country regarding material progress' (Pani, 1916: 9). Unfortunately, even despite the radical commitment of people like Molina Enríquez and Pani, this situation did not change substantially after the Revolution. Moreover, the 'dynamics of inequality' and the conditions of 'internal colonialism' characterizing independent

Mexican society were deepened in the context of a formally democratic regime (González Casanova, 1965b: 87–9), a process that despite the significant political transformations that followed persisted throughout the twentieth century and beyond. As shown in later chapters, this problem illustrates the slow process of substantive citizenship in Mexico.

After the Revolution: the challenge of citizenship

The post-Revolution development can be characterized synthetically as a process of continuing though never completed centralization of water control in public hands, best expressed in the creation of powerful federal institutions and, in the Basin of Mexico, in the expansion of Mexico City's hold over water resources beyond the basin's borders. However, neither increasing water control by the federal government nor the expansion of Mexico City's water availability brought immediate improvements for the living standards of the population. Even despite the crucial political decisions made by President Cárdenas (1934–40) to implement socially oriented water policies, until the 1940s essential water services in the metropolis ranked very low in the federal investment priorities. Moreover, though investment in urban water infrastructure grew rapidly since the 1940s this was not translated into the universalization of essential water and sanitation services, which only become a public-policy priority in the 1970s.

Water and institutional development

The thesis defended by the supporters of monopoly state control over water was that the colonial principles of public and royal law that sanctioned the public property of natural resources, including water, had been fused in a single legal body after Independence. These principles were later incorporated in Article 27 of the 1917 constitution. However, the actual enforcement of public control over water has been the object of protracted struggles since the early days of Revolution, when state water policies became centred in financing irrigation infrastructure and were captured by social sectors that controlled the key financial institutions. With the aim of reversing this situation, in 1926 President Plutarco Elías Calles (1924–8) created the first federal institution dedicated to water policy, the National Irrigation Commission (Comisión Nacional de Irrigatión (CNI)). The CNI became not just the main instrument for agricultural policy but also fostered the development of water science and knowledge and the systematic record of available water resources in the country (Aboites Aguilar, 1998: 106–27). The 'Callista irrigation' policies became an important instrument for the strengthening and legitimization of the revolutionary state in this period, although the bulk of the investment was concentrated in the northern states of Nuevo León, Coahuila, Chihuahua, Baja California, and Sinaloa.[9]

Another important line of institutional development concerned the effort to integrate the uncoordinated public offices dedicated to urban water services and place them under the Directorate of Sanitary Engineering (Dirección de Ingeniería Sanitaria (DIS)) created within the Department of Public Health of the federal government (Bribiesca Castrejón, 1975: 303–4). However, the impact of the DIS' policies was almost negligible, with total investment accounting for about five to six million pesos per year between 1924 and 1946 (DDF-SOS, 1975, Vol. 1: 461).[10] It seems that water and sanitation were not the highest priority for the earlier revolutionary governments (Wilkie, 1967: 169), which is clearer when we compare investment figures for irrigation that between 1926 and 1946 accounted for over 900 million pesos, an average of over 43 million pesos per year (Orive Alba, 1970: 67–92).[11] Nevertheless, in this period there was progress in the institutional development of urban water management, which also followed a pattern of increasing federal intervention at the regional and local levels. One the key instruments of this intervention was the Urban and Public Works Mortgage Bank (Banco Nacional Hipotecario Urbano y de Obras Públicas (BNHUOP)) created in 1933, which became the national government's vehicle for exercising financial and technical influence in local development, a policy that prompted widespread municipal resistance against the perceived intrusion of federal water experts in municipal affairs (Aboites Aguilar, 1998: 161–7).

President Lázaro Cárdenas (1934–40) continued the process of institutional consolidation with the enactment of a new National Waters Law (1934), the creation of the Water Consultative Board (1934) and of the Federal Police of Water Works (1935), and the passing of the Potable Water Public Service Law (1938) in the Federal District. The National Waters Law, for instance, reinforced the right of the State to reverse water grants made to private individuals and boosted the rights of small users, *ejidatarios*, and poor rural workers (Lanz Cárdenas, 1982: 68–9). He continued the trend of allocating the bulk of public investment in water to irrigation agriculture but aimed at enforcing at long last the revolutionary commitment to land distribution and by the end of his period in office had distributed 18 million hectares, expanding *ejidal* property from 15 per cent of cultivated land in 1930 up to 47 per cent by 1940 (Wilkie, 1967: 132–9). Also, Cárdenas redefined the role of the BNHUOP and announced increased investments in urban water infrastructure thus setting the standard for more progressive water policies (Aboites Aguilar, 1998: 161–2).

The institutional consolidation was furthered during the 1940s under the governments of Avila Camacho (1940–6) and Miguel Alemán (1946–52). State water control was strengthened with a 1945 reform to Article 27 of the constitution, enforced by law in 1948, which specified the previously ambiguous federal jurisdiction over underground water resources. More significantly, in 1946 the federal government created the Ministry of Hydraulic Resources (Secretaría de Recursos Hidráulicos (SRH)), the first example in the Western world of a public institution at the level of federal cabinet exclusively dedicated to water (Aboites Aguilar, 1998: 176–84), which became one of the leading examples of the growing role of the public sector in water management worldwide (Lee, 1999: 44). In 1947 the SRH launched Executive Basin Commissions aimed at developing the most important hydrologic basins of the country and started a massive dam building programme that by 1970 had expanded the storage capacity of water reservoirs from 16 to 125 billion cubic metres and the extension of irrigated land controlled by the Ministry to 2.8 million hectares distributed in 77 irrigation districts (CNA, 1993d: 40).

Despite the progress in the institutional consolidation of public water control, it was not until the early 1960s that the State introduced formal water planning activities, which only became established with the 1972 Federal Waters Law and the 1975 National Hydraulic Plan (PNH).[12] This development was furthered with the creation in 1976 of the Ministry of Agriculture and Hydraulic Resources (SARH) aimed at integrating water planning and operation into a wider policy framework with a holistic approach to water management. However, radical changes in the political environment introduced since the early 1980s and the financial restrictions caused by the 1982 debt crisis significantly reduced the impact of these initiatives (Perló Cohen, 1989: 40).

These changes taking place in the early 1980s were part of a radical transformation of the role of the state at the international level. The leading position of the public sector in organizing social and economic life that had been consolidated in the Western world since the 1930s became fiercely contested by the policies of deregulation, liberalization, and privatization adopted first in Chile, the United States and Great Britain and then exported globally. As discussed later in more detail, these policies sought not just replacing the state by the market as the key driver of economic development, but also transforming the foundations of societal governance by subordinating political and social considerations to the priorities set by international financial powers. The new policies had far-reaching implications for Mexican water policy, as they challenged the need for state intervention in the sector and attempted to reformulate the respective roles of the public sector and market interests in the governance and management of water.

Among the most important outcomes of these political transformations it is worth mentioning the creation in 1989 of the National Water Commission (CNA), which was entrusted with the integral process of water management, including the financial and budgetary aspects. The creation of the CNA was complemented by significant legal, political and administrative changes made in 1992 that included a radical revision of the Article 27 of the Constitution, and the enactment of the new Land Law and a National Waters Law. We address in more detail these changes and their political implications in later chapters.

Water and political power in the Basin

After the chaotic aftermath of the Revolution, the 1930s brought about significant institutional changes towards the consolidation of state water control in the basin, although the process has been characterized by frequent institutional overlapping and conflict. Water policy remained in the Department of Public Works of the Ministry of Communications and Public Works until the creation in 1932 of the General Directorate of Works of the Valley of Mexico (Dirección General de Obras del Valle de México (DGOVM)) within the same Ministry. Water supply and sewerage services became the responsibility of the Directorate of Public Works of the Federal District, which was taken over in 1933 by the General Directorate of Water Supply and Sanitation (Dirección de Agua y Saneamiento (DGAS)) and then incorporated in 1941 into the structure of the Federal District Department (Departamento del Distrito Federal (DDF)) (Perló Cohen, 1989: 25–7). However, the metropolitan water institutions have reflected the chaotic urban and industrial development of the MCMA, which in 1950 was composed of the Federal District and Tlalnepantla municipality and grew to include 10 additional municipalities by 1970 and almost double that number by the 1990s. Understandably, metropolitan water policies involving the governments of the Federal District and of the states of Mexico, Hidalgo, and Puebla plus the respective federal, departmental, and municipal bodies have been marred by institutional infighting, contradiction, and political conflict. For instance, despite the creation in 1992 of the Water Commission of the Federal District (Comisión de Aguas del Distrito Federal (CADF)) concentrating responsibility for the financial, operational, and administrative aspects, considerable overlapping remained with other bodies such as the DGCOH and the *delegaciones*, and with the State Commission of Water and Sanitation (CEAS) of the State of Mexico, responsible for water management in the conurbated municipalities.

The recognition of the need for integrated water policies at the basin level led to the creation in 1951 of the Hydrologic Commission of the Valley of Mexico's Basin (Comisión Hidrológica del Valle de México (CHCVM)), an inter-state body formed with representatives of the federal Ministry of Hydraulic Resources, and engineers of the governments of the Federal District, the states of Mexico and Hidalgo, the College of Civil Engineers (Colegio de Ingenieros Civiles (CIC)) and the Association of Engineers and Architects (Asociación de Ingenieros y Arquitectos (AIA)). The creation of the Commission expressed both the increasing territorial and jurisdictional complexity of water management in the basin and the growing importance of the water experts in the public sector. The Commission reflected the consolidation of 'administrative rationalism' based on the marriage between science, technology, and bureaucratic expertise (Dryzek, 1997). Although it had no executive powers, being a consultative body of the SRH directly controlled by the President, the Commission was organized with a conventional top-down hierarchical structure with no room for users' representatives, whether be farmers, industrialists, or domestic consumers. This situation remained unchanged until 1971 when it was replaced by the Water Commission of the Valley of Mexico (Comisión de Aguas del Valle de México (CAVM)), which in turn was taken over in 1989 by the CNA (Perló Cohen, 1989: 25–7, 45).

The flood control factor

During the 1930s reorganization, flood control, a never ending concern for the basin's population, was entrusted to the DGOVM that in 1932 revived a project started in 1929 for improving and expanding the capacity of the basin's drainage system. The project known as the Combined Deviation System consisted of a network of dams and tunnels to redirect river flows and was completed by the late 1930s. However, despite these efforts the city was struck by several flood events, twice in 1941 and again in 1942 and 1944. The gravity of the situation led President Avila Camacho to set up an Inter-Ministerial Commission in charge of the Basin's hydrological planning (Perló Cohen, 1989: 16–27). Again, in spite of these measures large floods in 1950–1 brought disaster and death affecting two thirds of the city, which revealed the extreme vulnerability of the Mexican capital. Although in 1954 President Ruiz Cortines' administration (1952–8) completed the second Tequixquiac drainage tunnel started during the Cárdenas period, other projects designed at the time and deemed essential for flood protection like the Eastern Interceptor, a 15-kilometre tunnel to collect and redirect the flow of 11 rivers, were not completed until 1960.

The magnitude of the 1950s floods prompted the design of a massive project involving the construction of a high-capacity drainage network located in the depth of the city's subsoil to overcome the impact of soil subsidence. The work later known as the Deep Drainage was only started in 1967 when the initial sections of the tunnels were laid, and the first stage was inaugurated in 1975 by President Echeverría (1970–6). Echeverría presented the work as 'one of the most significant of the century', and the government was proud to announce that it was built entirely with the resources of the Federal District (DDF-SOS, 1975, Vol. 3: 265).

The increasing centrality of water policy

Regarding water and sanitation in the metropolis, in the 1920s the Ayuntamiento resumed the expansion of the water supply network increasing the number of users to 22,500 in 1927. Although this represented an expansion of 80 per cent since 1914, the network only served a small fraction of the growing population that had passed the 600,000 mark by 1921 (Bribiesca Castrejón, 1975b: 314). As already mentioned urban water and sewerage were relatively low priorities in terms of actual investment until the 1940s. Paradoxically, the stage initiated in 1940 was marked by the retreat of the state-led urban planning activities characteristic of President Cárdenas' administration, and public efforts were concentrated in promoting the country's industrialization.

However, although expansion and improvement of water and sanitation systems in the city continued to be slow, the 1940s industrialization had far-reaching consequences for water management in the metropolis. The fast-growing water demand prompted the implementation of an old inter-basin water transfer project to import water from the Lerma River. Thus, Mexico City entered a new era by expanding its control over water resources beyond its jurisdictional borders, which added a new level of institutional complexity. The Lerma project was completed in 1951 during President Miguel Alemán's period, when public expenditure in water projects grew rapidly. During his presidency the state also assumed a more decisive role in urban water investment after recognizing that the provision of safe water and sanitation services could not be expanded without massive public support. Between 1946 and 1952 expenditure in the Federal District's water systems amounted to 50.2 per cent of the total investment in public works, of which 35.5 per cent were allocated to water supply works such as the Lerma transfer, the drilling of new artesian wells, the building of pumping stations for the drainage system, and the expansion of the urban networks of water supply and sewerage (see Table 3.2).

This trend towards higher investments in water infrastructure continued during the subsequent *sexenios*. Also, Mexico City's control over water resources located outside its jurisdiction was further extended, provoking the wrath of water users in the water exporting areas. For instance, President Díaz Ordaz (1965–70) decreed the appropriation of underground waters in the upper Lerma River basin for use in the Federal District despite the protests of local authorities, rural producers and other affected parties in the State of Mexico, which fuelled conflicts that continue until the present day. Moreover, the ever-

Table 3.2   Expenditure on public works in the Federal District. Presidency of Miguel Alemán (1946–52)

Works	Total Cost (pesos)	Percentage
Public services (lighting, pavement, and other works)	204,868	25.7 %
Public buildings, monuments	191,940	24.1 %
Water works	407,790	50.2 %
Total	797,598	100 %
Breakdown of water works		
El Desagüe	34,000	4.3 %
Sewerage	83,295	10.4 %
Lerma system	176,943	22.2 %
Water supply	106,552	13.4 %

Source: Perló Cohen (1989: 22).

growing thirst of the MCMA prompted new import ventures in 1976, when President López Portillo (1976–82) sanctioned the transfer of water from the Cutzamala River basin which required the construction of a highly sophisticated aqueduct system. This administration also implemented the *Colonias Populares* programme, which included a long-overdue expansion of the distribution network connecting about 2 million people to the water supply system. This trend in the MCMA was maintained in the early 1980s, during President de la Madrid's government (1982–8), with the further expansion of the network and with the construction of the southern branch of the Cutzamala aqueduct between 1983 and 1987.

The pace of investment in water systems was boosted since the late 1980s, as water policy occupied a central place in President Salinas de Gortari's period (1988–94). Between 1989 and 1993, the amount invested in potable water and sanitation in the country amounted to 13 billion new pesos, approximately 4.3 billion dollars, of which about 20 per cent was allocated to the Basin of Mexico (CNA, 1993d: 95). The budget for the period 1995–2000 was 41.4 billion new pesos, approximately 5.2 billion dollars, of which 29.5 per cent corresponded to the Basin of Mexico alone (CNA, 1995: 62). Undeniably, water control in the basin continued to have significant political relevance through the 1980s and 1990s, and we will explore further some aspects of this development in the following chapters.

Concluding remarks

This chapter has explored how human activities directed at the control and management of water resources have been intertwined with the changing configurations of social and political power in the Basin of Mexico. The need for restless human intervention to secure the protection of urban settlements against recurrent flooding has been one of the major challenges facing the basin's inhabitants over many centuries and there is no permanent solution in sight for this problem. Delivering water supply and disposing of wastewater have also required significant efforts since pre-Columbian times, and the decisions taken to secure the regularity and adequacy of these services have had far-reaching consequences in the environmental, ecological, economic, cultural and socio-political dimensions. The outstanding mastery of water science and technology deployed in the basin over the centuries has also made humans increasingly dependent on a particular water regime that has brought about largely unintended outcomes such as the drastic ecological transformation of the basin and the spiralling mortgage represented by the economic, financial, environmental, ecological and socio-political costs needed for sustaining life in the basin.

Water has occupied a central role in the development of power structures and configurations in the basin and the trends towards further state centralization of water control continue, as discussed in more detail in Chapter 5. Contemporary water politics in the basin are marred by contradiction and conflict cutting across state and society, redefining the divide between the public and the private, and more importantly from the perspective of this book, reflecting the structural transformation of the relationships between the Mexican state and its citizens. However, the increasing consolidation of water control in state hands did not bring about the universalization of the material improvements made possible by the unprecedented scientific and institutional progress achieved in the water sector since the late nineteenth century. This has compounded the reproduction and exacerbation of qualitative and quantitative social inequalities in the basin, which has fuelled protracted social struggles. In this regard, before entering the specific debate about the links between water and citizenship, the next chapter centres attention on the particular forms taken by the social struggle over water in the MCMA during the last two decades.

4
Contested Waters

'We have no choice but reacting because the authorities let us die from thirst, permit the voracity of the water vendors, and tell us that to get cheaper water we "must join the PRI".'—(**Neighbours from Ixtapaluca, Los Reyes-La Paz, Chimalhuacán, and Chalco, State of Mexico,** March 1986)

'We are a group of citizens organised as a civic force who drilled some wells to alleviate the thirst of the people in the face of the many unfulfilled promises of the authorities. We are committed to defend the wells from state takeover at any price.'— (**Chimalhuacán, State of Mexico,** March 1987)

'Unless the problem is solved, we will lynch the mayor, the head of the Council, who is a merchant of people's needs, and the boss of the water tankers.'—(**Cuautitlán Izcalli, State of Mexico,** August 1987)

Fragments from water struggles in the MCMA

This chapter shifts the temporal focus from the long-term to concentrate on the struggle over water in the MCMA during the last two decades of the twentieth century. We examine around 2000 events of water conflict that were identified through the classification of press reports during the period 1985–92.[1] These events are actions performed by individuals, families, groups, and institutions, in connection with different problems arising from the management of water resources or the provision of essential water services. Most cases recorded in the press, though, reflect the activities of domestic and small-scale users, as the intervention of large users such as industries or municipalities is normally hidden from public scrutiny and seldom reported. According to the empirical evidence, the immediate reasons moving the protagonists to act are multifarious and most events are discrete and unconnected, while the majority of the actors may be unaware of the multidimensional character of the overall process. Yet, by analogy with Clausewitz's model of war as a totality composed by a large number of discrete engagements, 'great and small, simultaneous and consecutive' (Clausewitz, 1989: 227), we argue that the apparently unconnected contests over water described here are part and parcel of a wider social confrontation that is autonomous from the individual will and reason of the actors. In our perspective, these events constitute an expression of people's reactions to the structural conditions underpinning the qualitative and quantitative inequalities that continue to exclude them from fully accessing the territory of citizenship.

In this regard, the territory of citizenship is composed of evolving bundles of rights and duties formally bonding all individuals within a given community, but actual access to it is the object of permanent and recurring social contests. Arguably, the protagonists of the individual battles summarized below can rarely grasp the whole picture, as most of these events are not interconnected and are scattered in space and time. This is compounded by the fact that the overriding techno-scientific rationality characterizing the management of water and water services has also contributed to render unobservable the social character of the process, which is often reduced to its technical–natural and bureaucratic dimensions. Unfortunately, the incursions of social science that have been most influential in the design of water policy since the 1980s have also tended to reinforce these negative trends, as the prevailing perspective has shifted the focus away from socio-political considerations to concentrate efforts in converting water into an economic good and re-centring the governance of water and water services around free-market principles. We come back to this debate in the last two chapters.

The context of the social mobilization over water in the MCMA

The environmental and ecological threats and hazards looming in the Basin of Mexico acquired renewed political saliency since the 1970s. For instance, the first Environmental Protection Law in Mexico was passed in 1971, together with the creation of the Under-Ministry of Environmental Improvement (Subsecretaría de Mejoramiento del

Ambiente (SMA)) within the Ministry of Public Health. As shown in the previous chapter, in the 1970s there were also significant institutional developments in water policy and management including the first National Hydraulic Plan (PNH) published in 1975 and the creation of the Ministry of Agriculture and Hydraulic Resources (SARH) in 1976. The PNH offered a study of the metropolitan water systems that took into account the interactions with hydrological, urban, and socioeconomic processes at the scale of the basin. Moreover, the authors asserted that most water problems in the basin were not merely technical in nature, but had also organizational, psychological and sociopolitical dimensions (Perló Cohen, 1989: 53), although this formal recognition of the multidimensional character of water management and policy was not sufficient to transform the prevailing technocratic tradition and develop a more holistic and interdisciplinary perspective.

The 1980s brought about unprecedented transformations, including the accelerated worsening of the urban living conditions in the MCMA and the radicalization of the social and political mobilization. The relative absence of organized political action around environmental problems characterizing the 1970s gave way to massive mobilizations in the early 1980s, which received a significant boost with the 1984 explosions in the San Juan Ixhuatepec oil refinery plant of Petróleos Mexicanos (PEMEX)[2] and the 1985 earthquakes that claimed thousands of lives. Although the mobilization about environmental problems had some antecedents such as the 1977 Green Brigades that opposed the widening of avenues at the expense of green areas, and other short-lived groups, it was only in 1983 that the first politically-defined ecological group appeared with the creation of the Coyoacán Ecological Association in a residential area of the Federal District, which was followed by groups throughout the MCMA. For instance, organizations like the National Ecologist Alliance, the Alternative Network of Eco-communication, and particularly the Group of 100 formed by artists concerned with the environmental deterioration of the MCMA, flourished in this period. In 1986, many of these organizations were incorporated into two umbrella institutions: the Mexican Ecological Movement and the Pact of Ecologist Groups (Aguilar *et al.*, 1996: 354–6). By the mid-1990s, the movement had experienced a significant growth with over 700 non-governmental organizations (NGOs) operating throughout the country around environmental problems.

Grassroots initiatives have been also important, and in fact urban mobilization around land and essential services has had a long tradition in Mexico that in modern times can be traced back to the tenant movements in late nineteenth-century Mexico City. The best known example in recent times is the Urban Popular Movement (Movimiento Urbano Popular (MUP)), later integrated into the National Confederation of the Urban Popular Movement (Coordinadora Nacional del Movimiento Urbano Popular (CONAMUP)), which originated during the 1960s in the rapidly growing adjacent municipalities of the State of Mexico. In addition, the mid-1980s urban disasters fuelled the emergence of neighbourhood organizations aimed at resolving the urgent needs created by the devastating effect of the earthquakes on the urban infrastructure, not least in the water supply systems. Some of these movements endured, like the Neighbourhoods' Assembly that became a leading political actor dedicated to representing popular concerns about housing, essential services and related issues in the MCMA.[3] In this context, the events over water have been a significant component of the urban mobilization.

Unsurprisingly, water occupied a central stage in the presidential campaigns during the 1980s and early 1990s. For instance, the candidate of the Institutional Revolutionary Party (Partido Revolucionario Institucional (PRI)) during the 1982 presidential campaign (and later elected President), Miguel de la Madrid Hurtado, put water at the centre of his political agenda, which included a series of popular consultations carried out by one of the party's think tanks, the Institute for Political and Social Studies (Instituto de Estudios Políticos y Sociales (IEPES)). On 5 January 1982, the IEPES, headed at the time by another future President, Carlos Salinas de Gortari, organized a meeting on 'Water and Development Planning' gathering water experts, urban and rural users, social scientists, and political functionaries.[4] The setting was the capital city of Chiapas, Tuxtla Gutiérrez, a state where the construction of massive hydroelectric dams had required the flooding of 100,000 hectares of croplands and the displacement of population, fuelling migration to the ill-serviced capital and other cities with the ensuing conflicts over urban infrastructure and service provision (PRI–IEPES, 1982: 11–12; Castro, 1992: Ch. 2). In the meeting, the presidential candidate sketched what soon thereafter would become a radical reorganization of the Mexican water sector:

> The serious flaws in our legal and administrative systems and the unfairness in the distribution of water for different uses ... have prompted us to elaborate a far-reaching policy programme aimed at promoting the rational use and preservation of water in Mexico.

This policy programme will be followed by the re-definition of the legal framework and of the administrative and institutional aspects (PRI–IEPES, 1982: 6).

Other contributors to the meeting expanded the framework of the new water policies being envisaged. For instance, Engineer Fernando González Villarreal, coordinator of the meeting and who would later head the National Water Commission (CNA) created in 1989, offered a revealing declaration of policy that illustrates the increasing awareness among water experts and functionaries of the multidimensional character of water problems:

> Water projects must be incorporated within a national water plan, where water infrastructure must not be the end but rather the means for improving people's health, achieving food self-sufficiency, diversifying our energy sources, and consequently enhancing the social well-being and the nation's development. However, the struggle over water does not end here, because achieving greater efficiency goes beyond the problems of physical infrastructure and also concerns the juridical-institutional framework and the users. Based on our Political Constitution, water management is carried out in agreement with the nation's interests, which must prevail over the local or regional and over those of individuals and groups. This implies that we must take into account not only the purely technical and economic factors but also those of ecological equilibrium and social justice. (PRI–IEPES, 1982: 21)

All senior participants in the meeting would later occupy top positions in the Mexican government, and had the opportunity to implement their proposals. This happened in the context of profound transformations in the international order, in which Mexico played a central role. Among these, the 1982 Mexican debt crisis became a milestone, foreshadowing major changes in the patterns of socio-economic development and public policy. Under President De la Madrid's administration (1982–8) Mexico began gradually switching to market-oriented economic policies, which required a significant shift in the composition of social forces that had historically supported the Mexican regime. In particular, the statist fractions were left outside the alliance in power, which brought about the first important challenge to the long-lasting primacy of the PRI, with the breakaway of leading members of the party in 1987.[5]

Most political parties running for the 1988 presidential elections also gave paramount importance to environmental and urban problems, and the 1987 presidential campaign of the PRI candidate Carlos Salinas de Gortari again put water at the centre. In a meeting held in Acapulco, Guerrero, on 2 December 1987, the candidate headed a debate on 'Water, a vital resource' which largely constituted a restatement of the Tuxtla Gutiérrez gathering (PRI–IEPES, 1987). However, the influence of the political changes that had swept through the country during the previous presidential period was reflected in the new emphasis given to two central issues: the need to create a national water authority, and the avowed commitment to change the status of water from public to economic good and to re-centre the governance and management of water around market principles. These issues became the keystones of water policy during President Salinas de Gortari's period in office (1988–94), when the institutional reforms inspired by the expanding neoliberal model were further deepened.

During the early days of the Salinas de Gortari administration, organized environmental activism declined, not least, perhaps, owing to the recruiting by the government of some of the leading environmental activists (Aguilar et al., 1996: 357)[6] and the political institutionalization of the ecological movement with the creation in 1991 of the Mexican Ecological Party (Partido Ecológico Mexicano (PEM)). In other respects, the Salinas de Gortari government accelerated the trend started during President De la Madrid's *sexenio* by introducing radical changes in the legislation and implementing deregulation, liberalization and privatization policies in vital areas such as the banking system, urban services – including water supply – and telecommunications, which we analyse later in more detail.

The events of social mobilization over issues such as the control over water infrastructures or the lack of access to water and sanitation services that we explore below took place in circumstances of rapid social and political transformation and rising awareness about the city's environmental problems. As discussed in Chapter 1, conventionally most of these events have been treated as being the result of technical or administrative failures, although the most extreme cases involving the destruction of property or personal attacks have been obviously treated as criminal offences. By and large, the links between these events and the emancipatory social struggles involving the democratization of the state and the expansion of substantive citizenship rights have been obscured or overlooked, and our objective is to examine the process in a different light to make observable the social character of the process.

Physical–natural cycles, social regularities

There are some characteristics of the water mobilization that may contribute to reinforcing the techno-scientific reductionism of conventional explanations. For instance, the temporal distribution of the
water events resembles the hydrological cycle. In a typical year, the frequency of actions increases sharply with the arrival of the dry season,
and then remains relatively stable until the rainy season brings some
relief. After a period of decline in the level of mobilization, the cycle
resumes with the arrival of the following year's dry period. Figures 4.1
and 4.2 provide a graphic reading of this situation, showing separately
total percentages for the MCMA, the Federal District and 16 adjacent
municipalities of the State of Mexico.[7]

However, although the charts suggest a clear interrelationship
between the seasonal climatic patterns and the water events, a closer
inspection raises important questions about the meaning and extent of
the correlation. For instance, in the light of the technical sophistication characterizing water management in the MCMA, the fact that the
metropolis imports water from beyond the basin's boundaries, and
looking at the high levels of coverage and per capita water distribution

Figure 4.1 Annual cycle of the events over water in the MCMA

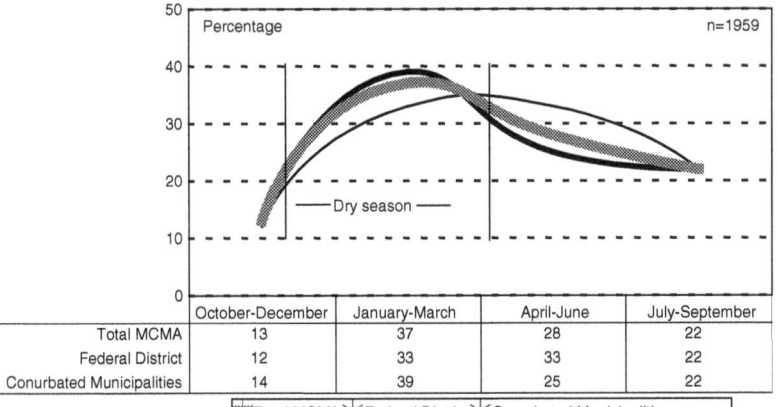

Mexico City Metropolitan Area (Percentage of events per quarter 1985-1992)

	October-December	January-March	April-June	July-September
Total MCMA	13	37	28	22
Federal District	12	33	33	22
Conurbated Municipalities	14	39	25	22

Total MCMA ▸ Federal District ▸ Conurbated Municipalities

Source: Elaborated from Torregrosa Armentia (1988–97).

Figure 4.2   Social and physical-natural cycles

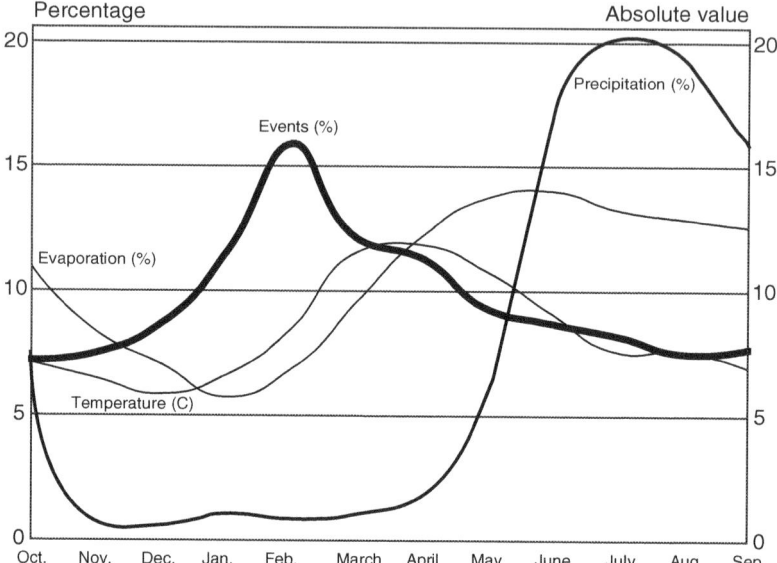

Mexico City Metropolitan Area (1985-92)

Sources: Elaborated from Torregrosa Armentia (1988–97); Instituto Mexicano de Tecnología del Agua (1996).

reported officially, the interaction between the seasonal rainfall regime and the sequence of the events merits further scrutiny.

In this connection, the evidence suggests that the association between the arrival of the dry season and the steep increase in social conflicts over water cannot be explained as being just the outcome of the 'natural' hydrological cycle. As expressed sarcastically by one of the protagonists of the events, 'in some urban quarters the dry season has been with us for over 15 years' (*Metrópoli*, 30 May 1989: 2). The dry season undoubtedly exacerbates water scarcity and the problems associated with it, but water scarcity is the outcome of interwoven and relatively autonomous physical–natural and social processes.

One indicator of the degree of autonomy of social patterns vis-à-vis physical-natural cycles is the differential weight of the social mobilization over water in the Federal District and in the neighbouring municipalities of the State of Mexico. As shown in Table 4.1, while the Federal District concentrates over 58 per cent of the MCMA population, only

Table 4.1   Relative weight of the events of conflict over water (comparative percentages). MCMA 1985–92

	Population	Events
Federal District	58.2	33.5
	(8,235,744)	(656)
Conurbated Municipalities	41.8	66.5
	(5,913,863)	(1303)
Total	100	100
	(14,149,607)	(1959)

Sources: Elaborated from INEGI (1991); Torregrosa Armentia (1988–97).

33.5 per cent of the recorded events of water mobilization happened in its territory. However, though the mobilization is more intense in the conurbated municipalities than in the Federal District, there exist large differences between jurisdictions. In the Federal District, over 46 per cent of the events were concentrated in three of the 16 delegaciones: Gustavo A. Madero, Iztapalapa and Tlalpan. Likewise, in the State of Mexico seven out of the 16 municipalities accounted for 73 per cent of the events: Ecatepec, Naucalpan, Chimalhuacán, Tlalnepantla, Atizapán, Netzahualcóyotl and Chalco.

This spatial distribution of the events may be connected with the process of demographic and urban expansion, as the delegaciones and municipalities concentrating the larger proportion of cases are also among the most affected by massive population growth since the 1960s. This is the case of Tlalpan, Iztapalapa and Gustavo A. Madero[8] in the Federal District, which recorded population increases of up to 1,000,000 people each between 1960 and 1980. Also, municipalities such as Netzahualcóyotl, Naucalpan, Tlalnepantla, Ecatepec, Atizapán, and Cuautitlán Izcalli had the highest rates of population growth between 1960 and 1980, which in the case of Netzahualcóyotl meant a net increase of over 1,200,000 people. During the 1980s, the most dynamic municipalities were Ecatepec, Chalco, Atizapán, Chimalhuacán, Tultitlán and Cuautitlán Izcalli, while Netzahualcóyotl and Tlalnepantla had a significant decrease (Bolos and Perdomo, 1990: 19–20).

However, the explanation of the conflicts over water cannot be reduced to the impact of population and urban growth. As discussed later, understanding the situation of defencelessness and extreme vulnerability affecting millions in the MCMA, not just in relation to water, requires the introduction of additional explanatory factors. We come back to this issue later, but let us first examine the structure of the water events.

The structure of the events

We analysed the water events looking first at their internal components such as the actors involved, their targets, the stated cause of the action, and the instruments employed. Then we aggregated the cases in different combinations according to key characteristics such as level of organization of the protagonists. Let us say that the sharpness of the analytical categories and components presented below is a necessary reduction for heuristic purposes, as we do not wish to reify the data presented in tables nor the individual examples listed later. We use the quantitative information to map the events and provide orders of magnitude that facilitate the understanding of the dynamics and directionality of the process, while the description of selected events offers a closer look into the multidimensional structure and interconnections of the struggle as a whole.[9]

The protagonists

Engagements imply the confrontation of two sides, an agent that takes the initiative and carries out certain actions against an opponent, an adversary. Let us call the actor that takes the initiative the 'protagonist'. The protagonists of our events range from individual members of the community without demonstrable links with groups or organizations, to highly structured and disciplined collective actors such as political parties, workers' unions or Non-Governmental Organizations (NGOs). However, it was not always possible to specify the identity of the protagonists or the nature of the organizations involved from the information provided in the press reports. Local associations and neighbours' committees, for instance, may be the outcome of self-organization in which people join forces in their search for the introduction or improvement of water services or in response to the complete interruption of the water supply for long periods. However, frequently the creation of organizations is also stimulated from above, either by the government, political parties, workers' unions, or foreign-funded NGOs, among other external agents.

In any case, the character of the protagonists must not be taken as given and static: on the one hand, self-organized actors can be co-opted or penetrated by more powerful organizations or state agencies, which can then influence and control, if not dictate the way to follow. On the other hand, top-down organizations designed to secure political control over popular movements can develop autonomous initiatives or, to put it in other terms, can also be co-opted by grassroots processes. This happened, for example, in some municipalities during the early 1990s with local officers of the National Solidarity Program (PRONASOL) launched by President Salinas de Gortari , who enjoyed a higher degree of autonomy from the centre, and sometimes became responsive to local causes, even joining or awakening centrifugal forces. Furthermore, depending on the level of analysis the same protagonists can become vectors of contradictory forces. In another example considered below in more detail, a local community from Ecatepec defended their right to keep control over a water system (a well and a network of household connections) that they had built when neither the state nor private entrepreneurs were interested in providing the service, and then managed and maintained it efficiently for many decades. Although theirs was a de facto decentralized, self-sufficient and community-managed water utility non-dependent on government subsidies, which in theory would fit in with the policies of administrative decentralization and civil society participation promoted by the government since the 1980s, in practice the authorities interpreted their refusal to hand over the water system as unlawful. What observed at the local level and in historical perspective was very likely a legitimate action of the community, observed at the basin level constituted for the authorities an act of opposition to the new policies directed at integrating water management activities under state control. This illustrates the multiscale and multidimensional character of the process captured in the water events.

Returning now to the character of the protagonists, although as shown in Table 4.2 two thirds of the events were performed by agents with some degree of organization, the number of cases carried out in apparently spontaneous circumstances, without an observable level of organization, is noticeable.

Interestingly, in contrast to the Federal District, where non-organized protagonists accounted for over 42 per cent of the events, in the neighbouring municipalities organized action was overwhelming with just under 76 per cent of the cases. Most of these actions were carried out by local protagonists, who accounted for over 60 per cent of the total number of events. In this respect, the breakdown of the data according to the level and type of organization of the protagonists

Table 4.2   Level of organization of the protagonists of the events of conflict over water. MCMA 1985–92

	EVENTS		
	Without organization	*With organization*	*Total*
Federal District	42.3	57.7	30.9
	(264)	(360)	(524)
Conurbated municipalities	24.2	75.8	9.1
	(260)	(814)	(1174)
Total MCMA	100	100	100
	(624)	(1074)	(1698)

Source: Elaborated from Torregrosa Armentia (1988–97).

reveals the central role played by local institutions such as neighbourhood associations or the local offices of political parties, workers' unions and other social organizations. This centrality of the local in the events is reinforced by the presence of municipal authorities and politicians, particularly in the State of Mexico, where they often appeared confronting state or federal authorities over water problems in defence of the specific interests of their communities. Moreover, non-organized protagonists, among which the role of women was paramount, were also mainly locally based.

However, the participation at the local level of regional and national organizations such as political parties, workers' unions or NGOs suggests that the scale of the events may well extend beyond the neighbourhood. For instance, even small community groups often appeared joining forces with peers from neighbouring colonies and quarters, a feature recorded with more frequency in the State of Mexico (20 per cent of the events) than in the Federal District (only 5 per cent of the events) (Bolos and Perdomo, 1990: 52–4). We shall later return to the protagonists, but let us now consider their targeted opponents.

The opponents

The antagonists in the water events have also wide-ranging identities and share the characteristic of being held accountable by the protagonists for water-related problems. Unsurprisingly, a large share of the events targeted local authorities and water utilities, although a significant number of cases were also directed to state and federal authorities, private organizations, and individuals (Table 4.3).

Table 4.3   Actors targeted by the protagonists of the events of conflict over water. MCMA 1985–92

	Federal District	Conurbated Municipalities	Total
Federal/state authorities	30.2 (81)	26.1 (112)	27.7 (193)
Local authorities	52.6 (141)	55.9 (240)	54.7 (381)
Other actors	17.2 (46)	17.9 (77)	17.6 (123)
Total MCMA	100 (268)	100 (429)	100 (697)

Source: Elaborated from Torregrosa Armentia (1988–97).

Most actions targeted municipal departments or the local offices of state or federal bodies such as the Ministry of Agriculture and Hydraulic Resources (SARH) or the Ministry of Urban Development and Ecology (Secretaría de Desarrollo Urbano y Ecología (SEDUE)). The category 'other actors' clusters people or organizations enjoying a degree of social power related to water and water services such as 'local leaders', 'urban speculators', the drivers of water trucks – both private and municipal – or local business people. These actors are targeted because the protagonists hold them responsible for real or perceived grievances such as massive clandestine water tapping by hotel owners, power abuses by municipal water distributors or overcharging for water by private vendors.

Interestingly, in an important number of cases the protagonists do not have a clear antagonist, a culprit or a well-identified opponent. For instance, in some cases the actors recognize that the solution to the problem is beyond the reach of the local authorities, bureaucrats and technicians and blame the 'current policies' or the 'economic situation' for the particular issues that moved them into action. In other cases, they mention 'natural' factors such as the 'drought', the 'excessive rain', the 'heat' or the 'parasites' as the causes of their complaints. In some circumstances the lack of identifiable targets may be an indicator of institutional crisis, as suggested by one case described later in which the protagonists could not identify who was responsible for providing water services in their neighbourhood, which was trapped in an inter-jurisdictional conflict between the municipality, the state and the federal government.

Reasons for action and instruments employed

Although 'water' is the obvious object underpinning the events, the immediate reasons given by the protagonists to justify their actions are wide-ranging and distinctive. For analytical reasons we have grouped the causes of the events in three main sub-dimensions: (a) actions to gain access to water or essential water services; (b) actions around deficiencies in the delivery of essential water services; and (c) actions involving the control over water resources and water infrastructure (Table 4.4).

The first group includes cases in which the action seeks to overcome legal, technical or administrative impediments precluding the access to water and essential water services. The second concerns problems such as the irregularity or poor quality of the services, unfair pricing, administrative and operational inefficiency, or water speculation. Finally, in the third group we singled out those events where the social and political aspects of water control become more evident such as competition for water sources, conflicts over the control of water infrastructure, or confrontations concerning the legal status of water which in the period under study the federal authorities were trying to change from public to private good.

Regarding the instruments employed by the protagonists, we identified five main categories: petitions, denunciations, mass mobilizations and parades, threats, and direct actions. In most cases the protagonists utilize a conjunction of different instruments when carrying out their actions, although the most common recourses were the petition and the denunciation, which convey different degrees of antago-

Table 4.4   Stated causes of the events of conflict over water. MCMA 1985–92

	Federal District	Conurbated Municipalities	Total
Gaining access to water and essential water services	32.1 (165)	28.2 (271)	30.0 (436)
Requesting improvements in technical-administrative standards	58.6 (301)	55.8 (525)	56.8 (826)
Controlling water and water infrastructure	9.3 (48)	15.4 (145)	13.3 (193)
Total MCMA	100 (514)	100 (941)	100 (1455)

Source: Elaborated from Torregrosa Armentia (1988–97).

Table 4.5 Instruments employed by the protagonists of the events of conflict over water. MCMA 1985–92

	Federal District	*Conurbated Municipalities*	*Total*
Petitions	5.3	5.3	5.3
	(14)	(24)	(38)
Denunciations	80.3	66.5	71.6
	(212)	(302)	(514)
Mass mobilizations/rallies	7.2	10.6	9.3
	(19)	(48)	(67)
Threats	5.7	9.3	7.9
	(15)	(42)	(57)
Direct actions	1.5	8.4	5.9
	(4)	(38)	(42)
Total MCMA	100	100	100
	(264)	(454)	(718)

Source: Elaborated from Torregrosa Armentia (1988–97).

nism. The petition is normally a formal request addressed to the authorities asking for the connection or restoration of water services. Although most cases are obviously directed to the local water and political authorities, often the petitioning is routed to higher-rank echelons and, typically, to the President of the Republic, reflecting both the frustration of the claimants and the long-lasting Mexican tradition that gives the President a fatherly authority even over domestic affairs.

The denunciation is the next step among the actors' tactics, and they normally resort to it when the petitions have failed to attract the attention of the authorities, though denunciations can also be triggered for other reasons such as exposing power abuses by water vendors or clandestine water tapping by industries or hotels at the expense of domestic users. There are two main types of denunciations: those directed to the authorities aimed at resolving a given situation, and those directed to the media with the purpose of raising public awareness of irregular situations and thus moving the authorities into action. The denunciation is by far the most common instrument employed by the protagonists in the recorded events, although there is an important difference between the Federal District where denunciations accounted for over 80 per cent of the events, and the conurbated municipalities, where the figure drops to 66.5 per cent. That most events took the form of the denunciation can be partly explained by the fact that the press was precisely the main vehicle used by protagonists to voice their demands and complaints over water issues in public during the period of study.

The third type of instrument employed is the public manifestation through parades, open meetings, and other forms of collective and mass mobilization that take place usually in the local *Zócalo* [main plaza], in front of government buildings, main roads, and other public spaces. The fourth type is the threat of further actions, normally a warning that direct action will be taken if there is no response within a given period of time. The content of threats range from implementing actions of civil disobedience such as non-payment of water bills and taxes, road blocking, and occupation of buildings to the kidnapping of water officers and vehicles, and the destruction of goods and infrastructure. The fifth and last type of instrument is the materialization of the threats.

There is a significantly higher occurrence of events involving mass parades, threats, and direct action in the conurbated municipalities than in the Federal District. This may be the outcome of the more extreme conditions of vulnerability affecting the provision of water services recorded in the municipalities or perhaps it may reflect the fact that protagonists of the events outside the Federal District find formal channels such as the petition and the denunciation much less effective. Also, this may be indicating the looser public control over water operations existing in the State of Mexico, which leaves water resources and services more exposed to political manipulation and factional power struggles between individual or collective water lords. This will be illustrated by the examples provided below and in forthcoming chapters.

A closer look into the events

The previous section offered a framework to facilitate the visualization of the overall process, its main trends, characteristics, and directionality. Here we will explore in more detail a number of selected events grouped according to the causes stated by the protagonists. This section will provide a richer description of the events that helps to grasp the multidimensional character of the struggle over water, including socio-economic, political, and ecological considerations. It also gives clues to identify otherwise unobservable interconnections between water and the development of citizenship, which we explore in more detail in the last two chapters.

Figure 4.3   Protest in front of the Senate Chamber, Federal District

Note and Source: The leaflet reads: 'WE WERE KIDNAPPED but not by delinquents; we were kidnapped by the Municipal Police of Pachuca ... for having committed the grave crimes of wanting sewerage, potable water, electric energy.' The leaflet also includes several declarations from children who were allegedly treated with violence and sent to prison. One declaration by a girl named Yutzel Roldán Valenzuela reads: 'Yes, we were sent to prison together with our parents because we painted a wall asking for water.'
Source: Photograph by Marco Peláez, 11 July 2001, reproduced with permission from *La Jornada*, Mexico City.

Events to gain access to the water services

Gaining access to essential water services, and especially drinkable water, prompted the actions of the protagonists in almost one third of the recorded events. As discussed in later chapters, that large numbers of people have to engage in often bitter and even brutal confrontations to gain access to essential water services exposes the flawed character of the mainstream reforms implemented in the water sector worldwide since the 1980s, including Mexico. In particular, it shows the fragility of the argument that the water crisis in urban areas is mainly the result of water being treated as a public good by an extremely magnanimous public sector. In fact, as illustrated by the situation in the MCMA, for millions water has always been a very expensive commodity, both in economic and political terms, subject to political and commercial speculation and to the severe 'discipline' of an unregulated market.

In this connection, the obstacles that people must overcome to gain access to essential services in the MCMA, and in particular water, constitute an intricate web of technical, legal, socio-economic and political factors. For instance, previous studies have shown that although provision of essential water services have been the highest priority identified by the communities for a long time, the authorities have often pursued other agendas, perhaps building roads and other infrastructures, oblivious to the demands of the population (Ward, 1986: 83). This type of situation recurred in many of the events, causing bitter conflicts sometimes even resulting in the loss of human lives.

In other cases, technical and legal obstacles constitute the main impediment to gain access to essential water services. For example, the chaotic urbanization process in the MCMA has led to many settlements being located in areas that are unsuitable or very difficult for the provision of networked water and sanitation services. In relation to legal and administrative concerns, unlike other services such as electricity, water utilities require a land title to connect new users and this has been a major bone of contention owing to the slow pace of land regularization in the MCMA (Garza and Damián, 1991: 35). However, there are many examples of non-regularized areas being provided with networked water services, such as the *colonia* San Miguel Teotongo in Iztapalapa, Federal District, which was created in 1972 through land invasions. Despite the irregularity in the land-tenure, in the early 1980s large areas of the *colonia* had been already connected to the municipal water network, which was the combined result of political patronage and popular mobilization (Schteingart *et al.*, circa 1989: 52–4). Let us explore now some of the examples taken from the events.

In July 1986, a group of neighbours representing about 2000 families from a 'gigantic ring of poverty' in Ecatepec, State of Mexico, resorted to make a public denunciation through the press, frustrated by the lack of attention to their long-standing petition for essential water services. As put by one of the protagonists, 'the local political authorities have refused to introduce water in our neighbourhood and they put the blame for this situation on other institutions such as the State Commission for Water and Sanitation, the Water Commission of the Valley of Mexico or the Municipal Directorate of Potable Water.'

A high-ranking municipal officer explained that 'the local authorities cannot deliver public services there, including potable water, because the land where the settlement is located is under federal jurisdiction'. In fact, the claimants had settled down alongside the Mexico-Laredo railway, a federal stretch within the municipal boundaries, and theirs was, in the quite graphic phrasing of the report, a *'ciudad perdida'* [lost city], a Mexican shanty town (*Metrópoli*, 25 July 1986: 8). This case illustrates another element in the web of impediments: the jurisdictional overlapping between state agencies that determines the existence of large 'grey' areas where the responsibility over public services is not resolved, which is worsened by the anarchic urbanization characterizing the MCMA.

The second example took place in November 1986, with the mobilization of about 100 neighbours from Tlalnepantla, State of Mexico, on the advice of a federal deputy from the Mexican Worker's Party (Partido Mexicano de los Trabajadores (PMT)). The protagonists held a rally and a sit-down in the esplanade of the municipal palace demanding the introduction of public services including water and sewerage, and the regularization of their land titles. According to them, since the creation of the settlements sixteen years before, and despite the fact that they were up to date with their taxes, their petitions for essential public services had gone unheard for many years. The demonstrators carried banners complaining 'If we pay our taxes, why don't we have water?' Local functionaries explained that the technical studies carried out by the municipality determined the unfeasibility of providing networked water in the area because the settlements were located in hilly rock areas where urbanization was considered technically and economically unsuitable (*Metrópoli*, 13 November 1986).

Often, the response of the authorities to situations like those illustrated above has been the regularization of settlements, either through legalizing land tenure or by moving whole *colonias* [urban quarters] to more suitable locations. However, while regularization is generally a notional necessary condition, it by no means ensures the provision of networked services to the claimants, and a large share of the population is served by municipal or private water tankers. This, in turn, paves the way for further confrontations, as water vending becomes an unchecked business under the control of powerful interest groups. Often, local and regional authorities collude with private entrepreneurs to exploit the benefits, especially during the dry and the rainy seasons,[10] which provokes bitter reactions from the population.

For instance, in December 1986, during the dry season, representatives of about 15,000 families from Ecatepec carried out actions against the municipal authorities through petitions, denunciations and threats. The protagonists restated petitions for the introduction of networked water services in their quarter, accused the municipal government of indifference to their previous demands and threatened to launch a campaign of rallies and parades to force a solution. They also complained that private water vendors were taking advantage of the situation by selling water at between 500 and 600 pesos per *tambo* (a container with an approximate capacity of 200 litres), respectively equivalent to 22.3 per cent and 26.7 per cent of a minimum daily salary at the time.[11] A few days before, about 1000 people had already marched to the municipal palace to complain that lower-rank municipal officials were applying high overcharges for connection to the water network. Furthermore, they alleged that this situation had lasted for two years during which their petitions had not been addressed and threatened to launch new actions the following week (*El Sol de Mexico*, 6 December 1986).

Another event, carried out in November 1988 by about 100 *colonos* from Chalco, State of Mexico, illustrates that even the pacific insistence on the introduction of essential water services can be a risky adventure for the claimants (see Figure 4.4). After organizing a five-hour blockade of the Mexico-Puebla highway to restate their long-standing demands for water services, they were given an appointment with the mayor 'at the old tollhouse' located in the same highway. However, in place of the mayor 'three trucks packed with policemen and civilians arrived who, rather than starting talks rushed at children, women, and elderly people who were mistreated and threatened with death if they persisted in their demands'. In the event, allegedly 15

Figure 4.4 Mazahua Indians from San Simón de la Laguna blockading a highway to defend their water rights, Mexico City Metropolitan Area

Source: Photograph by Carlos Mamahua, 11 November 1999, reproduced with permission from *La Jornada*, Mexico City.

persons were seriously wounded and two disappeared. The colonos claimed that their petitions went unheard because the mayor, whom they denounced as being the leading estate dealer in the region who colluded with urban speculators, was protecting powerful business interests that sought to control the land where they were located. The claimants asked for an appointment with the recently elected President, Carlos Salinas de Gortari, to request an investigation into the mayor's affairs since the state government had not taken any action (*Excelsior*, 1 December 1988: 3).

The above examples provide a picture of the otherwise opaque processes summarized in the first section. As these cases suggest, for many families the question of gaining access to essential water services is far from being a mere bureaucratic or technical procedure, not to say the exercise of a citizenship right. For millions in the MCMA, water has never been a public good freely distributed by a paternalistic state, as often described in mainstream accounts of the water crisis. In the extreme, the protagonists who dare to challenge the state and other power holders in their struggle for accessing essential services find themselves involved in wider confrontations. Our use of the model of war as inspiration for analysing the struggle over water is not merely a metaphoric resource, neither are the casualties.

In this connection, the structural conditions of social exclusion affecting a large share of the population in the MCMA find expression in the many different obstacles that people need to overcome in order to access essential water services, such as the illegality of the land tenure, the technical impediments to deliver services in unsuitable areas, the irresponsibility or dishonesty of public officials or the power abuses by public and private water vendors. The reactions exemplified in this chapter can be read as directed at breaking the exclusionary mechanisms and gaining access to a territory that is jealously protected from intrusion.

Events aimed at improving standards

The second group of examples concerns events where the protagonists are already regularized users of the water and sanitation services, whose actions are prompted by such problems as interruptions of the water flow, inadequate water quality, abusive increases in the price of water, lack of maintenance of the systems, unregulated water vending, political clientelism or inefficiency and dishonesty of public and private providers. This type of event was by far the most frequent, accounting for almost 57 per cent of the total number of cases.

In February 1987, at the peak of the dry season, a group of organizations claiming the representation of 1,500 families from Tultitlán, State of Mexico, rallied against the local mayor after three weeks of continued interruption of the water supply. Among the about 300 participants, there were members of the Organization of Towns and Colonies, the Federation of Settlers of the State of Mexico, the Proletarian Union of Settlers, and the National Confederation of Popular Organizations (Confederación Nacional de Organizaciones Populares (CNOP)). In addition to the mayor, they also targeted the private water vendors, some of whom were allegedly controlled by municipal functionaries, and charged them with negligence and with impeding the expansion of the water supply network owing to their vested interests in trading with water for private profit.

Their instruments were petitions, denunciations, threats and direct action. They demanded the immediate intervention of the state governor and of the President, and presented a plea with 17 points including the dismissal of the mayor, the re-establishment of the water supply, and the normalization of a long list of deficient public services such as solid waste collection, electricity, and security that had been contracted out to a private operator. Finally, they threatened actions of civil disobedience such as the non-payment of municipal taxes and, given the lack of response from the authorities, organized a permanent blockade with barricades of the highway José López Portillo, one of the main roads linking ten municipalities of the State of Mexico. The blockade lasted five days and caused a large-scale disruption of traffic affecting many thousands of travellers. The engagement was resolved with a partial agreement involving the state, the municipal authorities, and the private company. The re-establishment of the water supply and the commitment to maintain a regular service became the key concessions offered by the mayor, which served to calm down the situation, at least temporarily (*Ovaciones*, 23 February 1987: 7; *El Sol de Mexico*, 23 February 1987: 8; *Excelsior*, 23 February 1987: 9; *El Día*, 25 February 1987).

At the same time that the Tultitlán confrontation was calming down, in nearby Naucalpan furious colonos who identified themselves as members of the People's Revolutionary Movement (Movimiento Revolucionario del Pueblo (MRP)) were threatening to seize private water tankers if they were found selling water at a price higher than 500 pesos per *tambo* (approximately 22 per cent of a daily minimum salary). They also demanded that the authorities set price controls on water sold by private water vendors (*El Sol de Mexico*, 27 February 1987: 2b). Soon after that in Chalco, where water availability had fallen to around three litres per capita per day, desperate colonos were actually assaulting the water vendors, who were charging up to 600 pesos per *tambo* (approximately 27 per cent of a daily minimum salary) (*Excelsior*, 18 March 1987).

In an episode which occurred in September 1992, representatives of about 30,000 families from Netzahualcóyotl, State of Mexico, rallied to Los Pinos, the presidential residence in Mexico City. The claimants denounced that since the 1985 earthquakes the water flow had become irregular in about 80 *colonias*, but the situation had now become intolerable after six weeks of complete interruption of the water supply. They charged both the mayor and the head of the water utility with negligence and non-compliance with previous commitments, and accused municipal functionaries of taking advantage of the situation for private profit. According to them, water tankers of the National Solidarity Programme (PRONASOL), which must deliver water free, were selling it at up to 200,000 pesos per tanker (containing around

9,000 litres), which brought the cost of a 200 litre *tambo* to around 4,450 pesos, almost 37 per cent of the minimum daily salary of the time. They also claimed that the municipal authorities had recommended them to take water directly from the mains, but it was highly polluted and drinking it had caused the spread of gastrointestinal diseases and even cholera. As proof of their allegations, they handed over to the presidential representative a sample of the water which, in the words of the protagonists, 'the local authorities assure is clean but has the colour of tamarind juice' (*El Día*, 21 September 1992: 20; *El Financiero*, 22 September 1992: 26; *El Nacional*, 22 September 1992: 24).

Water speculation by private vendors who colluded with or were controlled by municipal officers, and steep increases in fees for networked water services were among the main issues triggering people's actions throughout the period of the study. In the descriptive words of the protagonists, the dry season provides the opportunity for the 'black market made with impunity with the white gold [water]' (*Metrópoli*, 23 March 1987). To provide an overall parameter of the situation, in 1990 users connected to the networked water supply were paying a monthly average equivalent to one and a half daily minimum salaries for their water bills.[12] In the examples given in this chapter, people buying water from municipal or private water vendors were paying prices many times higher, a situation confirmed by other studies in the MCMA and also comparable with similar cases in other developing countries.[13]

We also recorded several examples. For instance, in February 1986 neighbours from Naucalpan, State of Mexico, reported a massive interruption of the water supply affecting 500,000 people during a whole week. According to the protagonists, while the municipal water authorities were blaming the state water utility CEAS for the 'unexplainable' interruption of the water flow, both municipal and private water vendors were making huge profits by overcharging water deliveries. Allegedly they were selling water at between 60 and up to 100 pesos per *tambo* (respectively around 5 per cent and 9 per cent of the minimum daily salary), when 'the price should have been 40 pesos' (around 4 per cent of the minimum daily salary). Also, the price of a water tanker containing approximately 9,000 litres ranged from 5,000 to 10,000 pesos, which meant that a 200 litre *tambo* was being sold at between 110 and 220 pesos (respectively around 10 per cent and 20 per cent of a daily minimum salary). Tellingly, a group of housewives from the affected *colonias* 'threatened to defect from the PRI and join the Partido Acción Nacional (PAN) if the municipality did not regularize the water supply', which added to the evidence suggesting the existence of close links between water speculation and political clientelism in the MCMA (*Metrópoli*, 10 February 1986: 11).

Reports on related events carried out the same week in the municipalities of Naucalpan, Tlalnepantla, Atizapán, Tultitlán, Ecatepec and Coacalco help to complete the picture (*Metrópoli*, 12 February 1986: 11). Allegedly, municipal water tankers were neglecting popular neighbourhoods in favour of residential areas with, presumably, higher demand and capacity to pay higher prices. Likewise, the reports suggest that private water vendors were deviating water from the municipal network to refill their trucks and sell it at a profit and were blackmailing the *colonos*, threatening to stop water deliveries in the neighbourhood if they denounced the irregularities. The scarce water available had become the object of fierce competition between popular quarters, residential areas, industries and small businesses, while the latter were offering 'tempting tips' to both municipal and private water vendors in order to secure their water provision. Housewives complained that they needed to walk up to two kilometres to obtain a little water for their cooking and drinking needs. According to the reports, about 1,000,000 people were affected by the water shortage in this region alone (*Metrópoli*, 16 March 1986).

In some areas, like in Netzahualcóyotl where the community denounced the abuses of the water vendors, the latter fulfilled their threats and 'punished' the families by stopping water deliveries. Also, after six months of complete interruption in the networked water supply, during which the water bills continued to arrive punctually, many families had started to dig holes in the streets to take water directly from the mains. The streets were mushrooming with people carrying picks and spades to unearth the pipes, often fruitlessly as the mains were also dry. The neighbours decided to make a rally and meet the state governor to demand a definite solution to the 'fraud' (*Metrópoli*, 27 March 1986).

Other events included the mobilization of about 10,000 families from Ecatepec in February 1986, who filed an appeal of *amparo* against an increase of 700 per cent in their municipal water fees. The protagonists were reluctant to accept another increase while their water supply was only intermittent, with water available just for a few hours in the early morning (*El Nacional*, 26 February 1986). In another case, neighbours from Ixtapaluca, Los Reyes-La Paz, Chimalhuacán and Chalco announced plans for two rallies in March 1986, one to Mexico City and another to Toluca, capital of the State of Mexico, to protest against the lack of protection from 'the voracity of the water vendors' and the political manipulation by municipal functionaries who were asking them to 'join the PRI' if they wanted a fairer water deal (*Excelsior*, 18 March 1986).

Occasionally, the protagonists lost their patience, like those in Cuautitlán Izcalli on 11 August 1987, who marched to the municipal palace demanding the regularization of the water supply after two months of interruption. Housewives with babies, elderly people and neighbours carrying empty pails held a 'virulent rally' demanding water and threatening to lynch the municipal functionaries, including the mayor and the head of the water tankers (El Sol de Mexico, 12 August 1987). In the same municipality, in July 1991 the tone of the discussion had probably changed as the neighbours were threatening that 'if there is no water, there will be no votes', which illustrates the intimate connection between the delivery of services and political clientelism in the MCMA. A commission of delegates marched to the municipal palace to demand the normalization of water services, which had been extremely irregular for over one year. The commission complained that to have water, at least for running their toilets, they had resorted to drawing it from a neighbouring wastewater canal (*Excelsior*, 5 July 1991).

In this connection, another set of examples concerns the crucial impact of wastewater mismanagement and water pollution on public health. In January 1986, neighbours of Tlalnepantla directed a public demand to the state governor concerning the pollution of River Tlalnepantla. The river had become a wastewater canal and about 25,000 people were living on its highly polluted banks, and the claimants wanted the river piped (*Metrópoli*, 21 January 1986: 9). Another event took place in September 1992 to protest about the threat to public health posed by the extensive water pollution in Alvaro Obregón, Federal District, a jurisdiction also affected by recurrent flooding and landslides (*Ovaciones*, 4 September 1992: 6).

In Ecatepec, about 50,000 residents issued a denunciation to the press on February 1987 concerning the infiltration of the water network by wastewater from a neighbouring sewer. The population had stopped drinking water from the network due to the spread of parasitic diseases and had no other choice than buying expensive bottled water, which they had to pay for in addition to the normal water bills (*El Sol*, 9 February 1987: 2b; *El Universal*, 25 September 1992: 3). Similarly, in September 1991 a demonstration was held to denounce the lack of compliance with sanitary regulations by many of the almost

500 companies producing ice and bottled water in the Federal District. According to the allegations, uncontrolled ice and bottled water were provoking the spread of gastrointestinal diseases before the indifference of the health authorities (*Ovaciones*, 30 September 1991: 3a). This time the government intervened very drastically and closed down many of these enterprises, which were effectively found responsible for delivering unsafe water products.

In this regard, the environmental and public health impact of unsafe water supply, lack of drainage and sanitation, and inadequate disposal and treatment of wastewater is certainly one of the most serious problems in the MCMA. As stated in December 1986 by Francisco Camacho Lacroix, then president of the Medical Society of the Valley of Mexico, the MCMA was 'the most polluted zone in the country'. He also pointed out that the high records of infant mortality characteristic of the State of Mexico were mainly related to the lack of safe water, in particular in the municipalities of Netzahualcóyotl, Ecatepec, Tlalnepantla and Naucalpan (*Metrópoli*, 15 December 1986). Likewise, in October 1990 Francisco Escalante Martínez, director of the Environmental Commission of the Mexican Association of Occupational Health (Asociación Mexicana de Salud Ocupacional (AMSO)), denounced that 'the main causes of death in the metropolitan area are the gastrointestinal diseases provoked by water pollution and unsafe food' (*El Universal*, 10 October 1990: 3).

To complete this second group of examples, we include an event triggered by the recurrent flooding of the lower areas of the city, which continues to be a major challenge despite centuries of efforts directed at tackling the problem. In October 1992, as a result of a serious flooding affecting seven municipalities (Chalco, Netzahualcóyotl, Ecatepec, Tlalnepantla, Tultitlán, Coacalco and Atizapán), neighbour associations carried out blockades of highways, sit-downs in public buildings, and denunciations to the press demanding help from the authorities. In particular, the protagonists complained about the lack of maintenance of the drainage network (*Novedades*, 18 October, 1992: 22A). Shortly after, it was reported that several communities in Chalco had been flooded by wastewater, although in some cases the problem was already several months old. The families complained that little or no help had been received from the authorities (*El Universal*, 8 November 1992: 39). This problem is not exclusive to the conurbated municipalities, as according to the Commission of Public Safety and Civil Protection of the Federal District Department (DDF) there exist 70 *colonias* in the capital that are exposed to recurrent flooding, rock falls and landslides, especially during the months from June to September (*El Nacional*, 22 September 1991: 28).

This second set of examples illustrates the multidimensional character of the struggle over water in the MCMA. It casts light on the density, texture, and ramifications characterizing the interaction between users of the water services and the public agencies responsible for their provision. As observed, the web is made up of many other actors mediating the relation between users and public agencies, and includes corrupt public servants, private, social and political entrepreneurs and their organizations, water vendors and speculators, among others. We explore later the implications of these interactions from the perspective of citizenship, but let us first consider the last group of examples, which concern confrontations that take place around the social and political control of water resources and services in the MCMA.

Events involving the control of water resources and infrastructure

The third group of examples singles out those cases where the links between water and power are more transparent, and includes clashes over the control of water sources and water services between users, the authorities, private entrepreneurs or political factions. Many of these cases form part of processes briefly described in Chapter 3, such as the implementation of federal policies directed at securing public control over water resources or transforming the status of water from public to private good, which will be analysed in more detail later.

For instance, in June 1987, about 9,000 inhabitants from Ecatepec rallied to the main square to protest against the mayor's policy of 'municipalizing the water service which had been managed by the community for over 60 years'. The confrontation, according to the protagonists, had started two months earlier when 'the mayor, policemen, and other individuals' had dissolved a community gathering organized to discuss the administration of one of their wells. The protagonists alleged that the mayor was trying to enforce municipal control over a water system which had been built by the neighbours and which supplied at the time drinkable water to over 6,000 inhabitants, while uncontrolled private well owners were allowed to extract water for private profit 'under the blind eye of the authorities'. They intimated that a private company had a vested interest in controlling the well, and had paid the mayor 'a multimillion sum of money' to facilitate the process. The confrontation reached a violent character on 14 June, when during a massive meeting held again in the plaza four women were injured in a street combat fought with sticks, rods, stones and pipes. According to allegations, the real confrontation was between 'the people and the governing bureaucracy', as the PRI and the National Peasant's Confederation (Confederación Nacional Campesina (CNC)) had imposed on the community a 'fraudulent agreement to expropriate the well' (*Excelsior*, 12 June 1987: 25; *Metrópoli*, 1 June 1986: 11; *La Jornada*, 15 June 1987).

Another case happened in July 1986, when 'a group of *panistas* [members of the PAN]' from Atizapán, 'sabotaged the water supply' in response to the imminent take-over by the municipality of a water system that was under community control. In the words of the mayor, he was left with 'no other alternative but to take over the management and administration of the distribution system', and he added that the 'agitators' had been allegedly exploiting the water system for political recruitment and profit (*El Día*, 23 July 1986: 1a; *El Universal*, 18 July 1986: 20).

A similar event took place in March 1987 during the dry season in Chimalhuacán. A group of about 20 persons described as *panistas* seized an artesian well, another step in what had been a protracted struggle for the control of water sources and infrastructure in the region. According to one report, a water committee, allegedly under the control of *panistas*, had already seized four wells since 1985 and 1986. Now with five wells in their hands, the *panistas* controlled the water supply of about 1,000,000 people. This time, however, their action triggered the immediate response of several thousand *priístas* [PRI members] who seized the municipal palace and filled the plaza on 14 March 1987 'to prevent the PAN from taking complete control' over water. On the other side, members of the committee denied the allegations that the wells were controlled by *panistas*, and described themselves as 'members of the community, among whom there are obviously some *panistas*', and as 'a group of citizens from diverse political ideologies who organized themselves as a civic force and drilled some wells to alleviate the thirst of the people' after the many unfulfilled promises of the authorities. They announced their 'commitment to defend the wells at any price'. They also alleged that the state governor had 'invented a confrontation between *panistas* and *priístas*' to achieve the objective of taking over control of the wells, while there were about 2,000 clandestine wells functioning, most of them managed by private businesses, under the blind eye of the government.

The committee declared that they were not selling water for profit and, on the contrary, it was the authorities themselves who were taking water from their wells and selling it in other areas like the Federal District. The confrontation reached a peak on 17 March 1987 with the massive repression of the community by police forces sent by the state governor. The attack happened at 2am when about 50 patrol cars, 350 policemen and civilians covered with balaclavas shot, beat, tear-gassed and arrested men, women, elderly people and youngsters. According to the press reports, 27 people were wounded, some badly, 31 were arrested, seven disappeared, nine vehicles and some houses were damaged, and an opposition federal deputy was abused, robbed and illegally arrested. Finally, the state water utility CEAS took over control of the wells, although a few days later the defeated *colonos* marched to the Federal Chamber of Deputies to protest against the brutal attack and the municipalization of their wells, thus starting a new cycle of confrontation (*El Universal*, 14 and 20 March 1987, and 23 April 1987; *Excelsior*, 15 and 29 March 1987 and 23 April 1987; *El Sol de Mexico*, 19 March 1987; *Uno Más Uno*, 20 March 1987).

These events tend to confirm the allegations that water in the MCMA, particularly in the conurbated municipalities, is often controlled by political actors, and this notion was reinforced by allegations made by the Organization of Towns and Colonies and the Federation of Proletarian Colonies of the State of Mexico shortly after the repression of Chimalhuacán by state security forces. They argued that the United Mexican Socialist Party (Partido Socialista Unificado de México (PSUM)) controlled most water distributed in Tultitlán, while the PAN had maintained control over two wells in Chimalhuacán, even after the repression of 17 March. The PRI was allegedly the water boss in Naucalpan, Ecatepec and Tlalnepantla, 'where the neighbours who refuse to join their rallies have the water cut off in their colonies'. In other municipalities throughout the State of Mexico, the PAN, the Partido Socialista (PS), and the CNC also controlled water systems according to the allegation (*Uno Más Uno*, 20 March 1987: 10; *Excelsior*, 29 March 1987: 2e).

The type of events represented by the third set of examples accounted for over 13 per cent of the total number of cases, with a higher occurrence in the conurbated municipalities. The conflicts over water resources and infrastructure illustrated here are intimately related to issues of water governance, as they concern the definition of how water and water services are governed, by whom and for whom. In particular, it is worth highlighting the resistance encountered by the federal policies implemented since the 1980s aimed at enforcing state control over water resources, which shows that the long-term process of monopolization of water control by the state is still incomplete, fragile and highly contested. We come back to these issues later.

Concluding remarks

Undoubtedly, the main motivation for the actions of most protagonists of the events is to ensure a continued access to the essential services of safe water supply and sanitation. However, we have argued that the events cannot be explained away only by reference to their techno-bureaucratic or administrative dimensions, or to the impact of physical–natural or socio-demographic determinations on the management of water and water services. From our perspective, these events are part of a structural social confrontation to overcome the qualitative and quantitative inequalities preventing millions from full access to the territory of citizenship, a confrontation that is largely autonomous from the individual wills and reason of the protagonists. The autonomy of the process from its individual manifestations is clearer when analysed at the level of the combined result of multiple events happening throughout the complex spatial setting of the MCMA. Thus, the struggle over water cannot be reduced to the action of politically conscious protagonists, but must be also explored in connection with the largely unplanned political outcomes of the process. Unfortunately, the most influential interventions of social science in the fields of water policy and management since the 1980s have reinforced the already prevailing technocratic approach to these issues by playing down the social, political and cultural dimensions in the analysis.

In this connection, in the following two chapters we attempt to make a contribution towards re-establishing a balance by bringing forward other facets of water management and policy and re-orientating the analysis. We will now rejoin the long-term perspective of the book, momentarily interrupted in this chapter, to explore the interweaving between the formation of water rights, institutions, and practices and the development of citizenship rights.

5
Water and the Evolution of Citizenship

'All emancipation is a reduction of the human world and relationships to man himself. Political emancipation is the reduction of man, on the one hand, to a member of civil society, to an egoistic, independent individual, and, on the other hand, to a citizen, a juridical person. Only when the real, individual man re-absorbs in himself the abstract citizen, and as an individual human being has become a species-being in his everyday life, in his particular work, and in his particular situation, only when man has recognized and organized his own forces as social forces, and consequently no longer separates social power from himself in the shape of political power, only then will human emancipation have been accomplished.'—**Karl Marx**, *On the Jewish Question*

This chapter places the emphasis on the specific links between the control and management of water and the formation of citizenship rights in Mexico. Although by the mid-nineteenth century Mexico formally universalized civil and political rights of citizenship, in practice the ensuing historical process was characterized by the reproduction and expansion of qualitative and quantitative inequalities and the continued exclusion of the majority from access to substantive citizenship rights. We discuss first the conceptual links that can be established between citizenship and water, looking at the development of property rights over water – water rights – the governance of water resources and essential water services, and the access to water and sanitation as a social right. Then, we explore how water policies, institutions and practices became interwoven with the particular forms adopted by the long-term development of citizenship in Mexico.

The process of citizenship

In our discussion of citizenship we have taken into account the classical analysis of T. H. Marshall in his study of citizenship in Britain (Marshall, 1992). Although Marshall's arguments have become the object of much criticism and have also been reviewed and further specified over time, we believe that his seminal essay on the topic provides useful tools for the operationalization and study of the concept in historical perspective. He stated that:

> I shall be running true to type as a sociologist if I begin by saying that I propose to divide citizenship into three parts. But the analysis is, in this case, dictated by history even more clearly than by logic. I shall call these three parts, or elements, civil, political, and social. The civil element is composed of the rights necessary for individual freedom – liberty of the person, freedom of speech, thought and faith, the right to own property and to conclude valid contracts, and the right to justice. By the political element I mean the right to participate in the exercise of political power, as a member of a body invested with political authority or as an elector of the members of such a body. By the social element I mean the whole range from the right to a modicum of economic welfare and security to the right to share to the full in the social heritage and to live the life of a civilised being according to the standards prevailing in the society. (Marshall, 1992: 8)

The very optimistic tone of Marshall's essay reflected the post-war political environment of the late 1940s when the creation of the British welfare state, with the universalization of essential services such as health and education, represented for him the latest phase of the long-term evolution of citizenship rights in the country. In particular, Marshall argued that the institutionalization of social rights had abated qualitative inequalities – that is, inequalities of entitlements based on birth, ethnic origin or gender – which are incompatible with democracy and freedom. Moreover, by bestowing universal entitlement to the essentials of social welfare on all members of the community, social rights would have introduced 'a universal right to real income which is not proportionate to the market value of the claimant', thus reducing also quantitative inequalities (ibid: 7, 28). In turn, the entitlement to a share in the civilized life according to the prevailing standards of social well-being would have empowered all citizens to participate meaningfully in the economic, social and political process, as illustrated by the universalization of education, previously a preserve of the upper classes:

> The right to education is a genuine social right of citizenship, because the aim of education during childhood is to shape the future adult. And there is here no conflict with civil rights as interpreted in an age of individualism. For civil rights are designed for use by reasonable and intelligent persons, who have learned to read and write. Education is a necessary prerequisite of civil freedom. But, by the end of the nineteenth century, elementary education was not only free, it was compulsory. It was increasingly recognized, as the nineteenth century wore on, that political democracy needed an educated electorate, and that scientific manufacture needed educated workers and technicians. The duty to improve and civilize oneself is therefore a social duty, and not merely a personal one, because the social health of a society depends upon the civilization of its members. (Ibid: 16)

However, Marshall was also aware that the development of citizenship was marred by contradictions and driven by social confrontations. In this regard, he argued that the progress of citizenship is 'at war' with the capitalist system predicated on the existence and reproduction of quantitative, market-based inequalities. This is so because, although citizenship in a liberal democracy is instrumental to capitalism by providing 'the foundation of equality on which the structure of inequality could be built', in the long run the extension and enrichment of citizenship entails the potential for political emancipation and the abatement of market-based inequality (ibid: 21, 40). While civil and political rights may be a support for developing and sustaining capitalist relations, their scope may be checked by the expansion of social rights oriented by redistributive principles (Barbalet, 1993). Perhaps for this reason Marx, though doubtlessly aware about the shortcomings of citizenship in capitalist democracy, stated that the political emancipation achieved through the exercise of citizenship rights constitutes 'the final form of human emancipation within the hitherto existing world order' (Marx, 1975: 155).

However, the emancipation offered by citizenship within capitalist democracy is a territory fiercely protected from intrusion and, therefore, subject to protracted struggles which are multidimensional in character. This includes struggles over the definition of the boundaries and contents of citizenship as well as over the actual access to this jeal-ously preserved territory. In this regard, in his less optimistic writings of later decades, and in the face of unrelenting class inequalities, Marshall addressed the failure of the British welfare system as a defeat of the model of inclusive citizenship promoted since the 1940s (Marshall, 1981). His pessimistic evaluation of the actual progress of citizenship foreshadowed the far-reaching transformations that would affect British society since the late 1980s, when the very concepts of 'social rights' and universal access to essential services became under attack. In the new political environment, encapsulated in Margaret Thatcher's negation of the very notion of society, policies were directed at reversing the ideals of the 1940s and subordinating the rights of citizenship to the dictates of capitalist market principles. In the water sector, the new policies became embodied in the full-scale privatization of water and sanitation in England and Wales in 1989. We come back to this in Chapter 6, as the British case offers important lessons for understanding the main thrust – and internal contradic-tions – of the water policy models implemented worldwide, including Mexico, since the 1980s and their consequences for the development of citizenship.

Caveats and conceptual clarification

Before entering into the more specific discussion on water and citizen-ship in Mexico, let us highlight some important caveats and clarify some concepts. Although Marshall divided citizenship rights into three distinctive bundles for analysis, namely civil, political, and social, it has been argued that these categories are not mutually exclusive as there is considerable overlapping between the three (King and Waldron, 1988: 419). Also, over time there has been an inflation of cit-izenship forms including 'technological', 'ecological', and 'environ-mental', which has contributed to further specifying or even expanding the traditional categories laid out by Marshall to include, for instance, rights to information and informed consent, which are highly relevant to our discussion (Frankenfeld, 1992; Steenbergen, 1994; Newby, 1996; Mehta, 1998). Moreover, although Marshall was aware that the evolution of civil, political, and social rights was not linear and was subject to fluctuations and fallbacks (Marshall, 1992: 10), his argument that their development followed a temporal sequence has been widely criticized for its allegedly teleological approach (Giddens, 1982: 171; Mann, 1987: 340).[1] Other critics have argued that by giving social welfare the same status as political and civil rights Marshall obfuscated the difference between redistributive policy and citizenship, while ultimately he was not consistent with his own arguments and fell short of advocating the State's obligation to guarantee social equality (Klausen, 1995: 250–2).

These are important criticisms, and our discussion of citizenship avoids taking the categories elaborated by Marshall – and others after him – as fixed, exhaustive or mutually exclusive. Likewise, we do not argue that the recorded historical sequences in the formation of citizenship rights in Mexico or elsewhere have been the result of mechanical necessity or teleology. Following Norbert Elias' insights we argue that they formed part of a long-term process of structural change which has discernible directionality, whereby the establishment of human control over water in the Basin of Mexico was inextricably linked to the inter-human processes leading to the formation of specific power configurations, institutions and practices characterizing the development of citizenship in Mexico. Finally, although it is clear that Marshall himself was not politically consequent with the conclusion of his propositions, in the light of recent historical developments his work has acquired a somewhat radical character, certainly an unintended outcome of his work. In particular, as discussed in Chapter 6 Marshall became a target for neoliberal and neoconservative theorists since the late 1970s, which forms part of the epistemic–political dimension of the struggle over citizenship.

From another angle, the concept of citizenship is the product of the specific historical processes that led to the formation of modern nation states in Western developed countries. Rival bodies of thought have given strikingly different meanings to the concept, such as in the free-market Anglo-Saxon tradition compared to the social-democratic, radical, communitarian or republican versions, and they have also adopted multifarious forms in the political cultures and practices of different countries (Fraser and Gordon, 1994; Cohen and Arato, 1994). The conceptualization of these processes in the specialized literature reflects mainly the specific experience of Western Europe and the United States, which warns against the uncritical generalization of concepts such as citizenship to the developing world (Anderson, 1994). For instance, Western-style processes of state formation in what Crosby termed 'the Neo-Europes' and the mestizo countries emerging from the European colonization initiated in the fifteenth century, have been the uneven product of conquest, imitation, assimilation and recreation of European ideas and institutions. Thus, in Spanish

America the institutions of liberal democracy have been transplanted, imposed, copied and adopted since the nineteenth century, though this did not happen on a *tabula rasa*. In some cases like Argentina, Chile, and Uruguay, the new institutions evolved in recently established communities with a large population of European origin, while in Mexico the nineteenth-century liberal reforms were implemented against a background of more than three centuries of intricate interweaving of the Indian and Spanish forms of social organization.

Finally, geographical, cultural-historic and political cleavages are not the sole – nor perhaps the most important – factors in determining the meaning and content of citizenship. Citizenship changes over time within the same political community and, as Aristotle stated, 'the nature of citizenship, like that of the state, is a question which is often disputed ... the man who is a citizen in a democracy is often not one in an oligarchy' (Aristotle, 1948: 93). Paraphrasing and bringing up to date his insight, the borders of citizenship are a shifting zone. On the one hand, either peaceful or violent changes of political regimes frequently mean the redefinition of the content of citizenship and the consequent alterations in the quality and extension of citizenship rights enjoyed by a given community. On the other hand, although citizenship is in legal terms 'internally inclusive ... and externally exclusive' with regard to the formal community of rights (Brubaker, 1992: 21), in fact it is also internally exclusive regarding the quality of citizenship actually enjoyed by people. This applies to important sectors of the formal and legal citizenry who do not fully enjoy 'the standard of civilized life [and who] claim to be admitted to a share in the social heritage, which in turn means a claim to be accepted as full members of the society, that is, as citizens'. These claims for admission to the territory 'of basic human equality associated with full community membership' can take many forms, and constitute an integral part of the struggle for widening access to and deepening the content of citizenship (Marshall, 1992: 6, 45).

Water and citizenship: specifying the links

As shown by Marshall, the creation of property rights and its related institutions constituted a central element in the formation of modern citizenship systems, in particular civil rights (ibid: 8–10). In this perspective, property rights over water or water rights can be defined as a component of the civil rights of citizenship. In fact, ownership of water rights became a distinctive privilege of *ciudadanos* in New Spain, although citizenship in that context was restricted to the colonial elite of Spanish and Creole origin and some of its principles are not comparable with those of modern citizenship systems. Nevertheless, the struggle for transforming water from a privilege reserved to an oligarchic minority and making it universally available as a public good was not formally won until the Mexican Revolution, although the resulting promise of ensuring universal access to water and safe water and sanitation services is still unfulfilled for a very large number of Mexicans.

In this connection, water rights, a social relationship involving human-nature and inter-human interactions, have also been closely related to the development of political and social rights. Firstly, the principles and institutions associated with the definition and enforcement of these rights have been instrumental in the governance of water resources and water systems. Governance, a very recent concept also coined to capture processes largely stemming from developed countries, has come to occupy a central place in current international debates over water issues and we will address it more in depth in Chapter 6. Let us state here that, for the moment, we mean by governance the principles, values and institutions that determine how water is governed, managed and allocated, by whom and for whom, a crucial area of political decision from which most citizens have been historically excluded. Secondly, although not explicitly mentioned by Marshall, access to essential water services was a crucial part in the expansion of 'the right to share to the full in the social heritage and to live the life of a civilized being according to the standards prevailing in the society' that he identified with full membership of society, his broad definition of citizenship (Marshall, 1992: 6–8). Indeed, the universalization of water and sanitation in post-war Great Britain became a public priority not only for reasons of hygiene or health but also as a factor of economic growth, and it was finally achieved during the 1960s (Goubert, 1986; Hassan, 1998). However, it is worth noting that the notion that access to essential water supplies is a universal human entitlement can be traced back well beyond the development of modern citizenship systems, as it belongs to the heritage of human civilization.

Water, 'civilized well-being' and citizenship

The impact that the governance, management and allocation of water resources and water and sanitation services has on human well-being does not need much explanation. Firstly, water is the most essential life-sustaining element for human beings, 'cosmic juice', 'blood of the earth', 'life's matrix', 'real elixir' (Ball, 2000: 3, 21, 205). However, and secondly, a large proportion of threats and hazards to human life are related to the ways in which water resources are managed, which applies both to well-known water-related diseases such as malaria and schistosomiasis but also to broader health concerns including natural or anthropogenic chemical contamination of water supplies or catastrophic accidents such as floods (World Health Organization (WHO), 2003c). Thirdly, access to clean water supply and adequate disposal of excreta are considered to be a crucial factor in the sharp decline in infectious diseases achieved during the last two centuries in developed countries. One important reason for this is that, although infectious-disease mortality can be reduced by medical attention, a significant reduction in morbidity is only possible through preventive health policies in which safe water and sanitation are a basic requisite (Feachem, 1983: 25; United Nations Economic Commission for Europe (UNECE) and WHO-Europe, 2002).

However, despite the scientific and technological advances in the management of water resources and water and sanitation services, at the beginning of the twenty-first century around 1.1 billion people, 17 per cent of the world population, still have no access to safe drinking water, while 2.4 billion people or 40 per cent of the total, lack basic sanitation services (European Commission (EC), 2002a). It is estimated that over 5 million people still die each year from preventable water-related infections worldwide, with diarrhoeal diseases alone accounting for about 2 million deaths every year, mostly among children under 5 years of age from less-developed countries living in extreme poverty. Millions more are affected by illnesses caused by the intake of health-threatening substances naturally present in water such as arsenic which have delayed and long-term effects (EC, 2002b; WHO, 2003a; 2003b). Adequate management of water resources and services and universal access to water and sanitation, though, are only a necessary condition as their actual impact on human well-being is mediated by other considerations, among which crucial aspects of citizenship such as access to education and active engagement of the population in the governance of both water resources and services are paramount (Cairncross and Kochar, 1994; McGranahan *et al.*, 2001).

To a large extent, these observations refer to well-established knowledge already belonging to the heritage of modern civilization. For instance, by analogy with Marshall's comments on education, hygiene emerged as a main social concern in Europe since the late eighteenth century, and reached international dimensions in the late nineteenth century with the crusade for universalizing hygiene education and compulsory access to safe drinking water and sewerage launched by the sanitary movement. As Goubert put it, 'whatever their specialty or nationality, [the sanitary experts] were all very aware that, if the nation states wanted to protect their children, it was their duty to make the population healthy and strong to avoid the procession of avoidable diseases' (Goubert, 1986: 103–9). By analogy with Marshall's argument in relation to education, there was here no conflict with civil rights as interpreted in an age of individualism (Marshall, 1992: 16), for while education was considered to be a prerequisite of civil freedom, health – borrowing from Goubert – became 'an essential precondition for the strength of the nation' (Goubert, 1986: 111). The state needed not only educated citizens but also healthy soldiers, while industry also required a healthy workforce.

In this connection, Foucault conceptualized the expansion of the institutions of hygiene as forming part and parcel of what he called the 'police of the general health', the 'police of the social body'. He argued that these institutions were part of the 'web of microscopic, capillary political power' underpinning the emergence of capitalist social forms: the development of an industrial working force and a market economy, and the formation of national citizenship systems (Foucault, 1994a: 622; 1994b: 17–8). In intimate correspondence with these processes, water itself was increasingly acquiring the character of commodity, and in some countries like England, France, and the United States its diffusion fuelled the emergence of an important industry dedicated to the extraction, filtering, and distribution of water for human use. This, however, has not been a straightforward process and, particularly in the case of essential water supply and sanitation, the commodification process was punctuated by recurrent setbacks and even failure, as discussed in Chapter 6.

From another angle, rising public awareness about the benefits derived from using larger amounts of water on a regular basis also required significant efforts (Goubert, 1986: 23; Mumford, 1940: 423). As suggested by Norbert Elias:

> The impulse toward regular cleaning and constant bodily cleanliness does not derive in the first place from clearly defined hygienic insight, from a clear or, as we say, 'rational' understanding of the danger of dirt to health. The relation of washing, too, changes in

conjunction with the transformation of human relationships. Today, washing and bodily cleanliness are instilled in the individual from an early age as a kind of automatic habit, so that it gradually more or less disappears from his consciousness that he washes and disciplines himself to constant cleanliness ... for reasons of external compulsion. Regular washing with soap and water is another such 'compulsive action' cultivated in our society by the nature of our conditioning and consolidated in our consciousness by hygienic, 'rational' explanations. (Elias, 1994: 252, note 124)

However, even more daunting than persuading common people was the task of the health and sanitation movement to also convince the economic and political elites of the need for a social provision of water services, public health and sanitation, due to the prevalent understanding among those sectors that these services were only for people that could afford to pay for them. To a large extent, the programme of the health and sanitation crusaders was helped by the horrors caused by nineteenth-century epidemics, in particular cholera, which did not respect class boundaries in their ravages. In Britain, for instance, the cholera outbreaks of the mid-nineteenth century triggered the assumption that ensuring access to clean water and safe disposal of excreta for every household – at least in urban areas – was a binding moral duty for the community, and the Public Health Acts established that dwellings lacking safe water supply were unfit for human habitation (Ward, 1997: 6–7; McNeill, 1977: 271–4). However, translating these assumptions into actual policies and then effectively implementing them was only possible through decades of social and political conflict in Britain (Finer, 1997; Taylor, 1999; Hassan, 1998; Laski *et al.*, 1935; Millward, 1991; Luckin, 1986), while in the case under consideration, Mexico, change came eventually through a violent social revolution where conspicuous members of the sanitary movement played a central role.

Summing up, the links between water and an inclusive concept of citizenship involve a number of crucial aspects ranging from the development of property rights over water, to the institutions that govern the management of water resources and water services, and the interconnections between access to water and sanitation, citizen awareness and participation, and public health and well-being. The fact that a large share of the human population – as a rule the most vulnerable sectors – continue to suffer or die from preventable diseases or threats owing to the inadequate management of water resources or the lack of safe water and sanitation services shows that the struggle over the territory of citizenship is not just a metaphoric image. Rather, this long-term struggle continues to claim its victims in a tangible and quantifiable fashion. We will come back to the contemporary situation and to the relevant theoretical and political debate in Chapter 6, but let us now move on to the exploration of the long-term development of citizenship in Mexico in connection with the formation of institutions and practices that govern the control, management, and access to water resources and essential water services.

Water and the struggle over citizenship

The activities involved in the control and management of water resources, and especially the formation of water rights, were closely intertwined with the social and political transformation of New Spain into an oligarchic capitalist society by the end of the nineteenth century. However, this development was punctuated by multidimensional confrontations which we analyse here as components of the long-term struggles over the territory of citizenship. Firstly, the development of water rights offers an outstanding example of the temporal and spatial discontinuities that characterize the formation of property rights over the elements of nature, a crucial component of the civil rights of citizenship in modern liberal democracies. Secondly, the control and management of water resources and services in the basin has been characterized by the protracted failure to universalize the provision of safe living conditions, which is inextricably linked with the exclusionary and agonistic character assumed by the development of citizenship in the country.

In this regard, the ecological transformation undergone by the Basin of Mexico since the Conquest also entailed a radical transformation in the values, meanings and social practices associated with water, and particularly in the social relations mediated by the control and access to the resource. Water-related risks and threats, real or perceived, played a significant role in this development. For instance, the indigenous universe of socio-cultural, economic, political and aesthetic values associated with the lacustrine environment was displaced by the prevailing perception among the colonial elite that the lakes were a threat to public health and had to be removed. Likewise, the community values associated with water and land in the pre-Columbian period over time became superseded by the relentless monopolization of these resources by a relatively small number of private entrepreneurs. Nevertheless, this was not a linear process and the surviving Indian communities preserved much of their original water culture over the centuries, and some aspects of it have either remained the same or hardly changed at all until today (Dalton, 1990: 66–72; González Casanova, 1965a: 35; 1965b: 103–8; Garibay and Aboites Aguilar, 1994). In particular, the notion that common uses of land and water have priority over private forms has survived until today, not least because it became intertwined with ancient community traditions that also formed part of the Spanish legacy and were later inherited by the Mexican Republic.

Pre-Hispanic water management

Regarding water rights, scholarly consensus suggests that before the arrival of the Spanish conquistadores the Indians had well-defined water rights both for human consumption and for productive uses. However, water was a resource held in common, and private ownership of water was unknown or at best restricted to a minority of the population (Meyer, 1984: 18, note 26; Hundley, 1992: 23; Cano, 1991: 372). Moreover, it is not clear whether the rulers and noblemen themselves enjoyed private property rights over land and water as individuals or – as most evidence suggests – as recognition for their position during their period in office (León-Portilla, 1984: 23). Perhaps the case of urban water is the most controversial, as the king and noblemen enjoyed access to water carried by pipelines to their palaces. Also, some scholars have suggested that Aztec water sellers who distributed water from the Chapultepec aqueduct paid a fee (canon) to the king, although there is no historical evidence to back this hypothesis (Musset, 1991: 182).

Early colonial legislation supported the premise that water was a community resource shared among the Indians. King Charles V ruled that 'the same order that the Indians had regarding the division and allocation of waters be kept and practised among Spaniards' (Cano, 1991: 373) which consisted of allocating water freely and according to people's needs. The king also ordered that the Indians should have control and authority over those arrangements (Musset, 1991: 227). This was a relevant decision, as indigenous control over natural resources was overwhelmingly based on communal forms of ownership, and conflicts were resolved collectively. Water was a structuring factor of social power in the indigenous social organization and water rights were a crucial element for negotiation in their matrimonial agreements and territorial struggles (Gibson, 1964: 20–1; León-Portilla, 1984: 33; Burkholder *et al.*, 1994: 11; Brundage, 1972: 56–61).

Unfortunately, the laudable principles that led to the formal recognition by the king of the community-oriented water uses and customs of the Indians was not respected in practice, and Spanish settlers soon started a systematic process of expropriation of existing indigenous water rights.

In relation to water services and hygiene, archaeological and historical research has shown that cities had well-organized systems of water supply, sewerage, and cleaning of streets, plazas and canals (Cooper, 1965: 17). For instance, the city of Teotihuacán had roof and court gutters, sewerage pipes and underground canals to drain rainwater runoff (García Quintana and Romero Galván, 1978: 102). In Tenochtitlan, wastewater and rainwater were drained through gutters that crossed the city in a west–east direction and emptied into Lake Texcoco, a drainage system that continued to work until as late as the seventeenth century. Excreta disposal was also efficiently organized, and public pathways were provided with huts for the convenience of travellers; the accumulated waste was later transported in canoes and sold to be used in crop fertilization, leather tannery and salt production (Sahab Haddad, 1991: 155; García Quintana and Romero Galván, 1978: 103–4).

Notwithstanding these achievements and despite the resulting cleanliness of the city so praised by the conquistadores, water-related diseases were a major concern. Although their actual impact in that period is unknown, their importance is suggested by the cultural relevance given to these diseases among the Indians, whereby the shrine of Amímitl, god of fishing and aquatic hunting, in Cuitlahuac was the meeting place for those seeking relief from coughs, diarrhoea, dysentery, and rheumatism, while the Tlalocan, the paradise of Tlaloc, their ancient god of rain, was the natural place for those who had died from water-related infections (García Quintana and Romero Galván, 1978: 116–20). Moreover, the evidence suggests that epidemics often caused depopulation and abandonment of cities in pre-Columbian Mexico (Hernández Rodríguez, 1982: 150–3).

The colonial legacy

Colonial rule was imposed on a successful and well-organized water-oriented social formation, which challenged and resisted the invaders on many fronts, including the technical and legal dimensions of water control. However, as discussed earlier, the colonial development was also a process of cultural intertwining, which included the assimilation of elements from the subjugated civilization by the dominant. In fact, both Spaniards and Aztecs had a long historical experience of ethnic, social, and cultural synthesis. Spain had been invaded by disparate conquerors since the fall of the Roman Empire in the fifth century, including the Moors, and the Reconquest of the peninsula from Muslim political domination had finally been completed almost simultaneously with the arrival of the Spaniards in the Americas. All these cultures left an imprint on water traditions, uses, institutions and law (Glick, 1970; Meyer, 1984). Meanwhile, the Mexica Aztecs were but one of many cultures that had settled over the centuries in the Basin of Mexico, though they had the determination and ability to subordinate the rest, an achievement that had been consolidated only a few decades before the arrival of Hernán Cortés.

Given this highly dynamic socio-cultural context, the Spanish colonization had a syncretistic impact that can be traced in almost any aspect of post-Conquest development. For instance, the body of colonial law incorporated indigenous practices that have endured until our times in the water legislation and institutions (Lameiras, 1974: 183). However, not all Spanish traditions were compatible with the native ones and the divergent understandings of the values and status of water became a crucial factor in the struggles over the resource (Meyer, 1984: 20). In the end, the colonial process metabolized the indigenous legacy, evolving into a capitalist oligarchic order that engulfed the indigenous traditions, institutions and culture.

Water rights

The colonial development in the basin simultaneously sanctioned the large scale expropriation of indigenous water rights, and the expansion of private water rights vis-á-vis the preservation of collective and community rights over water. Community water rights were maintained in the Indian villages, which were protected by the religious orders from further pillaging and even extermination. Also, Spanish urbanization policies stressed the priority of communitarian concerns whereby water was considered a common good to which all *ciudadanos* were equally entitled. However, simultaneously the colonization of New Spain proceeded largely through the large-scale private appropriation of land and water resources. The legal apparatus slowly built through the expropriation of existing indigenous rights led, on the eve of Independence, to the monopolization of most land and water by a small Creole elite, whether in the form of private holdings or through the decentralized action of the religious orders which controlled directly or indirectly much of the land, urban property and water.

The struggle over water rights

The formation of water rights in the Basin of Mexico was far from linear and homogeneous, and was punctuated by permanent confrontations fuelled by different forms of indigenous resistance. Also, colonial rule was marred by contradictions between the Crown, the colonial authorities, the religious orders, and private entrepreneurs, which over time resulted in a chaotic system of de facto and ill-defined permanent water rights and widespread clandestine water use. In this connection, the colonization did not conform to the legal principles that formally protected indigenous water rights and gave priority to essential water uses by the community over individualistic appropriation of water for private profit. This situation exacerbated the process of social exclusion, especially of the large indigenous population of non-ciudadanos, and colonial water rights became an elite mark that over time evolved into de facto private water rights in the independent Republic (Musset, 1991: 182–92).

In principle, in Spanish water law, community rights had priority over those of the individual, which gave ground to the emergence of corporate forms of water rights (for example in irrigation districts, and towns) whereby private interests were subordinated to the common good. This tradition was compatible with the indigenous community-oriented water practices, which were preserved and even strengthened in some cases. In this regard, the main forms of water rights during the colonial period were the *mercedes* or *gracias* (water grants) extended by the Crown, authorizing the recipient to use a certain amount of water, while there were also other forms, such as the *sobrantes* (spare water), which allowed the holder of a water right to transfer or sell any unused allocation of water (Meyer, 1984: 137, 140, note 29). However, the contradictions in the colonial legal system generated confusion in the actual enforcement of the law, while the Crown's chronic financial bankruptcy led the king to allow wealthy individuals to colonize the territory at their own expense, which fuelled a process of private monopolization of land and water (Chevalier, 1963: 46–7). As a result, in practice private water rights often took de facto precedence over those of communities with the tacit acceptance of the authorities (Hundley, 1992: 26–8, 36–41).

A rich tradition of water law

In contrast with the long struggle to centralize water control in the Iberian Peninsula, public control over water in the colonies was enforced from the very beginning: in 1541 King Charles V ruled that 'pastures, woodlands, and waters be owned in common in the Indies' (Cano, 1991: 373). All land, water, and mineral wealth were part of the royal patrimony and could be alienated from Crown ownership only by the Crown itself or by properly designated authority (Meyer, 1984: 118–19). These principles were deeply rooted in the Hispanic legal tradition, whereby water – together with pastures and wood – was considered a community resource and responsibility. This understanding was based upon earlier Roman, Germanic, and Arabic traditions, and it was formalized in *Las Siete Partidas*, the thirteenth-century codification of Spanish Law by King Alfonso X. The main concern in these water traditions was securing the survival of human communities, a principle that acquired paramount importance in the mostly arid and hot Iberian Peninsula. In these circumstances, water also became a symbol of prosperity, and a highly contested resource that has probably caused more lawsuits than land conflicts in Spain (ibid: 20–1).

Unsurprisingly, water control was a crucial factor in the modern process of state formation in Spain, which involved not just recapturing the peninsula from the Moors but also the centralization of power in the Crown (Meyer, 1984: 21). The difficulties faced by the monarchs can be illustrated by the fact that the water prerogatives of feudal lords were only abolished in 1811, while formal public control over water was firmly established only in 1866 when the first Spanish Water Law came into force (Cano, 1991: 373). One crucial aspect of the struggle concerned the definition of the public and private spheres, as by tradition private water rights were only conceded on a temporary basis and were dependent on the context and circumstances: in conditions of scarcity the status of water could always be changed to re-establish equity among users. For instance, a holder of private water rights could not waste water if a neighbour was suffering from water shortage. A complementary tradition, going as far back as the Justinian Code (sixth century AD), sanctioned the status of water as a community resource for drinking, fishing, navigation, and similar uses, while high-consuming private activities such as irrigation and industry were subject to stricter control 'because it would not be wise that the benefit of all men be hindered by the interest of some individuals'. These principles were incorporated in *Las Siete Partidas*, the legal framework of early colonial rule, and this may explain why originally land grants in New Spain did not include water rights, which were only added many years later (Meyer, 1984: 108, 117, 188). This tradition was later confirmed by the *Leyes de Indias*, the compilation of Spanish American Law ordered by the Crown to systematize colonial legislation in the seventeenth century, which was completed in 1681 (Cano, 1991: 372–3).

The Spanish practice of considering water a common resource ultimately owned by the Crown was especially relevant in colonial urban centres, which in the view of the royal strategists were the main instruments for expanding and consolidating territory (Morse, 1984: 70–9). In this tradition, municipalities were seen as the agents of the Crown and urban water was treated as a community resource and responsibility which passed from the monarch to the people as a corporate body (Hundley, 1992: 39, 41). However, the law also recognized private water rights, establishing a balance between community and individual rights but also contributing to the confusion characterizing the practical implementation of the legal principles (Meyer, 1984: 156).

In this regard, besides developing community-oriented water institutions, Spaniards had also learnt that water was a source of private wealth and social power. It is not surprising, therefore, that the actual water practices brought about a model quite removed from their more community-aware water traditions. In particular, the introduction of private ownership and its institutions alongside water uses oriented at private profit wrought a transformation in the character of the struggle over water control (ibid: 19).

The contradictions between legal principles and actual practices

As discussed in previous chapters, on the eve of the Conquest most water sources in the basin had already been tapped and brought under human control, and therefore the concession of water rights by the Crown necessarily implied the expropriation of existing rights. As a result, the Indians soon lost control over their water resources and had to seek permission to use water from the Spaniards, which became a major source of conflict. Although formally the authorities agreed that legitimate Indian possession ought not to be jeopardized, the real practices showed no respect for the formal principles. Spanish settlement involved the removal and relocation of indigenous communities, and the evidence shows that the colonial authorities sanctioned the factual expropriation of the Indians with legal formalities. Very frequently, high-ranking colonial officers used their power to encroach on Indian possessions for private benefit, while others managed to buy existing water rights from Indians at very low prices through manipulation but maintaining the legal façade (Gibson, 1964: 272–80). Moreover, although the religious orders acted as the main protectors of the Indians, in practice they too often short-changed the natives in matters of land and water. Despite the fact that the Indians resorted to legal actions within the colonial system, and a *Protector de Indios* (Indian's Protector) was appointed to represent them in courts, in most cases Spanish justice failed to protect them from pillage and expropriation (Meyer, 1984: 60–3).

The Indians waged important legal battles to protect or recover their water rights from the early colonial days, resorting to principles recognized in Spanish water law such as 'prior appropriation' to argue that they had used the water before the Spaniards arrived. For instance, the Indians of Coyoacán and Tacubaya immediately brought lawsuits for the restoration of possessions appropriated by Hernán Cortés. In the 1540s, the *encomendero* Gonzalo de Salazar took away the water used by the community for drinking and irrigation to power his own textile mill, and although the Indians swiftly launched a legal action it was only in the 1550s that the Real Audiencia accepted the community's case (Gibson, 1964: 79–80, 273). This however, was one of a few exceptional cases, as the Indians were mostly on the losing side. For instance, in 1587 the Indians sued the Spanish miller Antonio Pérez who had redirected the river Cuautitlán for his own use leaving the community without irrigation water, but the Real Audiencia sustained the right of the miller (Strauss, 1974: 147–54). In other cases, Indians were required to submit their water titles to the authorities in order to substantiate their claims, but then the titles were never returned (Meyer, 1984: 60; Gibson, 1964: 50–4).

Another major bone of contention involved the appropriation of fishing jurisdictions, which the Indian communities had as clearly demarcated as land jurisdictions. For instance, in Ecatepec fishing waters had the status of community property among the Indians, and the income produced formed an integral part of the pre-Conquest tribute system. However, Spaniards encroached on the Indian fishing territories by every available means, including armed actions of intimidation, and the conflicts went on until the eighteenth century when the invaders eventually displaced the natives from their best fisheries (Gibson, 1964: 339–43). To a certain extent, the struggles over water rights abated since the seventeenth century as a consequence of the massive appropriation of Indian lands and the relocation of the herding industries outside the Valley (Chevalier, 1963: 280–1).

In historical perspective, the struggle had a predictable winner. Although the legal framework and the official royal policy were supposed to respect the Indians' rights, there was a large gap between formal institutions and actual practices. In Chevalier's words:

> Unfortunately, natives did not always understand the exceptional importance of the [legal sanction of land and water rights], in the sense that it would make expoliations and other abuses irrevocable. It was generally quite easy to pull the wool over their eyes; their 'natural fecklessness', in the words of one inspector, did the rest. What was really serious was that injustices no longer arose from the law's ignorance of de facto situations; the law, owing to the peculiar, definitive nature of settlements, itself was sanctioning injustices. In a country governed by jurists, this was a commitment pledging the word of future generations (ibid: 273–4).

Summing up, the formation of water rights during the colonial period was an important component of the process of territorial and political domination, which took the form of a monopolization of land and water in the hands of a reduced elite of *ciudadanos* by the end of the colonial period. The ensuing confrontations were not reduced to the conflicting water interests of whites and Indians, but rather involved the clash between opposing principles and practices, and between contrasting traditions of human-nature and inter-human relationships. On the one hand, the practical consequences for the human communities involved were dramatic, because – as shown below – water became increasingly a social privilege in the hands of a reduced elite while the majority of the population became deprived from the concomitant benefits of water-related health and well-being achieved by the prevailing standard of civilized life of the time. On the other hand, however, colonial water law became the vehicle of universal principles converging from diverse traditions, whereby water for essential human uses has been historically considered a community resource and responsibility. This principle and the tradition that bestows on the state the duty to preserve the interests of human communities in the allocation of water resources, were among the key elements inherited by Mexican water law after the Independence. These issues would continue to be at the centre of social and political confrontations for years to come.

Water and human well-being

As already mentioned in Chapter 2, water-related diseases played a crucial role in the conquest of Tenochtitlan-Tlatelolco by Cortés, and most scholars agree that they were also the principal factor in the sixteenth-century collapse of the indigenous population. According to Crosby, smallpox was perhaps more decisive as a weapon than gunpowder 'because the indigenes did turn the musket and then rifle against the intruders, but smallpox very rarely fought on the side of the indigenes' (Crosby, 1994: 200; McNeill, 1977: 75–6; Musset, 1991: 115). Smallpox, measles and typhus came to the Americas with the conquistadores and found fertile ground in the immunologically defenceless indigenous population. And if disease continued to help the Europeans it did not happen due to indigenous ignorance. For example, during the 1576 smallpox epidemics, the Indians resorted to a sort of bacteriological war of resistance when they sought to transmit the plague by polluting the water supply with infected corpses[2] and baking bread with blood taken from infected victims. The tactic failed, and the colonial authorities reinforced police regulations to prevent the Indians from polluting water and food destined for the consumption of Spaniards (Márquez Morfín, 1994: 109).

From a broader perspective, the disease regime established in post-Conquest Mexico was part of the changing pattern of disease dissemination brought about by the worldwide European expansion since the late fifteenth century (McNeill, 1977: 216). In the Basin of Mexico, it led to the striking collapse of the indigenous population, which may have fallen by as much as 73 per cent between 1519 and 1597 (Whitmore, 1992: 119).[3] However, morbi-mortality patterns cannot be explained away solely by biological factors, and the sociogenesis of these phenomena – anticipated long ago by empirical practice and intuition – has been elucidated by recent research. The evidence shows that smallpox, measles, yellow fever, epidemic hepatitis, typhus and pneumonia decimated the population of Mexico City on a regular basis from the sixteenth century onwards, and they affected in particular those neighbourhoods where the poor were concentrated (Márquez Morfín, 1994: 169). Unsurprisingly, historians have also found that epidemics and famines very often coincided throughout the whole colonial period (Malvido, 1982).

In relation to this, the geography of water-related morbi-mortality was almost the mirror image of the spatial configuration of water supply services, which in turn contributed to shape the intra-urban social segregation characteristic of the colonial city. For instance, in the sixteenth century, the Indian quarter of Tlatelolco was one of the worst affected by lack of safe water, and this caused the spread of disease and a noticeable rise in the mortality rate. A complaint presented in 1592 reports that the quarter's population had been halved over a 50-year period, from 6000 to 3000 inhabitants, and people were moving to other areas of the city such as San Juan and San Pablo, although these were also affected by chronic water deficiencies (Musset, 1991: 152–3). On the opposite side, as discussed in Chapter 2, since the seventeenth century the building of new aqueducts and water supply networks favoured the western quarters, where the Spaniards chose to settle, leading to the further decline of the eastern side where the poor were concentrated.

Although the historical record shows that the authorities were concerned with improving sanitary conditions (Gaceta de México, 1731: 338–40; 1732: 458; 1735: 720; 1738: 980), over time Spanish policies became mainly geared to the satisfaction of the elite's needs and preferences. Consistent with this trend, in the late colonial period the building of new works seems to have been mainly concerned with private water uses rather than with community needs and, for example, new aqueducts were constructed to supply water for haciendas while the old communal systems were left without adequate maintenance. According to Gibson, in the eighteenth century the Texcoco water conduits were broken, the Coyoacán and Xochimilco aqueducts fell into ruin, and although the structure of the Tembleque aqueduct remained intact, the water level had fallen and it carried no water (Gibson, 1964: 347).

Interestingly, some descriptions by Mexican chroniclers of late seventeenth century Mexico City depict an urban environment characterized by cleanliness, which contrasts quite sharply with descriptions of the prevailing conditions in European cities of the time. For instance, while drainage systems in London were deficient and people used to rid households' human waste by throwing it into the streets, Mexico City would have enjoyed almost exceptional conditions of tidiness at that time (Lanning, 1985: 352). However, the historical evidence suggests that this idyllic situation could only have been enjoyed by a small elite in the few blocks that composed the best-built areas of the city centre. The many policies and regulations drafted on paper seem to have had little effect on the city's reality. Water pollution was a major problem, as suggested by the municipal records of recurring contamination of the aqueducts by agricultural, industrial and domestic waste. Likewise, wastewater disposal was a permanent public nuisance, as also was the pollution of canals and lakes which often were used as dumps for all sorts of waste including Indian corpses, offal, human excreta and the like (Musset, 1991: 158–66; Cooper, 1965: 9–15).

The enlightened late eighteenth-century urban policies designed by viceroys Bucareli and, particularly, Revillagigedo certainly brought about important innovations. When Viceroy Revillagigedo took office in the late eighteenth century, the unsanitary conditions of the city were appalling, and he launched a radical campaign to clean the streets, plazas, drainage canals and other public spaces, and improve the quality of the urban water supply, and also introduced strict measures to enhance the sanitary education of the population. Although Revillagigedo's policies prompted a sharp decrease in illnesses and deaths and were formally endorsed by his successor Branciforte, the improvements did not last and soon the old practices were resumed (Lanning, 1985: 352–6; Gaceta de México, 1791b: 367–8). In fact, many of the ordinances drafted by Revillagigedo were never enforced, and the Viceroy himself was attacked and brought to trial in 1794 by the Ayuntamiento owing to his radical reforms (Cooper, 1965: 36).

From another angle, the fact that the city had been built on a lakebed caused serious problems, including the constant threat of flooding in the rainy season and the difficulties for building efficient drainage systems. Moreover, the impact of the lacustrine environment on public health was the object of heated debates among the colonial scientific community in the late eighteenth century. For instance, medical experts of the time blamed epidemics on the decreasing level of the lakes, which would have increased the dryness of the atmosphere, and they noted that epidemics precisely occurred during the dry season (Gaceta de México, 1789a: 334–5; 1789b: 342–3). They argued that the best way to control epidemics was to preserve large surface water bodies (Gaceta de México, 1789c: 355), and consistently associated epidemic-free years with higher levels of humidity in the atmosphere, due to such factors as 'a hard winter' and 'excess of fog' (Gaceta de México, 1790a: 7; 1791a: 249–50). Nevertheless, an outstanding event that happened on the eve of the war for independence in 1810, contributed to the consolidation of the prevailing views that informed the desiccation policies. In that year the drainage systems of the city collapsed and according to the records the population was so overcome by fetid odours that the authorities commissioned an urgent investigation. The main conclusion was that the polluted lakes were responsible for the situation, and that they should be drained completely (Lanning, 1985: 357–8), a view that would also prevail after Independence.

It is worth noting that eighteenth-century public-health experts in Mexico City showed considerable awareness of scientific discoveries being made in Europe, and suggested their application to the improvement of public hygiene and sanitation (Gaceta de México, 1784: 63–4). Methods for the purification of river water, and techniques for cleaning sewers to control fetid odours, for instance, were a common issue in the specialized literature of the time (Gaceta de México, 1790b: 39; 1792: 139–40). Despite this, epidemic and water-related diseases such as digestive disorders were a major cause of death, and in particular of infant mortality. In fact, the adoption in Spanish America of the scientific advances made in Europe was, with few exceptions, a very slow process that usually took one or two generations to take hold. Also, the hierarchical structure of colonial power centralized in the viceroy and ultimately in the king, prevented the establishment of efficient systems of public health and response to extreme urgencies. For instance, during the smallpox epidemic of 1779, actions were mostly left to the charity of the authorities and of powerful members of the community, while petitions for royal funding to treat the sick in the Indian quarters and poor neighbourhoods went unattended (Lanning, 1985: 360, 369–71).

In a way similar to water policy, responsibility for sanitation and public health rested with a wide range of overlapping and sometimes competing authorities. These included the Ayuntamiento and the Royal Board of Medicine (Protomedicato), but also the viceroy and the Church, and the latter traditionally held control of hospitals and cemeteries. Therefore, there was no central authority clearly in charge, which largely accounted for the characteristic duplication of efforts, indecision, and confusion recorded (Cooper, 1965: 16–17, 40–6). An illuminating evaluation of colonial sanitation policies was offered by Viceroy Revillagigedo in the final years of colonial rule. He asserted that 'if in the government of New Spain there might have always been proper attention given to the matter of public health, then the frequent epidemics ... would not have occurred' (quoted in Cooper, 1965: 36).

After Independence

Independence from Spain (1821) did not mean a real break with the colonial model, as colonial-like power relations were maintained by the 'locally-bred colonists' of the oligarchic elite (Tannenbaum, 1965: 52). In formal terms, though, the independence brought about many formal changes in the organization of Mexico City's public life. For instance, Article 188 of the 1814 Apatzingán constitution set as a State duty ensuring 'the healthiness and comfort of the citizens'. However, in practice, basic water and sanitation infrastructure and public health were a low priority during most of the nineteenth century. In this connection, with the exception of small sections of the city centre around the Plaza Mayor, which had the best quality buildings and urban services, the living conditions in nineteenth-century Mexico City were unsanitary in every conceivable respect. Lack of access to water, let alone safe water, and sanitation was the standard, especially in the northern quarters that had been almost deserted for this reason. The impact on human health was enormous, as illustrated by the situation in the areas of Peralvillo and Santa Ana, which lacked urban infrastructure, and where the recorded average age of death was 23 years in 1840 and 13 years in 1851. Also, although global improvements in medical knowledge and practice radically reduced the incidence of old plagues such as smallpox, the lack of water and sanitation compounded by the extremely precarious living conditions of the majority contributed to the persistence of old diseases such as typhus, malaria and dysentery, and provided a fertile seedbed for new diseases like cholera (Márquez Morfín, 1994: 169–70, 245–6, 263–4).

In this connection, the 1833 cholera epidemic that by a sad coincidence erupted together with the Civil War became a landmark in several respects. In particular, the epidemic triggered a pioneering set of sanitation policies coordinated with the emerging public-health movement in Europe and the United States. However, the resulting improvements in drinking water supplies, sewerage and sanitation were strictly geared to the well-off sectors of the population that could afford the cost, which deepened the prevailing social segregation. This situation did not change much during the rest of the century, and even the impressive water engineering innovations of the Porfirian period only delivered water services to a privileged sector of the population while the majority continued to be exposed to preventable old diseases such as typhus, the major cause of morbi-mortality in pre-revolutionary Mexico (Márquez Morfín, 1994: 45–6, 263–8, 283–4, 289, 292).

The making of citizens

From another angle, independence both liberated and renewed old centrifugal social forces, which underpinned the division of the power elite into two irreconcilable factions, centralists against federalists, conservative Catholics against liberal anticlericals. This confrontation was part and parcel of the tragic sequence of civil war and external intervention that characterized much of nineteenth-century Mexico. In the process, the enforcement of a modern system of private property rights over land and water became a central objective of the liberal project intended at creating new foundations for citizenship in Mexico. However, in the process, the expropriation and exclusion of the majority at the hands of the oligarchic state would be exacerbated to unprecedented levels.

The post-independence historical development was characterized by the transplantation of European, and especially Anglo-Saxon, ideas and institutions. As in the rest of Latin America, Mexico became an experimental field of social-engineering processes directed at dismantling the corporate systems of property embodied in the Church possessions and the Indian villages, and fostering a process of individualization and modern citizenship through the creation of individual property rights over land and water. Liberal social fractions strove to eradicate the Church and Indian forms of corporate property, but their efforts were defeated in the 1830s and 1840s and it was only in the mid-1850s that they would have a chance to enforce their project. In 1855 the Minister of Justice Benito Juárez abolished clerical immunities, and in 1856 the Minister of Finance Lerdo de Tejada produced the famous disentailment law also known as Ley Lerdo, by which the Church had to sell off all its urban and rural real estate. Finally, these laws were incorporated into the 1857 constitution, which also extended civil and political citizenship rights outside the limits of the oligarchic elite. It was the first time after the aborted 1814 Apatzingán constitution that liberal rights of citizenship such as private property rights or the right to vote and be elected were extended to all Mexicans, excluding only vagrants and criminals (Bazant, 1994: 14–19, 36).

However, there is a firm consensus among scholars that the liberal policies were doubled-edged. As an ideal, the liberal programme copied the model of colonization based on a large class of pioneering small landowners of European origin following the example of the Neo-Europes, in particular the United States. In practice, the actual social process reaffirmed the colonial pattern of extensive appropriation of land and water by big landowners, who tellingly were among the main supporters of the liberal reforms (Bazant, 1994: 37, 50; Katz, 1994: 51, 56–7). In this regard, the nineteenth-century intra-elite struggles between monarchists and republicans, federalists and centralists, Church and State, widened the gap between the oligarchy and the lower classes.

The large-scale enforcement of individual property rights was not the outcome of consensus, even among the elite of ciudadanos in power. It was rather the result of bloody civil wars and cruel repression of the majority of second class ciudadanos and non-ciudadanos, as the liberal attack on the Indian villages and Church institutions fuelled the reappearance of rural conflict (Tutino, 1986, 1988; Katz, 1988b). The swift Porfirian modernization (1884–1911) carried the process of social exclusion to unprecedented extremes, transferring most communal lands to private accumulators and leaving about 90 per cent of the peasantry landless by the end of the regime (Katz, 1994: 94).[4] As a Mexican political philosopher put it, 'citizenship is not a spontaneous event, neither is individualism', and the whole process took the form of 'a war to create citizens' (Escalante, 1992: 40–1). Eventually, it led to the bloodiest and largest-scale social confrontation of twentieth-century Latin America, the Mexican Revolution (1910–17).

Water and the redefinition of the private–public divide

As discussed in Chapter 3, the nineteenth-century privatization of water rights was the counterpart of the trend towards further concentration of water control in state hands. In a broader perspective, the wide consensus about the need for state intervention and regulation to create and preserve the conditions for capitalist development was neither restricted to the Mexican scene nor to water policy, and was rather part of a historical cycle involving widespread state intervention in most aspects of social organization in the face of a growing disbelief in the classical liberal tenet about the self-regulating capacities of the market (Polanyi, 1957).

Regarding water rights, the process was partly fuelled by the high degree of legal uncertainty inherited from the colonial period and worsened by the political and administrative disorganization that followed Independence. Increasing competition for water prompted the modernization of water management and policy through innovations in water science and engineering and the regularization of the legal framework for the allocation of water rights. In a first stage, the task was assigned to private companies, but private efforts failed to deliver and this provided grounds for a tacit consensus on the need for state centralization of water control within the otherwise irreconcilable fractions of the elite. This convergence of interests permeated the debates during the Porfirian period (Kroeber, 1994: 99–101).

For instance, while defending private enterprise big landowners and businessmen such as Oscar Braniff promoted state action for regulating river use, implementing land distribution and building and administrating large dams, and argued for complete state control over irrigation water. They wanted to ensure that the available water was allocated to efficient producers capable of using water rationally, and also favoured state action for creating water markets where water rights would be freely tradable transforming water into a mobile factor of production like money, labour or equipment to be allocated by market mechanisms under the regulatory control of the State (ibid).

From within the state apparatus, functionaries such as Andrés Molina Enríquez, while favouring co-operation between the private and public sectors argued that the State should take the leading role given that the large scale of the projects envisaged was beyond the reach of private entrepreneurs. He argued that the tradition of Spanish water law whereby the Crown was the sole owner of water, land and woods, including the principle that any alienation of Crown property was, at least in theory, subject to restitution, had been integrated into Mexican law after Independence. However, owing to poor administrative records there was no accurate information about water rights holders, water sources or volumes granted, and Molina Enríquez advocated the need for a new water law based on the colonial and Mexican traditions to regularize the situation (Molina Enríquez, 1964: 176–95).

Since the 1880s the federal authorities had assumed the task of confirming already existing water rights, replacing the old colonial titles by new ones, and assessing the availability of water for future users. In 1888 the government had enforced a new Water Law which provided the framework for the confirmation of existing water rights either based on legal title or continued use for more than ten years. However, the law also enforced federal ownership over non-navigable rivers, which encroached on existing private rights over these water bodies and caused big controversies. In the early 1890s, the intervention of the State in a conflict over water rights in the river Nazas involving US and British companies against local hacendados established a landmark precedent, whereby the Republic was confirmed as the legal owner of the rivers and the sole authority with power to grant water rights (Kroeber, 1994: 122).

Nevertheless, the incorporation of these principles into water law was the subject of heated debates, as reflected in the repeated failures to regularize water rights in successive laws passed in 1894, 1896 and 1902. The situation was finally reversed with the 1910 Federal Water Law, influenced by the 1879 Spanish Water Law,[5] which secured State control over federal waters by restating the colonial legal categories of 'public domain and general use' and vested in the State the power to confirm existing water rights and to grant new ones. The law also confirmed and further specified the traditional scale of priorities for the use of federal waters, whereby domestic use and public services for human settlements had the status of public good and were given precedence over irrigation, production of hydroenergy, and industrial uses (Herrera y Lasso, 1994: 132–41, 206–7; Aboites Aguilar, 1998: 88).

Summing up, the regularization of water rights in the late nineteenth century was part and parcel of the radical liberal policies that formally universalized civil and political citizenship in Mexico and simultaneously exacerbated the actual levels of social and political exclusion. In the process, however, the status of common good and priority use attached to essential human water consumption – truly a universal human heritage – was confirmed and formalized in the water legislation of the modern Mexican state. Thus, the internal contradictions of liberal citizenship, particularly between individual civil rights and the collective entitlements sanctioned by social rights, converged with the long-term confrontations between community-oriented and individualistic forms of water use and practices. Moreover, this happened in the context of increasing monopolization of social power and resources in the hands of the oligarchic state, of which the centralization of water control was part and parcel. The ensuing Mexican Revolution both formally reversed and practically reinforced some of these trends and processes.

'A revolution for land and water'

One of the most significant offshoots of the Mexican Revolution (1910–17) was the formal decision to reverse the large-scale expropriation sanctioned by the liberal policies through legalizing collective (corporate) rights along with individual property rights over land and water and thus setting a framework for the redistribution of these resources (Knight, 1990: 170). It was done through legalization of the ancient corporate institutions of property embodied in the *ejidos* and *pueblos* under the juridical principles of Spanish colonial law in an otherwise largely advanced liberal democratic constitution. The constitution embodied contradictory conceptions of the role of the State and of the relations between the State and its citizens. In the new model, the relationship between individuals and the State became mediated by corporate bodies (the organized peasantry, the unions), which created a form of collective citizenship. As Tannenbaum pointed out:

The Constitution had therefore created two classes with special rights in the body politic: agrarian communities (ejidos) composed of agricultural peasants on one hand, and unions composed of labourers on the other. These two 'moral persons', special creatures of the law, have been encased in an essentially individualist constitutional framework. (Tannenbaum, 1965: 116)

Concerning land and water, Article 27 restated the colonial principles whereby collective rights had priority over individual. The Mexican State replaced the Spanish Crown, becoming the sole owner of land and water and bestowed with power to grant users the right to the usufruct of the resources but retaining the capacity to reverse this action and cancel the rights granted to protect the public interest. Furthermore, Article 115 gave water services the character of public good and granted the public sector, in particular municipalities, a leading role in their governance and management. This policy, prompted by leading members of the sanitary movement, was aimed at reversing the appalling conditions caused by the lack of safe water and sanitation.

In this connection, at the beginning of the twentieth century the sanitary conditions in the city were disastrous. Only a fraction of the streets were paved, cleaning and sweeping was limited to paved areas, water supply and sewerage continued to cover only the old central quarters, and unsanitary practices continued to be widespread in the population (Márquez Morfín, 1994: 330–1). The need to improve this situation became a major topic for reformers and enlightened minorities, some of whom became leading revolutionaries like Engineer Alberto Pani. Writing in the middle of the Revolution, Pani carried out a comparative analysis between Mexico City and other world metropolises including São Paulo, Barcelona, Birmingham, Kiev, and Sidney, and concluded that the Mexican capital was 'certainly, the most unhealthy city in the world' (Pani, 1916: 19). Pani found that digestive diseases, particularly diarrhoeas and enteritis, had been the first cause of mortality in the city between 1895 and 1912, accounting for over 32 per cent of total deaths, and suggested that the main causes underlying this pattern of mortality were inadequate diet and water services (ibid: 23–5).

Pani's writing contained virulent attacks against the oligarchic regime of Porfirio Díaz, which he condemned for its disregard for human life. However, suggesting the existence of a community of experts beyond political divides, he quoted a former Minister of the

Higher Council of Public Health during the Porfiriato, Rafael Norma, who had asserted the obligation of the State to protect its subjects 'procuring the extinction and preventing the propagation of epidemic or endemic-epidemic diseases' (ibid: 140–1). Pani's efforts to create a federal department in charge of sanitation to foster the massive introduction of hygiene and sanitation in educational curricula and make sanitary prevention compulsory in the most affected urban centres (ibid: 142–52, 191) were eventually fulfilled when the 1917 constitution established the Council of Public Health.

Notwithstanding these significant changes brought about by the Revolution, access to essential water and sanitation services continued to rank low in the scale of priorities of most post-Revolutionary administrations, which was reflected for instance in the recurrent ravages caused by preventable water-related infections. In this regard, during the Revolution there were at least two typhus epidemics (1914 and 1915), and one of smallpox (1916). These were followed after the Revolution by the Spanish influenza (1918), with a devastating mortality rate estimated at 20 per 1000,[6] smallpox again in 1922 and 1938, and further typhus epidemics in 1934 and 1938. In fact, periodic water-related epidemics would remain a feature for decades to come (Fujigaki and González Galván, 1982). Epidemic outbursts, however, reflected structural processes. Writing in 1927, Engineer Miguel A. de Quevedo asserted that the country's situation with respect to the water services was appalling owing to the insufficient infrastructure, lack of maintenance and absence of sanitary awareness. In the mid-1930s, analysts confirmed that water-related intestinal parasitic diseases continued to be the most important factor of mortality in the country, which had one of the highest infant mortality rates in the world (Ceniceros, 1935: 29–38).

Improvements continued to be very slow during the 1940s, when the official infant mortality rate (children dying before their first birthday) was on average over 100 per thousand born, compared to a rate of about 30 per thousand in the United States, Denmark and England at the time. Although shocking, these figures already represented a significant improvement over the 50-year period starting in 1900, when one out of four (or, perhaps, three) children born died (Benavides *et al.*, 1953: 649–51). Nevertheless, water-related diseases remained the most important cause of mortality until the 1970s (Fujigaki and González Galván, 1982).[7]

Thus, although the revolution formally reversed the process of exclusion and laid the basis for granting universal access to the territory of citizenship, in practice a yawning gap opened between legal forms and political practices (Foweraker, 1996: 79). The institutionalization of citizenship rights was not sufficient to counteract 'the internal dynamics of inequality' characterizing the post-Revolutionary development (González Casanova, 1965b: 87), which continued to exclude a large share of the population from the full exercise of citizenship rights. In fact, enforcing Article 27 became the object of protracted struggles throughout the twentieth century (Bartra, 1978; Hewitt de Alcántara, 1978; Bartra, 1985; García de León, 1985; Tutino, 1986; Oswald *et al.*, 1986; Gordillo, 1988; Knight, 1990), and the project of universalizing essential water and sanitation services did not make substantive progress until the 1970s (Wilkie, 1967: 169; Perló Cohen, 1989).

Once again, the reconciliation of the 'imagined citizen' drawn in constitutional documents with concrete human beings proved to be a slow and endless process (Escalante, 1992). We may recall here Marx's insight on an analogous discussion:

> All emancipation is a reduction of the human world and relationships to man himself. Political emancipation is the reduction of man, on the one hand, to a member of civil society, to an egoistic, independent individual, and, on the other hand, to a citizen, a juridical person. Only when the real, individual man re-absorbs in himself the abstract citizen, and as an individual human being has become a species-being in his everyday life, in his particular work, and in his particular situation, only when man has recognized and organized his own forces as social forces, and consequently no longer separates social power from himself in the shape of political power, only then will human emancipation have been accomplished. (Marx, 1975: 168)

No doubt, Marx's notion of human emancipation implies superseding the ultimately alienating character of the liberal conception of citizenship, which he was confronting in the mid-nineteenth century. Ever since, emancipatory struggles have substantially transformed the boundaries and contents of the territory of citizenship, and access to it has also been conquered by ever-growing numbers of human beings. In the Mexican case, in retrospective, enjoyment of citizenship has been greatly expanded compared with the situation prevailing on the eve of the Revolution. And yet, in the twenty-first century, even the limited emancipation offered by citizenship continues to be inaccessible for a large share of the population. We continue this discussion in the last chapter.

Concluding remarks

The governance and management of water and essential water and sanitation services are intimately related to the exercise of citizenship. This connection, however, is not straightforward and this chapter has presented some of the key interrelations that can be established between water and citizenship by examining the historical evidence in the light of theoretical insights. This evidence shows how, in the long-term, water policies, institutions and practices became intertwined with the highly exclusionary forms of citizenship that developed in Mexico, a situation that was not entirely reversed by the Mexican Revolution and still underpins the persistence of extreme qualitative and quantitative inequalities in the country.

As suggested earlier, the emancipation offered by citizenship within capitalist democracy is a territory fiercely protected from intrusion and subject to protracted social contests over both the definition of the boundaries and contents of citizenship and over the actual access to it by those who – borrowing from Marshall – 'claim to be admitted to a share in the social well-being, to be accepted as full members of the community, as citizens'. These social contests adopt many forms and are multidimensional. The next chapter focuses in more detail on the epistemic and political dimensions of the struggle, in the light of contemporary processes.

6
Water and the Territory of Citizenship

'Barbarism ... is rather a by-product of life in a particular social and historical context ... barbarism has been on the increase for most of the twentieth century, and there is no sign that this increase is at an end. First, the disruption and breakdown of the systems of rules and moral behavior by which *all* societies regulate the relations among their members and, to a lesser extent, between their members and those of other societies. Second ... the reversal of what we may call the project of the eighteenth-century Enlightenment, namely the establishment of a *universal* system of such rules and standards of moral behavior, embodied in the institutions of states dedicated to the rational progress of humanity.'—**Eric Hobsbawm**, *Barbarism: A Users' Guide*

The previous chapter addressed the contradictions between the formal enunciation of rights, such as the universal right to water and essential water-related services, and the real practices that render formal entitlements meaningless for vast majorities. In this regard, the formal sanctioning of the access to water and essential water services as universal public goods in Article 27 of the 1917 Mexican Constitution, which in practice was never achieved, is an excellent example. The constitution not only proclaimed the universal right to a share in the social wealth, but also gave the state a leading role in endowing individuals and social groups with the means to exercise effective command over essential goods and services such as water and sanitation. However, as discussed earlier, despite the laudable principles adopted in the charter, and of the paternalistic policies that followed, the factual post-revolution development was characterized by 'the internal dynamics of inequality' (González Casanova, 1965b: 87). This process eventually precluded a large part of the Mexican population from full access to these essential goods and services and, indeed, to the territory of citizenship.[1]

In this chapter we explore Mexican water policy in the light of the epistemic and political confrontations that underpinned its evolution since the late nineteenth century. The main focus will be on the development of a model of water governance grounded on the principles of social citizenship and state leadership that were formalized in the 1917 Constitution, and on the recent radical attempts to cancel the principle of social citizenship and reorganize that model around free-market policies such as the commodification of water and water services. Although the epistemic confrontations have often been presented as an opposition between state-oriented and free-market-oriented models of society, from the perspective of the struggle over citizenship there is a need to examine critically the underlying antagonisms. The crucial confrontation, the chapter argues, is between inclusionary models of social organization – marred by inescapable internal contradictions, tensions, and limitations as they might be – and the systemic exclusion of human beings from accessing the territory of civilized life, which has been exacerbated by the free-market reforms implemented since the 1980s.

Water and citizenship in twentieth-century Mexico

As previously discussed, the 1917 Constitution sanctioned a state-led model of water governance by adapting the colonial principles that gave priority to the status of public good and essential human uses over private interests, although it also recognized a plurality of models for the allocation of land and water rights including private, collective and public forms. In this particular sense, the Mexican case was highly idiosyncratic, not least because the radical changes came about as a result of a violent revolution. Nevertheless, from an overall perspective the Mexican experience was in fact part of a worldwide development characterized by growing state intervention in almost all aspects of socio-economic and political activity. This trend led to the organization of the governance of essential public services around powerful and hierarchical state bureaucracies, a process that accelerated after the First World War when the public sector became increasingly involved in the development of basic infrastructure, including roads, ports, dams, canals, public services like water, electricity, telecommunications and the provision of collective consumption goods (Swyngedouw *et al.*,

2002: 127). In Western Europe and the United States, this process was fostered by the 1929 Great Slump and the subsequent period of recession, which brought to an end the confidence in self-regulating markets and consolidated the trends towards increasing state regulation (Polanyi, 1957: 142). Moreover, the state-led efforts for appeasing the socially and politically explosive situation in the 1940s further strengthened the role of the state in eliminating mass unemployment – epitomized in Keynesian economics – and universalizing basic welfare provision as incarnated in the Beveridgian welfare state theorized by Marshall in relation to the social rights of citizenship (Hobsbawm, 1994: 94–7).

In relation to water, the process took the form of an increased centralization of the management of water resources and related services in the hands of national states, with the creation of public bureaucracies such as the Bureau of Reclamation and the Corps of Engineers in the United States or the Ministry of Hydraulic Resources (SRH) in Mexico (Lee, 1999: 44). The ensuing tradition of 'administrative rationalism', borrowing from Dryzek (Dryzek, 1997: 63–83), became dominated by experts in engineering, environmental science and related fields, who played a key role in water governance and in the development of modern water management systems. The expansion of water supply and sewerage services became increasingly a matter of state priority not only for reasons of hygiene or health but also for economic growth, and became the object of large-scale subsidies and stricter standards.

First in Europe and the United States, and later in other regions including Latin America, the model of water management based on unregulated private monopolies that had prevailed since the late eighteenth century gave way first to the implementation of tighter regulation and control of private operations and, since the late nineteenth century, to the eventual municipalization and posterior nationalization of the services (Schultz and McShane, 1978; Goubert, 1986; Warner, 1987; Hassan, 1998; Ogle, 1999; Castro *et al.*, 2003). This happened because a widespread consensus arose among the economic and political elites that the need for expansion and improvement of the systems, so patently highlighted by the devastating water-related epidemics of the time, could not be entrusted to private operators because of their limited technical and financial capacities, overall poor performance record, and their narrow profit-oriented interests. In Great Britain, for example, water and sanitation services were progressively subject to tighter regulation and municipalization since the late nineteenth century, and became fully nationalized by the end of the Second World War (Hassan, 1998).

In Latin America, the national states assumed a leading role in the expansion of water and sanitation since the early twentieth century, a trend that was accentuated by the economic crisis of the 1930s. Also, alternative forms of private initiative (as opposed to state-led) such as co-operatives, mutual associations and not-for-profit ventures became important drivers for the development of public services, water included. In Mexico, the post-Revolution administrations set in place a stricter legal and regulatory framework, which curtailed the privileges enjoyed by the previously unregulated private water monopolies and gave the federal government a stronger position to supervise their performance. Eventually, public efforts to improve water and sanitation led to the take-over of inefficient or under-performing private companies, as happened in the cities of Torreón in 1918, Tampico in the 1930s, San Luis Potosí in the late-1930s, and Monterrey in 1945 (Márquez Morfín, 1994: 330–1; Birrichaga Gardida, 1997: 95–100; Connolly, 1997: 95–6; Aboites Aguilar, 1998: 157–67; Bennett, 1995: 33–7; Suárez Cortez, 1998). This process, however, was not always translated into actual expansion and improvement of these services.

While in developed countries the state-led model of water governance was successful in meeting the targets, as in England and Wales where universal coverage was achieved by the 1960s, in most developing countries the state failed to attain similar results. As already noted before, in Mexico a substantial expansion of water and sanitation services had to wait until the 1970s, and even today access to safe water services remains a privilege enjoyed by a relatively small fraction of the population. From another angle, the state-led model of water governance, based on the marriage between hierarchical bureaucratic structures and scientific expertise developed a highly technocratic approach – borrowing from Dryzek, 'leave it to the experts' – that left little or no room for citizen participation or for the exercise of democratic control over the process (Dryzek, 1997: Ch. 4). In this tradition of administrative rationalism, citizen participation has been understood as expected obedience to decisions taken by the experts. This is relevant for our study of water policy since the 1980s, as we found that civic disagreement with official water policy, not to say open conflict as discussed in Chapter 4, is often treated by the authorities as insubordination, disobedience. Despite the introduction of notions of social participation in water planning and policy since the late 1970s, traditionally citizens have not been expected to discuss water policy and with few exceptions what is expected from them is compliance with government policies. As put by a former General Manager of the National Water Commission (CNA) in the state of Chiapas:

> The CNA is trying to break the paternalist culture: water systems are repaired or new systems are built; then, people are told what the tariffs are, and they have to respond accordingly, otherwise we cannot work. There are several cases where we have carried out the works and now people are refusing to pay. We have already informed them that if they do not pay the government will withdraw its support for the municipality and will seek to recover the debt. In any case, it will be the population that pays or otherwise they will have no water. (Stamatrio, 1992, Sources, Interviews)

These words must not be misunderstood or decontextualized. The engineer interviewed was describing the enormous efforts being done to provide water services in one of the worst-serviced regions of the country, and there were very important achievements of the CNA in Chiapas, which were certainly praiseworthy. However, although the quote cannot be taken as representing the collective position of Mexican water experts and functionaries, it illustrates the fact that the notion of 'participation' traditionally held by the authorities is in fact equivalent to 'expected obedience'. This is the product of the prevailing top-down approach to state-society interaction characterizing the tradition of state-led governance. Nevertheless, as shown in Chapter 4, citizens do disobey and state initiatives to enforce control over water resources and services continue to be marred by low legitimacy and weak citizen involvement. This situation, however, has characterized water governance in Mexico during the twentieth century, which we discuss next.

Re-ordering water governance

Notwithstanding the strict state control over water formally sanctioned by the 1917 Constitution, in practice key areas such as water abstraction remained largely uncontrolled throughout the twentieth century. In this regard, critics of the state-led model of water governance in Mexico have argued that although Article 27 of the constitution was complemented by successive water laws in 1929, 1934, 1972 and 1992 aimed at fostering its implementation, none of them offered a clear definition of water rights or provided adequate guarantees for right-holders thus creating uncertainty and promoting overexploitation of the resource (Roemer, 1997: 99, 289). Indeed, clandestine water extraction has been the rule in Mexico, and different attempts at bringing water withdrawal under effective state control have repeatedly failed. Since the late 1970s the state made renewed attempts at enforcing public control, and a system of fee-paid abstraction rights was enacted in the 1982 Federal Rights Law. In 1985, this law was revised and complemented by the Law of Contribution for Improvements by Public Works in Hydraulic Infrastructure, which sought to recover federal investment in the water sector from the users. In practice, however, these laws were never enforced due to political and administrative obstacles (ibid: 106). Nevertheless, these initiatives foreshadowed the renewed attempts to consolidate state control over water that led to the creation of the CNA in 1989, the radical changes made in 1992 to Article 27 of the constitution and the introduction of a new National Water Law in the same year.

These institutional changes were part of an effort to re-order the governance of water and water services, a process characterized by apparently contradictory trends such as the simultaneous attempt to consolidate state water control and the introduction of free-market mechanisms such as private water rights and the progressive commodification of networked water and sanitation services.

The case of water resources

The 1992 Water Law sanctioned the creation of a Public Register of Water Rights aimed at regularizing all users of federal waters, including rivers, lakes, and underground aquifers (Articles 30–7). Users in possession of water rights conceded under the legislation in force before 1992 would have to surrender their titles and apply to the CNA for new abstraction rights that would be time-limited, have volume restrictions, and be subject to abstraction fees, all of which would be periodically reviewed and updated. Similar provisions were introduced for the management of wastewater disposal.[2]

However, these attempts by the Mexican state to establish a more effective control over water also encountered many obstacles and strong opposition. During our interviews with CNA officials in 1997 it became apparent that the enforcement of the new system of water rights was widely resisted by users. For instance, only 1 per cent of industrial water users in the country had registered to obtain legal rights for water abstraction and wastewater disposal by mid-1997.

Likewise, in the MCMA only 62 users were recorded in the Public Register under the heading Public Urban Use, although the actual universe in the Federal District alone was in the order of around 60,000 large users (those consuming at least 60 cubic meters per month) which included over 3100 industries (NAS, 1995: Ch. 6). Strictly speaking, most users in the MCMA were extracting water illegally under the 1992 Water Law.[3] Thus, claims made in 1992 by water functionaries that the new law expressed 'the will of all Mexicans' proved to be, at best, controversial.[4]

In fact, this overwhelming resistance of the users to the new policies prompted the CNA to moderate their treatment of illegal users and to adopt a more lenient approach. Although the 1992 Water Law had already decriminalized clandestine water abstraction and replaced prison sentences as envisaged in the 1972 law by economic punishment or, in extreme cases, the cancellation of the concession (PRM, 1992b: 65–9), by 1995 the CNA decided that even these softer penalties were unenforceable and offered facilities and compensations (for example levying fines) to persuade users to regularize their situation and enter voluntarily into the Public Register.[5] Similarly, concerning the disposal of wastewater, industrialists were able to obtain significant concessions from the Ministry of Environment, Natural Resources and Fishing (Secretaría de Medio Ambiente, Recursos Naturales y Pesca (SEMARNAP)) in the enforcement of the new tighter standards for industrial effluents. This weakening of the legal framework for industrial discharges had strong repercussions across the border, where an assortment of environmental groups and other actors threatened legal action against Mexico for violating the environmental standards agreed under the North American Free Trade Agreement (NAFTA).[6]

The case of essential water supply and sanitation

As discussed in earlier chapters, in the specific area of water supply and sanitation the reforms can be traced back to the 1980 administrative decentralization, which transferred responsibility for these services from the federal level to the state governments. This policy was complemented by the 1983 revision and extension of Article 115 of the constitution, which for the first time clearly assigned responsibility for local public services, including water, drainage and sanitation, to the municipalities. However, the decentralization policies failed, not least because of the financial difficulties experienced by the country in the aftermath of the 1982 debt crisis. As a result, the much-needed expansion of the services was significantly slowed and service standards worsened in a large number of cases, especially in intermediate urban centres (Torregrosa Armentia, 1990: 50–6). It was in this context that the events over water discussed in Chapter 4 took place.

The process of reform received a new impulse under President Salinas de Gortari, with the creation of the CNA and the 1992 reforms to the constitution and the new water law. The main thrust of these policies was to set the conditions for the privatization of urban water systems. Thus, in late 1991 Engineer Fernando González Villarreal, CNA's Director, reported to the Commission of Agriculture and Hydraulic Resources of the federal Congress that the government was studying the feasibility of privatizing water and sanitation services (*Excelsior*, 11 September 1991: 1; *Uno más Uno*, 11 September 1991: 1). In January 1992 González Villarreal confirmed the imminent privatization of the services to the Commission of Hydraulic Affairs of the Chamber of Deputies (*Tribuna*, 15 January 1992: 1b; *Summa*, 15 January 1992: 8), and in September 1992 the authorities announced that some aspects of water services management in the Federal District would be contracted-out to private companies. The director of the newly created Water Commission of the Federal District (CADF), Carlos Casasús, stated then that 'the Mexican government has privatized, so far, more than one thousand public companies. It is now the turn of the municipal services, including water' (*Excelsior*, 27 September 1992: 5; Casasús, 1992). Finally, in 1993 the CADF signed contracts with four transnational consortiums to initiate a three-stage project aimed at transferring the provision of essential water services in the Federal District to the private sector. Among the first tasks assigned to the contractors was the elaboration of a complete register of users, the regularization of water metering and billing, and the reduction of leakage.[7]

Contested waters

To a large extent, the radical changes in water governance and management since the 1980s were both the expression of undergoing social conflicts as well as the trigger of new confrontations over water and water services in Mexico. As already mentioned, the policies directed at enforcing state control over the abstraction of water resources and the disposal of wastewater encountered strong opposition, especially from large users, to the point that the stricter regulation envisaged in the new law was in practice unenforceable. Likewise, as illustrated in Chapter 4, related policies directed at establishing state control over water systems built decades earlier by local communities at a time when neither the state nor private operators were providing the service caused great upheavals and bitter social confrontations. For instance, government initiatives to enforce the new fee-based abstraction rights in the case of water systems managed by local communities were confronted with widespread civil disobedience. As a CNA functionary put it:

> To charge for water, we need first to raise awareness among water users. But, imagine the case of a community that has been drawing water from a *fuente de vida* [life's source] such as a spring, a *noria* or a well since long ago. How can we pretend to go and start charging this people for that water without first explaining the reasons, without helping them to understand what we are doing and why? They feel that the spring is theirs, isn't it? Although the Constitution states that water belongs to the nation, how can anybody approach this community and say 'Well, now you must pay for this water because it belongs to the nation'. It will be very difficult to convince them! (Aguayo y Camargo, 1997, Sources, Interviews)

And yet, this was exactly what was happening, as the state tried to enforce public control over water systems across the basin in ways that were perceived as illegitimate by the citizenry. Moreover, the reforms carried out in the early 1990s were formally aimed at creating a 'new water culture' to replace what the government termed an 'ingrained dependency culture' that had prevailed during the twentieth century, whereby the state would have played the role of a paternalistic bene-factor and water would have been provided free of charge (CNA, 1990: 16). As eloquently stated by the water authorities in 1993, the new water culture being promoted implied that 'water has ceased to be a free good and from now on it is a resource which has an economic value, and society must pay for it' (CNA, 1993c: 11; Rogozinsky, 1993, 1998). However, this experiment of social engineering sidelined some basic facts such as that cultures cannot be changed by decree, that water values are multidimensional and incommensurable, that the eco-nomic dimension is not reducible to its market expression,[8] and that water had actually not been a free good as stated by the government. We come back to this later.

From another perspective, the formal institutional reforms also faced strong resistance, as shown by the fact that the 1992 Water Law was only passed after thirty-eight amendments to the original project. The political opposition in Congress argued that the law proposal was aimed at favouring the monopolization of water by private companies, especially by the large building contractors specializing in water infrastructure. They described the law project as a 'manual of procedures to facilitate the granting of concessions to the private sector' rather than a proper water law, as allegedly the original text did not contain a single reference to essential water management activities such as water conservation and reuse or environmental protection, and did not establish any provision for the defence of users' rights (*El Universal*, 12 November 1992: 11; *El Nacional*, 12 November 1992: 13; *Diario de México*, 12 November 1992: 3a).

Perhaps, the extent of the social and political opposition to the new policies can be best illustrated by the fact that the term 'privatization' was virtually suppressed from the public domain. Already during the debates originated by the new Water Law, government officials changed their language in response to allegations made by the political opposition that the government was privatizing the water services.[9] Not surprisingly, when we carried out our interviews with water authorities and private water operators in 1997, the recurrent answer of the interviewees was that 'there is no privatization of water services in Mexico'. Moreover, the four private consortiums that were granted service contracts in the Federal District were operating in public under the name of the CADF to disguise their identity. Privatization had become a forbidden word owing to the social and political conflicts stemming from the policy.[10]

In the words of a functionary, 'these policies have not been totally accepted by the population and will need a period of maturation' (Aguayo y Camargo, 1997). In practice, users responded by withholding payment of water bills in protest for what they considered excessive tariff increases; others resorted to destroying the newly installed water meters or otherwise disrupting the activity of the private operators through the occupation of buildings, the taking of water utility workers as hostages, and other actions discussed in Chapter 4. At least one of the private companies was keeping a detailed record of the attacks against their staff and property.[11] In 1997, the authorities introduced new regulations to allow legal procedures against offenders with the creation of an administrative police in the Federal District (*Diario Oficial de la Federación*, 11 April 1997: 60–70). The legal manager of one of the private companies explained that under the new provisions they would be able to obtain administrative and political support to prosecute water offenders, which in the case of non-payment of water bills would result in the disconnection from the service.

However, the prospect of prosecuting offenders, and especially disconnecting people for non-payment, added further controversy. In the opinion of a CNA functionary, disconnecting people was not part of the Mexican tradition and was not in the official agenda. He also commented on the potential impact that disconnection could have on the health of the population:

> Many health problems in the country are already linked to the lack of water, and if the government interrupts the service it will only cause further problems. The cost of disconnecting families and individual users from the service of potable water would be terrible ... I think that it would be grave from a health standpoint. One thing is to recognize that from an administrative and financial point of view water is a service which must be paid for. However, to disconnect people there must be a careful procedure to find out the causes of non-payment and to know what the conditions of the affected family are, why they could not pay. And these are very complex problems to deal with. (Aguayo y Camargo, 1997)

The concerns expressed by our interviewee were shared by many others. In the context of water privatization, disconnecting domestic users from essential water supplies is the logical consequence of transforming water services from public to private good in order to make feasible the exclusion of non-payers.[12] However, several questions arise from this development. To what extent have water and water services been actually transformed into commodities by the 1992 reforms? Were water services a public good delivered for free by a benefactor state before the reforms, as claimed by the government? Had not these services been already commodified prior to the reforms? Has the policy of creating private property rights over water succeeded? Have water markets developed as a result of this policy? More importantly, have these policies brought about the promised results in terms of higher efficiency of the services and improvement of social well-being? Not all these questions can be answered here because this research ended in the early 1990s when the policies were launched.[13] Nevertheless, as seen below, the enunciation of these problems is relevant to orientate the rest of the discussion presented in this chapter.

Essential water services and the sociogenesis of scarcity

As shown earlier, daily per capita water distribution in the MCMA is well above the internationally accepted standards for household needs (such as drinking, washing, and cooking) estimated at 100 litres.[14] This volume of water available in the MCMA contrasts drastically with the '40 litres of safe water per person per day' that the UN Agenda 21 programme set up in 1992 as a global goal for year 2000[15], which was unfortunately missed by the international community. However, analysing water use at a high level of aggregation such as average per capita distribution conceals the existence of inequalities in the access to the service. In this regard, although the average water availability in the MCMA is almost twice that required by international standards for meeting essential human needs, access to water is strikingly uneven among neighbourhoods and families, and in the poorest colonias water consumption per capita per day is at best 20 litres.[16] In contrast, the well-off consume piped water at rates that run into the hundreds of litres per capita per day in discretionary uses such as gardening, watering lawns, and swimming pools (NAS, 1995: Ch. 6). This situation is aggravated by the fact that between 30 and 50 per cent of the water supply in the MCMA is wasted due to leaky pipelines and faulty installations, which accounts for a large share of the water extracted from underground aquifers.[17]

It can be argued that the fact that millions of human beings in the MCMA experience water scarcity is not the direct outcome of hydrogeological and technical constraints or, as mainstream water policy theorists argue, of the failure to treat water as an economic good in order to exclude non-payers from consuming it. Regarding the first, as already shown, the actual water volumes made available in the MCMA largely exceed the daily amounts needed for essential human use. In relation to the second, in the MCMA water has been a scarce and expensive commodity since long ago, especially for the poor, but this scarcity has been socially constructed.

Borrowing Amartya Sen's conclusions about the analogous problem of famine, 'scarcity is the characteristic of people not having enough ... it is not the characteristic of there not being enough. While the latter can be the cause of the former, it is one of many causes' (Sen, 1981: 1). In Sen's perspective, the key for understanding why people starve must not be sought in the aggregated figures of food availability per head as in fact famines occur without any decline in food output or availability per head. Rather, he argues that independently of its particular causes (droughts, floods, inflation, economic recession and so on) a famine reflects widespread failure of entitlements on the part of substantial sections of the population, which can be the outcome of many different causes. In short, the main problem is not the average level of food availability, but rather the capacity that individuals and families have to secure access to the food they need, what he termed the 'acquirement problem' (Sen, 1990: 36–7). Therefore, Sen argued that independently of the current food output per head in a given country, if a person's entitlement[18] does not give him or her command over enough food that person will starve. Likewise, changes either in the endowments (for example due to alienation of land, or loss of labour power during sickness) or in the person's entitlement mapping (for example fall in wages, rise in prices, loss of employment and so on) could lead that person to lose command over the essential amount of food (and other commodities) needed to survive. For this reason, Sen stressed that food per head is a misleading indicator in the rational analysis of famine, as in fact the intensification of hunger in many parts of the world has occurred hand in hand with a steady rise in food output. What counts in his argument is how people gain command over essential commodity bundles (Sen, 1990: 35–7).

Sen's argument about the interdependence between food output per capita and starvation casts light on analogous problems identified in the access to essential water supplies. The fact that water-related diseases continue to be one of the main causes of morbi-mortality in the MCMA, although the actual water volumes made available would be sufficient to meet the essential human needs of the population, is a case in point. In this regard, it is noticeable that although the economic impact of buying water on the poorest families is well known, water is not included in official estimations such as the cost of products in the recommended food basket.[19] This is an indication of the ambiguous character of water, officially considered to be a public good, a free good provided by a benefactor state that has to be transformed into a private good, a commodity. In fact, despite that the process of water commodification is incomplete, that urban water in the MCMA is largely subject to political rationality and that, particularly in the Federal District, non-market systems of water allocation such as heavy subsidies operate, for the majority water has since long ago become an expensive private good.

Returning to Sen's insights, the possession of endowments, for instance property rights over certain assets, does not ensure the enjoyment of entitlements on a regular basis because in a capitalist society the interaction between endowments and entitlements varies over time and it can even disappear. For instance, formal rights can be bestowed on people, like the right to work, to shelter, to good health, to water. These rights can be formalized in a country's charter or declared to be a universal human right, but this endowment does not guarantee people the sustained entitlement to have access to suitable jobs, housing or essential water services. The passage from endowments to entitlements is affected by a number of variable factors, which can even include the temporary or permanent loss of the initial ownership and deprive people of their entitlements.

In this connection, the evolution of social rights of citizenship described by Marshall represented a particular solution to the unacceptable inequalities resulting from the mismatch between endowments and entitlements characterizing life in a society predicated on the premises of the self-regulating market. Social rights, in the context of capitalist democracy, are notionally intended at reversing the inequalities that preclude large majorities from accessing the essential goods and services required for enjoying full community membership, the territory of citizenship. Marshall's take on this debate was a reformist one, but in historical perspective it has acquired a radical touch. It was also part of a wider epistemic–political confrontation that has entered a new phase since the 1980s.

The epistemic–political contest: mainstream water policy in action

The water sector reforms implemented in Mexico since the 1980s were part and parcel of the mainstream water policies being implemented worldwide. These, in turn, were intimately related to the transformations taking place in the intellectual and political environment that had prevailed during much of the twentieth century. In this connection, the consolidation of the state-led model of water governance since the late nineteenth century had been accompanied by ongoing intellectual and political confrontations. At the theoretical level, the movement towards increasing regulation of private-sector activities and state take-over of essential services found expression, for instance, in the conceptualization of 'market failures' proposed by welfare economists to explain situations where market solutions do not sustain an efficient allocation of resources. These economists prescribed state intervention to correct for market failures such as the existence of natural monopolies, externalities or public goods, which constituted a radical revision of the classical tenet of the self-regulating capacity of the market defended by laissez-faire economics.[20] In relation to essential water supply and sanitation, these arguments sought to explain the failure of the nineteenth-century private water monopolies and provided a powerful argument to give the state the leading role in the governance and management of these services. Also, the development of regulation to protect the 'public interest', entailing formal standards and codes of conduct for private enterprises, emerged out of the need to establish control over the unregulated private provision of goods and services in the face of increasing public unrest since the late nineteenth century. Although liberal interpretations of this movement towards increasing regulation argued that it was an antiliberal conspiracy and an attack against political democracy, the social and political forces spearheading state intervention were wide ranging and included prominent liberals and convinced free-market supporters seeking to preserve the functioning of capitalist markets. In fact, the reactions against the negative impact of laissez-faire policies embraced all aspects of social and economic life, with calls to enforce stricter standards for food and drink quality and prices, compulsory vaccination, taxation for developing water and gas supply networks, the banning of child labour and the torture of workers, among many other issues (Polanyi, 1957: 144–50).

However, the concepts of social welfare, market failure and public interest emerging from the intellectual and political debate that accompanied the consolidation of state-led governance were soon questioned from different quarters (Newbery, 1999; Lee, 1999), and in the extreme the critique has taken the form of a blunt denial of the very notions of market failure and public interest (Zerbe and McCurdy, 2000). Still, the critics did not succeed in mounting a significant challenge with practical consequences until the 1970s, when radical changes in the global economy created a favourable environment for the return of free-market policy models.

These changes included an increase of world trade up to the levels reached before the First World War, the expansion of foreign direct investment in most developed economies, the growth of transnational companies, and the internationalization of capital flows, which led to the abandonment of the world trade regime sanctioned by the creation of the Bretton Woods institutions in 1944. First the decision by the United States to abandon the dollar–gold convertibility in 1971 and shortly after the cancellation of the fixed-exchange-rates regime in 1973, underpinned a cycle of global economic crises manifested particularly in unprecedented levels of international debt and extreme volatility of currency values and commodity prices. Perhaps, the new intellectual and policy environment that was becoming dominant became more transparent when the Organization for Economic

Cooperation and Development (OECD), led by the governments of the United States and the United Kingdom, formally abandoned the Keynesian economic principles in 1979–80 by implementing and promoting far-reaching reforms based on a 'neoliberal' set of policies including deregulation, liberalization, and privatization (Leys, 1996). Soon after, these policies that had first been tested by United States free-market theorists in General Pinochet's Chile during the 1970s became the new global paradigm by the 1980s. As put by one contemporary observer of the process:

> As a result of the growing support these ideas are gaining among politicians and economists and the translation of these ideas into policy, some commentators are already characterizing the 1980s as the decade when 'the market mechanism returned to favour. (Burink, 1987: 161)

The arguments informing this revival of 'market-driven politics' (Leys, 2001) have ranged from the 'the intelligent deployment of market mechanisms to achieve public ends', proposed by moderate pro-market reformists to the free-market extremism that argues for the creation of private property rights and unregulated markets in all sectors of activity, including water (Dryzek, 1997: 102).[21] Although there are substantial differences between moderate and radical pro-market reformers, these authors share a set of beliefs that can perhaps be expressed as the principles of neoliberal water policy. In a nutshell, these principles are:

(a) Water resources should be allocated through the market; that is, private water rights should be created replacing any existing forms of common, collective or public rights, and they should be freely tradable.

(b) Water services have to be transformed into an economic good, a private good that has to be bought in the market; non-payers can be excluded from accessing them; the notion that these services are a public or social good must be abandoned.

(c) Water services should be provided by private operators, which are inherently more efficient than public ones; if possible, water services should be self-regulated by market mechanisms and state intervention should be minimized if not altogether cancelled.

(d) Water services are not a natural monopoly, as claimed by the defenders of state intervention; most operations can be opened to competition; if high transaction costs make competition difficult, a privately-owned water monopoly is preferable to a public one; keep regulation to a minimum or cancel it altogether.

(e) Water users should be transformed into customers, and right-holders into property owners and consumers.

Not all free-market reformers would probably share these principles to the full extent of their meaning and practical implications. However, each one of these principles can be exemplified with the actual policies implemented in the water sector worldwide since the 1980s, including Mexico.[22]

From another angle, these principles have been often presented as based on solid economic theory, suggesting that they provide technical tools which are politically neutral, while they are in fact the result of a combination of arguments and ideology derived from different bodies of thought, in particular free-market liberalism, neoclassical economics, public choice and property rights theory (Roemer and Radelet, 1991; Commander and Killick, 1988; Leys, 2001). In particular, pro-privatization thinkers have recognized that the principle asserting the superiority of private over public ownership has no grounds in economic theory (Nellis and Kikeri, 1989: 663). Moreover, it is widely accepted that the revival of free-market policies has not been as much the result of theoretical rigour and evidence-backed arguments as it has been the outcome of an ideological change that replaced the state by the market as the key driver of economic development (Atherton and Windsor, 1987: 94), a process that has been associated with 'a clear rightward shift in political opinion in Europe and North America' (Commander and Killick, 1988: 316).

Perhaps, the political character of the neoliberal policies mainstreamed since the 1980s, not just in the water sector, does not need much demonstration, as there is mounting evidence of the direct action taken by OECD countries through their government departments, aid agencies, lending policies, or through the programmes designed and implemented by bilateral and multilateral institutions (Commander and Killick, 1988: 314). The combination of pressure and persuasion implemented by these actors was ingenuously described by a pro-privatization author, who suggested that:

Pressure has been 'applied on developing countries by international organizations such as the World Bank, International Monetary Fund (IMF), and the US Agency for International Development to pursue the policy of privatization as a part of a package of economic reforms [quoting]'. In order for the leaders of the developing countries to see privatization as their best alternative, they have to be trained and educated in this field through seminars conducted by scholars and practitioners who have know-how in this field. (Dinavo, 1995: 51)

Ostensibly, this agenda has met with great opposition from different quarters, a reaction that has often been explained as the result of ideological prejudice if not blunt ignorance on the part of developing countries. As put by a USAID representative commenting on the leading role that the agency was taking in promoting privatization into the 21st century:

> The US Agency for International Development is defining future directions for privatization assistance based on the experience of the last 15 years, from a modest start in Latin America to the recent crescendo dominated by assistance to formerly Communist states. In the countries of Central and Eastern Europe and the former Soviet Union, the privatization of state-run enterprises and the dismantling of state monopolies are critical to these nations' transition to free markets. Poorer countries and governments ideologically resistant to opening their markets – largely in sub-Saharan Africa, the Middle East, and South Asia – will need continuing technical and policy support, as well as new, creative interventions. (Farley, 1997: 10)

No doubt, a large share of the extensive range of papers, articles and books published on this topic in recent years has been the result of this educational crusade. As eloquently stated by Joseph Stiglitz:

> In setting the rules of the game, commercial and financial interests and mind-sets have seemingly prevailed within the international economic institutions. A particular view of the role of government and markets has come to prevail, a view which is not universally accepted within the developed countries but which is being forced upon the developing countries and the economies in transition. (Stiglitz, 2002: 224–5)

In this regard, mainstream public policies since the 1980s have been underpinned by the free-market liberal tradition which identifies civil society with the market, a space characterized by the free concurrence of self-interested individuals, and considers citizenship as limited to the realm of civil and political rights. Correspondingly, the prevailing neoliberal framework rejects pluralist and communitarian notions of civil society, understood as the realm of reciprocity and solidarity, or social-democratic traditions such as the notion that universal access to essential services is a social right of citizenship. Nevertheless, these confrontations between rival theoretical bodies and political cultures remain hidden in the official discourse adopted in mainstream public policy, which is normally presented as a politically neutral, technically oriented toolkit for reform.

For instance, a large literature has been developed reflecting on the transformations experienced in the governance of natural resources and related services, including water, since the early 1980s. Some authors have argued that there has been a shift from the state-led model of governance based on 'state monopoly' towards a new system that would be characterized by conditions of 'pragmatic pluralism' (Esman, 1991). Perhaps, one of the main contributions of this body of literature has been the acknowledgement of the multi-layered and multi-sector character of management regimes dealing with complex socio–natural processes. According to these authors, contemporary governance systems include the classic forms of hierarchical organization and authority embodied in the state but also, and increasingly, elements of private-sector management regimes driven by market competition, and 'civil society' dynamics that are reliant on voluntary association, reciprocity and citizen participation (United Nations Development Programme (UNDP), 1997; Picciotto, 1997; Streeck and Schmitter, 1985).[23]

Accordingly, the model of multi-scale governance would be characterized by a combination of hierarchical structures, participatory dynamics, associative action, and market mechanisms, and would be based on a culture of dialogue, negotiation, active citizenship, subsidiarity and institutional strengthening. This is not just a subject of abstract academic discussion and the debate has rather far-reaching consequences in the field of public policy and, for that matter, in the transformations that we are discussing in the field of water governance and management. Among other issues, this model has been translated into an ideal-type version (Figure 6.1) suggesting that current mainstream policies (deregulation, liberalization, privatization) would be underpinning a beneficial transition from the traditional state-centred model of governance to the new conditions of pragmatic pluralism characterized by partnerships between the state, the private sector, and civil society.

Figure 6.1   The ideal-type model of governance of the mainstream literature

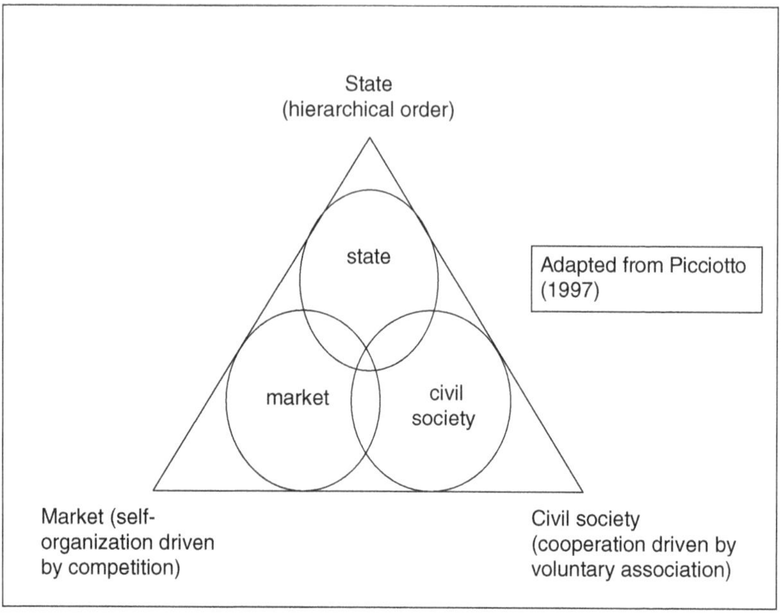

With regard to water and sanitation, it is all too evident that there is a need for effective democratic governance if the universalization of the access to these essential services is going to be achieved (Asian Development Bank (ADB), 1995; Buse and Walt, 2000; EC, 2000, 2002b; Global Water Partnership (GWP), 2002, 2003; Camdessus, 2003). However, it can be argued that mainstream water policies implemented under the umbrella of this idealized understanding of governance have in practice contributed to the increased alienation of common citizens and exacerbated existing inequalities of power, especially in developing countries. In this perspective, the mainstream understanding of governance has contributed to legitimating the subordination of political and social processes to the requirements of capitalist accumulation in the framework of a technocratic model of development where the valuation of nature in market terms has been imposed as the dominant language (Martínez Alier, 2002) through what some authors have termed the 'conjugation of the market fix with the technological fix' (Martins, 1998: 104–5). Often, this process has caused the roles of the state and of ordinary citizens in defining, protecting and promoting the public interest to be whittled away by the worldwide push towards blunt privatization and public sector commercialization. In most cases, and contrary to the predominant rhetoric, these policies have in practice delivered neither improved services nor greater control by ordinary people over the former public sector. Instead, they have allowed corporate interests to increase their hold on the main levers of economic power (Martin, 1994), which has caused retrogression in the difficult process of expansion and enrichment of substantive democracy and citizenship.

The shifting boundaries of citizenship

In his analysis of British history, Marshall argued that the principle of universal access to a modicum of social welfare, which he identified with the social rights of citizenship, had been originally developed in the early stages of capitalist development and consolidated by institutions such as the Poor Law and systems of wage regulation which later 'sank to vanishing point in the eighteenth and early-nineteenth centuries'. These policies were reversed and defeated in the battle against free-market forces. He suggested that in the twentieth century a reestablishment of these rights was in the making through the development of the social services (Marshall, 1992: 14–17).

In perspective, by arguing that welfare provision was a crucial component of citizenship, Marshall offered a framework for the defence of an inclusive conception of citizenship (King and Waldron, 1988: 422). It is this understanding of social welfare as a universal entitlement that became the target of neoliberal and neoconservative theorists, who consider public welfare institutions to be economically damaging and a source of moral corruption. According to these authors, Marshall has been used as an authority to justify the view that any erosion of the welfare system represents an erosion of citizenship rights (Saunders, 1993: 61). They have also argued that the welfare institutions created a dependency culture which must be replaced by an enterprise culture in which people's access to provisions is gained by individual effort, and the role of the state be reduced to offering emergency help for those unable to care for themselves. In the words of Lawrence Mead, emphasis should be placed 'beyond entitlements' and rather on the social obligations of citizenship: thus, restating early nineteenth-century conceptions, welfare provision should depend on people's readiness to work and not merely on the assumption of a universal right to full community membership (Mead, 1986). Although there is no denial that a dependency culture has emerged from the particular policies associated to welfare systems in many countries, the emancipatory potential of citizenship in the context of capitalist democracy has been significantly curtailed by the neoliberal solution of dissolving social rights into marketable commodities and replacing the rights of the citizen by the 'sovereignty of the consumer' (Saunders, 1993: 57, 60).

This process forms part of the ongoing struggles over the contents and shifting boundaries of the territory of citizenship (Figure 6.2). As discussed before, the classic rights of citizenship include civil rights (the right to own property, to enter valid contracts, and to have access

Figure 6.2   The shifting borders of the territory of citizenship

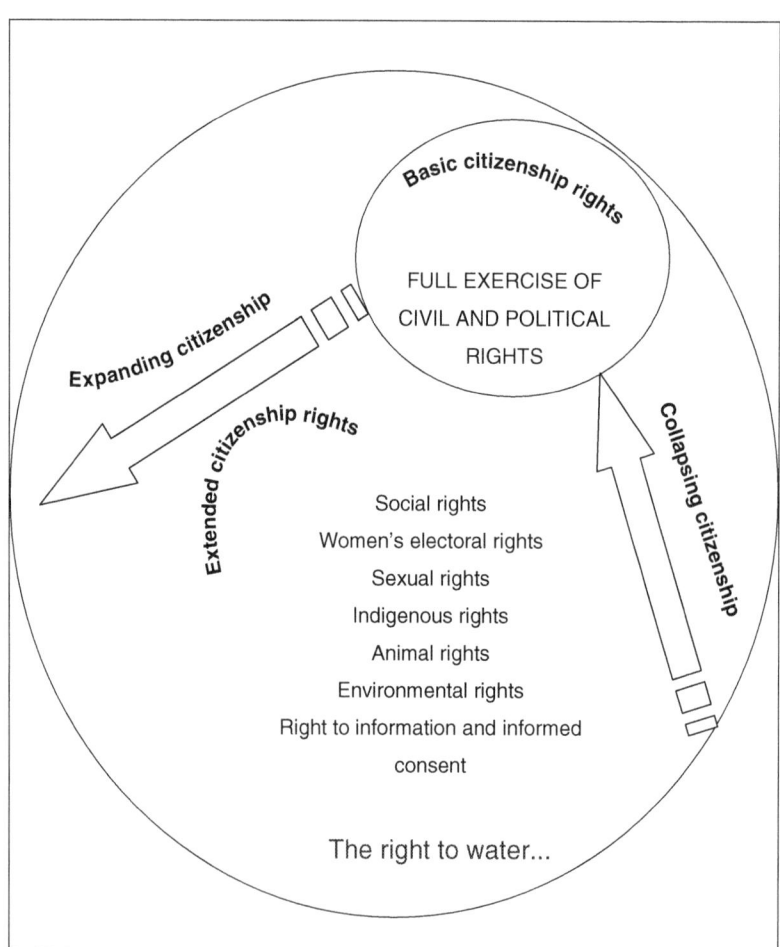

to fair judicial procedures for the administration of justice) and political rights (the right to be elected or to elect others for government). Social rights (for example, the right to universal education or health care) already represented an expansion of the territory of citizenship consolidated during the twentieth century.

On the one hand, struggles to expand the boundaries of this territory have brought about the further specification of existing rights and duties and the inclusion of new ones. For instance, in the specific case of water, several connections can be made with the traditional categories of citizenship (Table 6.1): water (property) rights can be considered a specification for the civil right to own property; the rights and duties involved in the governance and management of water resources and services is part of the sphere of political rights; and the universal right to essential water and sanitation services belongs in the group of social rights. On the other hand, and in addition to this expansion of the boundaries of citizenship, the process has also entailed the progressive inclusion of growing numbers of human beings, as for instance

Table 6.1   Links between citizenship and water

Citizenship rights	Water-specific links
Civil rights (property rights, judicial protection)	Water rights, water equality, formal justice arrangements
Political rights (democratic exercise of power)	Democratic water governance, participation
Social rights (civilized standards of well-being)	Universal access to water and essential water services
Extended conception of citizenship, specifying:	
Right to information and informed consent	Right to information about how water resources and services are managed (for instance, compliance with environmental standards by water managing bodies; quality of water services, and so on), and governed (how are water resources and services governed, by whom, and for whom; transparency of information allowing democratic accountability and control)
Intra- and trans-specific and temporal rights and duties	Socio-ecological justice and human stewardship

with the extension of electoral rights to women during the first half of the twentieth century. However, both the boundaries of the territory and the scope for accessing it are also subject to reversion and collapse, as illustrated by the suppression of civil and political rights during dictatorships and other authoritarian processes, or in the eventual expulsion of citizens who had gained access to the territory in periods of expansion, as in the dismantling of the institutions of social rights resulting from the neoliberal reforms implemented worldwide since the 1980s.

In this regard, when we examine the reordering of the system of governance that has taken place through the mainstream policy reforms implemented since the 1980s, taking the water sector as an example, we find that the market has been given a leading role in the governance complex vis-á-vis the other nominal components, the state and civil society. In this regard, the mainstream debate on governance has provided a theoretical and ideological framework to the unprecedented and unchecked expansion of market mechanisms to almost all spheres of human interaction (Martins, 1998). This reification of the 'market imperative', which according to some authors forms parts of a concerted attempt to establish ideological and political hegemony (Swyngedouw, 2000), has taken precedence to the point that in many countries, especially in the less developed world, the state and civil society can barely counterbalance or keep in check the operation of private water operators. In many cases, these policies have in practice delivered neither improved services nor greater control by ordinary people over the former public sector. Instead, the shift from state-centred to market-centred governance has facilitated the monopolization of power and resources by corporate interests to the neglect of the rights of the citizens, even in their reduced role as consumers (Solanes, 1999: 45). For instance, the evidence shows that unchecked market-centred water governance, coupled with the dismantling of the public sector fostered by the neoliberal reforms, has prompted an institutional crisis due to the withdrawal of crucial information (for instance, water management data) that was previously in the public domain and has become the property of private corporations (Dourojeanni, 1999).

Although these negative trends have been already identified and are the subject of the wide-ranging debates taking place around the world (GWP, 2003), in practice the prevailing model continues to alienate and exclude substantive citizen involvement. Current policies formally acknowledge the multi-scale and multi-polar character of modern governance systems but they are predicated on the pre-eminence of free-market interests. Thus, converting public services such as essential water and sanitation or health care in private for-profit businesses has become the main driver of development, but the overall consequence has been an exacerbation of inequality and social conflict.[24]

From another angle, although citizen participation was certainly absent in the repertoire of administrative rationalism, the highly technocratic and state-led model of public service governance that prevailed almost unchallenged until the 1980s, in the current mainstream model inspired by free-market politics the citizen has been erased and people's participation has been reduced, for the most part, to their role of passive consumers. In fact, the evidence shows that participation often means willingness to accept decisions already taken with little or no consultation. These policies are creating an imbalance resulting in the weakening of local governments and civil society structures, which have lost any capacities they had acquired in the past to actually exercise democratic control over the running of essential public services in most developing countries.

Unsurprisingly, reactions against policies that undermine public and social control over water and water services, like those captured in our research, have been largely neglected or played down in the mainstream literature. However, the unbalanced expansion and strengthening of capitalist forms of private accumulation at the expense of the public interest does not happen in a social vacuum (Schmidt, 1993). Therefore, it is not surprising that mainstream water policies are meeting strong resistance and have fuelled renewed social conflicts worldwide (Bond, 1997; Savedoff and Spiller, 1999; Guha and Martínez-Alier, 2000; Martínez-Alier, 2002; Public Services International Research Unit (PSIRU), 2003; Castro and Laurie, 2004).

Summing up, the far-reaching reforms introduced in the water sector since the 1980s have been addressed here from the perspective of the long-term struggle over the territory of citizenship. Although these policies have been often presented and implemented as a neutral, non-political instrument to foster better governance and democratization, in practice they are grounded on the principles of free-market liberalism, which reflect a particularly narrow understanding of citizenship and democracy. The boundaries of citizenship have historically been a shifting zone, and the late twentieth century revival of free-market liberalism constitutes an attempt to move the territorial boundaries backwards reducing the scope for substantive democracy and emancipation. The long-term and contemporary contests over water studied in this work have provided an excellent empirical field to examine the forces at work and the dynamics of the process.

Concluding remarks

The formal granting of a universal right to essential water supplies and related services to every Mexican-born person enshrined in the revolutionary 1917 Constitution was an unprecedented historical achievement in the struggle over the territory of citizenship in the country. In historical perspective, it formed part of a worldwide process by which the benefits of the scientific and technological progress in the management of water resources and services were made available to ever larger numbers of human beings. Since the late nineteenth century, this expansion came to be considered a social duty and promoted by a broad spectrum of social and political actors that gave the state a leading role in placing the pursuit of social welfare above narrow social interests. In turn, this expansion of citizenship within the framework of capitalist democracy formed part of the universalization of the system of 'rules and standards of moral behaviour, embodied in the institutions of states dedicated to the rational progress of humanity' (Hobsbawm, 1997: 253–4).

However, access to the territory of full citizenship has been always innaccesible to large numbers of humans, as illustrated by the fact that still in the early twenty-first century preventable water-related diseases continue to be the main cause of disease and death in Mexico and in most developing countries. As pointed out by Hobsbawm, the project of the Enlightenment, to the extent that it represented a potential for human emancipation, has been set back in many respects by the progress of barbarism and the disruption of the principles, standards and institutions oriented towards the universalization of human progress (ibid). In this connection, the neoliberal attack on the institutions of social citizenship, formally predicated on the need to tackle the failures of the state-led model of governance and management, have exacerbated the conditions of social inequality and undermined the principles of inclusionary citizenship and democracy. Nevertheless, these negative trends are confronted at different levels, from the mobilizations and street battles over specific water problems explored in Chapter 4 to the more sophisticated epistemic and political contests waged in academic and similar spaces of reflection, analysis and political action. As hinted by Marx, this struggle over the territory of substantive citizenship still constitutes a confrontation over the final form of human emancipation in the context of the existing world order (Marx, 1975: 155).

Conclusion

This book has attempted to bring out the import of social struggle and power configurations for understanding the interweaving of social and physical–natural processes. However, we sought to avoid the reification of the empirical manifestations of the struggle, as our interest has been to deploy the concept as a heuristic device to capture the multidimensional and long-term character of the processes under consideration. Therefore, although the research was triggered by our interest in understanding the meaning of the conflicts over water recorded in the Basin of Mexico during the 1980s and 1990s we have placed these events in the wider context of the struggle over citizenship.

In this regard, the reasons moving the protagonists of the water conflicts to act were multifarious, most of these events were discrete and unconnected, and most actors may have been unaware at the time of the multidimensional character of the process and of the unintended implications of their purposeful action. Yet, by analogy with Clausewitz's notion of war as a totality composed by a large number of discrete engagements, great and small, simultaneous and consecutive, we have argued that these apparently unrelated contests are part and parcel of an evolving social confrontation that is autonomous from the individual wills and reason of the actors. It is part of the struggle over the territory of citizenship, a territory composed of unfolding bundles of rights and duties formally bonding all individuals within a given community but in practice punctuated by structural exclusions and, therefore, the object of permanent and recurring social contests.

Comprehension and understanding of the multidimensional character of the process has been hindered by the overriding techno-scientific and bureaucratic rationality characterizing water governance and management which has historically contributed to render unobservable the social character of water. Unfortunately, the incursions of social science that have been most influential in the design of water policy since the 1980s have also tended to reinforce this unbalanced understanding of water problems. Thus, the far-reaching water-sector reforms informed by these policies have strengthened technocratic tendencies in water governance and management and continue to shift the focus away from fundamental socio-political considerations. In consequence, problems ranging from widespread water inequality and poverty to depletion of aquatic ecosystems are reduced to their techno-scientific and bureaucratic aspects and therefore diagnosed 'technical' fixes like converting essential water services into private goods or re-centring water governance around 'non-political' free-market princi-ples. Our work attempts to provide a framework for overcoming this prevailing reductionism and to contribute in developing meaningful transdisciplinary coordination across the natural and social sciences in order to better grasp the multidimensionality of the processes involved.

In historical perspective, the incorporation of individuals into citizen status has formed part of the long-term integration of human beings into wider units of social organization – borrowing from Norbert Elias – a process which, although subject to fluctuations and setbacks, has over time led to the expansion and enrichment of the territory of citi-zenship. For instance, we cannot doubt that today the proportion of people born in Mexico that can claim full rights as Mexican citizens is enormously larger than, for instance, on the eve of the 1917 Revolution. However, these long-term tendencies are not irreversible and are rather punctuated by the continued exclusion of large numbers of humans from full access to this territory, and by the outright expul-sion of others who had managed to gain access to it during favourable battles. The confrontations over water recorded in the Basin of Mexico during the last two decades of the twentieth century are an excellent illustration of this multidimensional process: the intensification of water policy reforms that continue to alienate citizens from the exer-cise of democratic rights has been answered back not just with defen-sive actions to prevent further exclusion from the territory of citizenship but also with offensive tactics directed at expanding the scope and depth of substantive citizenship and democracy.

Although this research has focused on a particular area of social and political activity, water governance and management, the conclusions are further supported by processes taking place in other fields. In this regard, since the late 1980s Mexican society has experienced significant social and political transformations, which led among other issues to the breakdown of the single-party system that had dominated the country's political life since the late 1920s. In this and other important ways, at the turn of the twentieth-first century Mexicans have certainly extended and deepened the contents and scope of citizenship in their country. Nevertheless, for most Mexicans, the actual mid- and long-term consequences of this development are unclear because the posi-tive advances made in the field of electoral rights have been offset by the lack of progress and even reversal in other areas, such as in the combat against water inequality and poverty and the attempt to make water governance and management in Mexico more transparent and accountable to the citizens.

The Mexican example casts light on the problems arising worldwide from protracted water inequalities that preclude millions of human beings from accessing the goods and services deemed essential for survival and full community membership. The failure of the state-led model in most developing countries to guarantee universal access to the essentials of civilized life has created an unacceptable situation that certainly justifies radical action. However, in the light of the historical evidence, there is no ground to expect that the radical neoliberal policies implemented since the 1980s will provide the much needed answers. Would the enactment of private water rights and the liberalization of water markets contribute to stop the depletion of aquatic ecosystems as claimed by mainstream theorists? Would the expansion of weakly regulated or unregulated private water monopolies in water and sanitation bring about universal access to these essential services for the unserved world population? Would the neoliberal model of water governance help to deepen the process of democratization, as claimed by some of its leading advocates? How could a system predicated on the cancellation of basic citizenship rights be the vehicle of human emancipation through substantive citizenship and democracy? How could policies oriented at giving financial and business interests unchecked control of the global governance game enhance the life chances of the disadvantaged in developing countries?

Despite the formal recognition in these policies of the need for active citizen participation in water governance and management, in the current context participation continues to be understood as expected obedience to decisions already taken, which is the approach to citizen involvement that has prevailed in the techno-scientific tradition of the sector. Unfortunately, top-down and paternalistic practices were reinforced during the twentieth century by the increasing specialization undergone in the different fields of water expertise and by the abandonment of the wider perspective of the world that characterized earlier generations of water experts. Even then, there exist alternative approaches to the techno-scientific rationality prevailing in this field, and there is a growing number of positive experiences of transdisciplinary coordination in water research and action that give centrality to the fundamental problems of water inequality, injustice and substantive democracy.

From another angle, it would be relevant to further investigate the processes analysed here in a comparative perspective as they have taken place in other countries and cultures. Beyond the particularities and even idiosyncrasies of the Mexican case, how did water rights and the right to water evolve in other social figurations? Even where water control has not been as politically important as in the Basin of Mexico, what are the common patterns that can be identified in the relationship between the formation of techno-bureaucracies and the models of state-citizen interaction? And how are the current processes of water sector liberalization implemented worldwide transforming the rights of the citizens and the prospects for substantive democracy in each particular case? In the eventuality that the social forces behind water liberalization could realize their objectives, how would that affect the universal right to a fair and safe share of water recently enshrined by the international community as a human right and the achievement of the UN Millennium Development Goals?

As a final note, from our observations in the field of water governance and management we have confirmed the worrying trends already found in many other areas of activity: not only that we are still far from reaching all-inclusionary social systems, but also that we are not even reaching consensus about the desirability of such an outcome. In the current circumstances of reversal of the values of universalism, the defence and further conquest of the territory of citizenship has become a truly radical, in the sense of going to the roots, endeavour. However, although we recognize that in the present historical stage emancipatory struggles take the form of a struggle over the territory of citizenship, we do not reify this process because current citizenship systems, as mechanisms for inclusion and exclusion, cannot deliver all-inclusive membership. We cannot foresee what the exact course of the future of humanity will be or what other forms of sociopolitical organization will emerge or are already emerging, but we hope that this research can make a contribution to the emancipatory struggles oriented at developing new, more inclusionary social forms oriented by the principles of substantive democracy.

Notes

Introduction

1. The concept of 'governance' was first developed for the study of corporations and later adopted in political science to conceptualize shifting configurations of political power. In specific reference to water, governance has been defined as the 'range of political, social, economic and administrative systems that are in place to develop and manage water resources, and the delivery of water services' (GWP, 2003). We discuss governance in more detail later but let us be precise here that water governance includes the processes and institutions that determine how water is governed and managed, by whom and for whom, a crucial area of political decision from which most citizens have been historically excluded.
2. We will refer repeatedly to water resources and water and sanitation services as distinct. Unless stated otherwise, the terms 'water and sanitation services', 'water services' and similar expressions refer to the provision of essential domestic water supply and sewerage.
3. We will refer often to 'mainstream' water policies meaning the initiatives of deregulation, liberalization and privatization of water resources and services implemented by the international financial institutions (for example, World Bank), aid agencies and governments of the OECD countries since the 1980s. We will also refer to 'mainstream social science', by which we mainly mean the body of literature – especially in economics and policy-oriented political science – that has informed these far-reaching initiatives.
4. The concept of 'observable' encapsulates an epistemological position: the object of knowledge is not given but it is rather the result of the action of knowing carried out by a particular subject. Both the action and its outcome, the observable, are determined by preexisting cognitive structures. See Piaget (1978): 43–6; 1977: 342–6.
5. An adequate reference list would be too long. For a more comprehensive account of the scholarship on the topic, see Knight (1990).
6. See Orive Alba (1970), Kroeber (1994), and Aboites Aguilar (1987) on irrigation history; Aboites Aguilar (1998) on water sector development, and Lanz Cárdenas (1982) on the history of Mexican water law. See Palerm (1990) and Musset (1991) on pre-Columbian and colonial water history, and CEHOPU (1991) and Hoberman (1980) on the history of water engineering, architecture, and technology.
7. See, for instance, Foweraker and Craig (1990), Fox (1990), Escalante G. (1992), Whitehead (1992, 1994a, 1994b, 1995), Cornelius et al. (1994), Foweraker (1996), Joseph and Nugent (1994), Aitken et al. (1995), Roberts (1995). The classic analysis by González Casanova (1965b) remains an important reference.

1 The Social Character of Water

1. The MCMA encompasses the Federal District (16 *delegaciones* [departments]), and the adjacent municipalities of the State of Mexico. The number of adjacent municipalities varies according to different authors, but for the purposes of this research we consider 17 municipalities.
2. This is the average amount required to meet basic needs such as drinking, washing and cooking, while only one litre is required for drinking every day (Clarke, 1991: 19).
3. Engineer Fernando Gonzalez Villarreal speaking during the 1982 presidential campaign of the Institutional Revolutionary Party (PRI). In the late 1980s Gonzalez Villarreal became the head of the National Water Commission (CNA), PRI-IEPES, 1982: 21.
4. For data on service coverage and mortality rates see Tables II-4a, b and V-1 to V-3 in the Appendix (www.staff.ncl.ac.uk/j.e.castro/WPCAppendix.doc).
5. For data on water prices in the MCMA during the period of study see Tables IV- 9 and 10 in the Appendix (www.staff.ncl.ac.uk/j.e.castro/WPCAppendix.doc).
6. These policies have been challenged on technical, social and political grounds across the globe, leading to the collapse of many projects during the 1990s. See Bond, (1997), World Bank (1998), Basañes *et al.* (1999), PSIRU (2003), Crespo Flores, Laurie, and Ledo (2003).
7. Extraction includes consumption but not all water extracted is consumed, as in the case of water used for the generation of hydroenergy that is accounted for as 'extracted' but most of which is returned to the water source.
8. The water balance is calculated as the annual average water volumes resulting from 'surface runoff' (+), 'natural aquifer recharge' (+), 'artificial aquifer recharge' (+) and 'consumption' (-) (CNA, 1995: 7).
9. For a detailed account of this broad tradition see Redclift and Benton (1994); Benton (1996); Foster (2000); Martínez Alier (2002).
10. Strictly speaking, *usuario* refers to customers who hold an account with the water utility (homeowners, commercial users, and so on) and not necessarily to the actual people using the water under that account. The term is used frequently in a loose and general way to refer indistinctly to the universe of water users disregarding their legal situation with the water utilities. *Demandantes* are those who do not have access to water and sanitation services and put forward demands to be connected.
11. Interestingly, legal land tenure is deemed essential for the provision of water and sewerage but not for other services such as the energy supply (Garza and Damián, 1991: 31).
12. *Ejidal* land is land allocated under the agrarian reform programme, where plots (*ejidos*) are owned collectively.
13. Just to mention a few pioneering works on this subject: Eckstein (1977); Ward (1986); Garza and Schteingart (1984); Benítez and Morelos (1988); Schteingart (1989); Varley (1996).
14. This has been also reported by different authors, see Aguilar (1988); Schteingart *et al.* (no date [circa 1989]); Garza and Damián (1991); Varley (1993).

15. Analogies between war and other social processes, even those perceived as 'peaceful', abound in the literature. For an analogy between war and processes of human control over nature from a historic-sociological perspective, see Schmidt, 1993: 39.
16. The concept of holochronic analysis was advanced by T. Carlstein with reference to the study of socio-natural processes defined as '*systems in motion* and *systems of 'flows' in time and space*' [italics in the original]. Carlstein, 1982: 22–3, 300.
17. This certainly makes sense if we refer to the historical changes brought about in the Mexican political scene during the early 1990s, especially the 1992 radical changes to the Revolutionary Constitution.
18. As already explained, we explore here the long-term development of citizenship. We have to keep in mind, therefore, that the meaning of the concepts of citizenship and citizen has evolved over time. In this regard, although as explained in later chapters modern citizenship did not arrive in Mexico until the nineteenth century, the concepts of *ciudadanía* (citizenship) and *ciudadano* (citizen) were also part of the Spanish colonial tradition (see Morse, 1972). We use the term precisely to convey the message that the development of citizenship in Mexico was a long-term process that did not start with the liberal reforms of the mid-nineteenth century.
19. This has been part of a worldwide push towards the privatization and commodification of urban services, including water and sanitation, which has been actively promoted as the best strategy 'to improve the efficiency of infrastructure services, extend their delivery to the poor and relieve pressure on public budgets' (World Bank, 1998: 1; Savedoff and Spiller, 1999) while at the same time improving social equity (Inter American Development Bank (IDB), 1998: 120). We address these issues in more detail in Chapter 6.
20. Carlos Salinas de Gortari during his presidential campaign (PRI-IEPES, 1987: 11).

2   The Sociogenesis of Water Stress

1. We mention here only some regions to illustrate the extreme contrasts being discussed. Mexico is divided into 5 development regions (South-Southeast, Centre-West, Centre, Northeast, and Northwest) and 13 hydrological regions. See CNA, 2001: 44–76.
2. Average water availability is defined as the sum of the averages of surface runoff plus aquifer recharge (CNA, 2001: 73–4; 2002: 23).
3. The basin was first opened in the early seventeenth century, although the drain was not completed until 1900.
4. Different authors include a variable number of *municipalities* in the 1990s: 26 according to Garza and Damián, 1991: 22; 21 in Aguilar *et al.*, 1996: 307, and in Rowland and Gordon, 1996: 177.
5. Artificial cultivation islands made of a structure of reed covered with fertile mud and anchored to the bed of the lakes with wooden posts.
6. On the concept of socio-technical system, see Pfaffenberger (1992).

7. The Xochimilco canals are almost the only surviving areas of the original lake system. They are now under UN protection and have been declared a Mankind Heritage by UNESCO in 1987.

8. The collapse of the basin's population during the sixteenth century must have had an impact on water resources at the basin's level, perhaps through a significant reduction of water abstractions and of the pollution of water sources by wastewater. However, our discussion here is mainly concentrated on the urban area of Mexico City, where the impact of depopulation on water resources must have been counterbalanced by expanding water uses as described here.

9. Names designing street water vendors and municipal employees in charge of distributing water in the Basin of Mexico today. *Piperos* are the drivers of water tankers (*pipas*), while *burreros* [donkey men] use donkeys to carry water containers.

10. *Encomienda* was the system used for allocating Indian labour to Spanish overlords (*encomenderos*) during the early colonial period.

11. An analysis of the technological debates sustained can be found in Hoberman (1980). See also Gurría Lacroix (1978); Musset (1991) pp. 313–65.

12. 'Syncretism' as used here does not entail positive or negative connotations either regarding the direction and sequence of the process or the character-istics of the outcome. It does not suggest any teleological progression of his-torical stages either leading to the degradation of an original and pure state or to the completeness of an ultimate social model. However, we also prefer 'syncretism' to 'symbiosis' in order to conceptualize the process under dis-cussion. G. J. Cano, for instance, has termed 'symbiosis' as 'the process of legal and technical synthesis in the water sector in Spanish America' (Cano, 1991: 371). Also, Sanders and Price used this term with reference to the link between irrigation agriculture and the evolution of states in Central Mexico (Sanders and Price, 1968). However, I believe that syncretism is more appro-priate in order to avoid biologicist connotations. Symbiosis means 'Association of two different organisms (usually two plants, or an animal and a plant) which live attached to each other, or one as a tenant of the other, and contribute to each other's support. Also, more widely, any inti-mate association of two or more different organisms, whether mutually beneficial or not' (*The Oxford English Dictionary*, 1989, Vol. XVII, pp. 450, 451). By contrast, syncretism meant originally a social interaction between otherwise opposed human groups who become amalgamated to face a common threat or challenge, which seems to fit better the processes under review (for a useful overview of 'syncretism', see Shaw and Stewart, 1994).

13. Pearson would play a central role in Mexican politics during the 1890s and 1900s, through his participation as public works contractor (see Connolly, 1997, especially pp. 193–297).

14. In interviews carried out by the author in May 1997, water experts from the private water companies currently operating in the Federal District asserted that the official estimations that water losses amount to 30 per cent of total water delivered in the MCMA are untenable and that the actual figure is much higher. See 'Selected Interviews'.

15. Tables Table II-2, II-4a, and II-4b in the Appendix provide more detailed information (www.staff.ncl.ac.uk/j.e.castro/WPCAppendix.doc).

16. Literally, 'lost cities', Mexican jargon for shanty town.

3   Water and Power in the Basin of Mexico

1. Marx had stated that 'Climate and territorial conditions ... constituted artificial irrigation by canals and waterworks, the basis of Oriental Agriculture. This prime necessity of an economical and common use of water, which, in the occident, drove private enterprise to voluntary association, as in Flanders and Italy, necessitated in the Orient where civilisation was too low and the territorial extent too vast to call into life voluntary association, the interference of the centralizing power of government.' Marx, New York Daily Tribune, 25 June 1853, quoted in Avineri, 1969: 90.
2. For a detailed discussion on this issue, see: Bailey and Llobera (1981). Also see Peet (1985); O'Leary (1989).
3. For a theoretical criticism on Wittfogel's theory, see Bailey and Llobera (1981): 107–233. Also: Jones (1981): 8–10; O'Leary (1989): 235–61. Other authors also offered an empirically grounded criticism of Wittfogel's generalizations. See, for example: Leach (1959); Geertz (1980); (1993): 327–41; Glick (1970): 1–7; Pérez Picazo and Lemeunier (1990): 21–38.
4. Michael Meyer made a similar argument in his legal and social history of water in northern New Spain concerning the organization of irrigation systems (Meyer, 1984: 18).
5. For a consideration of the *científicos* and their role in the formation of modern Mexico, see Córdoba (1973). Some of the outstanding personages in this movement are considered in Sáez (1980).
6. The *Laguna* water conflict was not solved until after the revolution. Meyers (1977) offered a detailed study of the conflict.
7. The case of Lake Chalco is an outstanding example (Tortolero, 1994, 1996). Another relevant case, outside the Basin of Mexico, was the expulsion of the Yaqui Indians from their well-watered lands in Sonora (see Kroeber, 1994: 165–73).
8. Although this constitution was aborted it set important legal precedents.
9. The investment in irrigation represented 1.6, 4.2, and 7.4 per cent of the total public expenditure in 1926, 1927, and 1929 respectively (Aboites Aguilar, 1987: 30–5). See also Meyer (1994): 201.
10. These figures must be read with caution because the source does not provide a basis for ascertaining if these are nominal pesos or pesos of 1947 when the reference is made.
11. Pesos of 1966.
12. For a detailed analysis of the 1975 National Hydraulic Plan and related policies, see Herrera Toledo (1997): 6–53.

4   Contested Waters

1. The collection of reports covered 19 newspapers and magazines published in the MCMA during the period of reference. The reports were classified and subject to statistical analysis, which included controls to avoid repetition owing to multiple reporting of the same event. The database was prepared

by the Water and Society team at the Latin American Faculty of Social Sciences (FLACSO) and the Mexican Institute of Water Technology (IMTA), of which I have been a member since 1990 (Torregrosa Armentia, 1988–97). I also used material from previous research on water struggles in the Mexican cities of Tuxtla Gutiérrez and Ciudad Juárez (Castro, 1992). Although the events cover a crucial period of the recent history of the Mexican water sector, the fact that the database ends in 1992 means that crucial aspects such as the public reactions to the particular form of water privatization implemented in the MCMA since 1993 were not captured here. Nevertheless, we refer to some aspects of this important development in chapters 5 and 6.

2. On 19 November 1984, the blaze in the oil plant of PEMEX, located in the State of Mexico and popularly known as San Juanico, killed over 500 people and caused extensive damage to the city's infrastructure.

3. The endurance of the movement and its presence in the water struggles is noticeable. For instance, according to representatives of the private water companies working in the Federal District since 1993, the Neighbourhoods' Assembly represented by *Superbarrio* (a masked wrestler from a popular TV programme), was leading the occupation of buildings and other forms of protest against the water utilities on a weekly basis (from interviews with the Technical and Legal managers of a private company operating in the Federal District who requested strict confidentiality, Interviews, May 1997).

4. A public consultation was held prior to the meeting in Mexico City on 22 December 1981 (PRI-IEPES, 1982: 11).

5. This led to the creation of the centre-left Party of the Democratic Revolution (PRD) headed by Cuauhtémoc Cárdenas, son of former President Lázaro Cárdenas.

6. In fact, co-option of non-partisan leaders and formation of new grassroots leaders was a crucial strategy of the Salinas government, whose most valuable recruits were perhaps those coming from the historical core of the 1968 student movement and from autonomous popular organizations such as CONAMUP (Dresser, 1994: 152–6). See also Knight (1994): 39–40; Lustig (1994): 79; Moguel (1994).

7. For a detailed breakdown of data see Appendix, Tables IV-1 to IV-5 (www.staff.ncl.ac.uk/j.e.castro/WPCAppendix.doc). It should be noticed that the data for climatic patterns (precipitation, temperature and evaporation) cover the period 1975–88 while the events were recorded in the period 1985–92. We assume that the climatic patterns have not experienced substantial changes during the period of our research, for which climatic data were not available when the study was carried out.

8. However, according to the 1990 Census, during the 1980s the *delegación* Gustavo A. Madero reduced its population (INEGI, 1991).

9. In the following sections we refer to information that is presented in more detail in the Appendix, Tables IV (www.staff.ncl.ac.uk/j.e.castro/WPCAppendix.doc).

10. During the peak of the dry season competition for water worsens which leads to higher prices and abuses; during the rainy season, very often whole neighbourhoods are cut off as water vendors stop serving large parts of the

city where access roads are disrupted by the weather conditions (García Lascuraín, 1995: 132).

11. Tables IV-9 a and b in the Appendix (www.staff.ncl.ac.uk/j.e.castro/ WPCAppendix.doc) provide a list of examples of water prices recorded from the press reports. Table IV-10 also in the Appendix gives the nominal and real values of the minimum daily salary for comparative purposes. Although this information should be read with caution owing to potential errors in the press reports, it provides an overall adequate description of the situation. The high fluctuation in prices and the price values recorded are consistent with results published by authors who carried surveys of water pricing in the MCMA during the same period (see García Lascuraín, 1995). In our comparison of water prices with nominal minimum daily salaries we have taken into account that the values given in Table IV-10 of the Appendix correspond to the month of December each year. Therefore, water prices during the first semester are compared against minimum daily salaries of the previous December: for instance, water prices from March 1987 are compared with minimum daily salaries of December 1986.

12. This was the national average in 1990 for domestic users assuming a daily water consumption of 200 litres per household (Saavedra Shumidzu *et al.* 1991: 30).

13. See, for instance, García Lascuráin (1995) for the MCMA; Swyngedouw (1995, 1995b, 1997, 1999), for a similar study in Guayaquil, Ecuador.

5 Water and the Evolution of Citizenship

1. David Held has rejected Giddens' criticisms and offers a different reading of Marshall's historical account. Held (1989): 166–70; see also Turner (1986): 45, 46.

2. As mentioned in Chapter 2, the contamination of water supply was one of many weapons employed by the Indians in their protracted resistance against colonization. See also Llamas Fernández (1991): 190.

3. Actually, this author, who based his calculations on a wide array of sources, gives this as his most conservative estimation.

4. The real extension of this process, however, is still a controversial subject. See for instance, Knight (1990) vol. 1: 96–7.

5. The 1879 Spanish Water Law was the model for most Latin American countries, and remained unchanged in Spain until the enforcement of the 1985 Water Law (Cano: 1991, 374–82).

6. For a revision of different estimates of the mortality rate of the 1918 influenza epidemic, see Knight (1990) vol. 1: 422.

7. See Tables V-1 through V-3 in the Appendix (www.staff.ncl.ac.uk/j.e.castro/ WPCAppendix.doc).

6 Water and the Territory of Citizenship

1. We cannot do justice here to the ongoing debate about the real character of the Mexican Revolution. See, among others, Aguilar Camín and Meyer

(1993); Knight (1990); Hart (1987); Tutino (1986); Guerra (1985); Brading (1980); Katz (1981); Meyer (1973); Womack (1969; 1991).

2. This new system of water rights was further institutionalized through the Water Rights Federal Law passed in December 1996 (PRM, 1997).

3. In 1991 the CNA estimated the number of clandestine wells in the country at about 20,000, in addition to the illegal extraction of water from other sources like rivers (*Uno más Uno*, 21 June 1991: 19). In the same year SARH officers denounced the proliferation of clandestine wells in Chalco and Texcoco (*El Universal*, 15 July 1991: 39). Other examples from the press reports consulted show public officers from Coacalco, Chimalhuacán, Texcoco, and Chalco, claiming that in the Valley Cuautitlán-Texcoco alone there were over 2000 clandestine wells, most of them in the hands of industrialists, hotel owners and businesses (*Excelsior*, 12 August 1987: 1). See also 'Unpunished drilling of water wells in marginal zones of Cuautitlán-Texcoco' (*Excelsior*, 12 March 1987).

4. Declaration made by the former President of the Commission of Hydraulic Resources of the Chamber of Deputies, Fidel Herrera Beltrán (*El Nacional*, 24 October 1992: 11).

5. A Presidential Decree issued on 11 October 1995 ruled the 'granting of administrative facilities and the condonation of contributions to users of national waters'; a second decree issued on 11 October 1996 widened the categories of users to be benefited by the condonation (*Diario Oficial de la Federación*, 11 October 1995: 7–13; 11 October 1996: 25–31).

6. 'SEMARNAP Quietly Scuttles Key Environmental Regulation: On October 23 [1995], Mexico's *Secretaría de Medio Ambiente, Recursos Naturales y Pesca* (SEMARNAP) quietly announced an immediate and dramatic loosening of its environmental-impact assessment (EIA) requirements. A number of US environmental groups are considering filing a complaint with the North American Commission for Environmental Cooperation, based on the environmental side agreements' injunction against lowering environmental standards in order to attract or retain investment' (BorderLines, 1995).

7. See Martínez Omaña (2002) for an account of the private consortiums. Also, Appendix (www.staff.ncl.ac.uk/j.e.castro/WPCAppendix.doc), Table V-1.

8. On value incommensurability in relation to ecological processes, see Martínez Alier (2002): 267–71.

9. For instance, the CNA's director repeatedly intervened in public to make a distinction between private sector participation and privatization: 'The administration of water will not be re-privatized; water is a property of the nation. Fernando J. González Villarreal assured that the private sector will be allowed to participate' (*El Universal*, 9 April 1991: 15); 'Water will not be privatized and the nation will maintain the property of this vital resource, assured the Director of the National Water Commission (CNA), Eng. Fernando González Villarreal' (*La Jornada*, 22 September 1992: 37). Similar statements were made by other functionaries seeking to calm down the political debate over the radical changes introduced by the Constitution and the new Water Law. 'The external assessor of the National Water Commission, Urbano Farías met deputies from the Commission of Hydraulic Resources. In answer to the queries of legislators from the Partido

Popular Socialista (PPS), Partido de la Revolución Democrática (PRD), and Partido del Frente Cardenista de Reconstrucción Nacional (PFCRN) ... the functionary said that the project is totally consistent with the constitutional principles and that water would not be privatized' (*Novedades*, 20 September 1992: 10a; *El Heraldo de México*, 20 September 1992: 3a; Farías Hernández, 1993: 3–32); 'The initiative of the National Water Law is not aimed at privatizing the resource because it is a good of the nation .... This was manifested by Manuel Contijock, Sub-director of Hydro-agricultural Infrastructure of the National Water Commission' (*La Afición*, 14 September 1992: 3).

10. See 'Sources, Interviews'. Some of the interviewees requested anonymity.
11. This information was provided by the legal manager of one of the private companies under the request of strict confidentiality. The manager of another private company asserted that the main resistance to the new policies of water metering and billing came from the middle classes (Eng. Michael Phillip Jones Taylor, see Selected Interviews).
12. This is confirmed by similar experiences of privatization where disconnecting domestic users for non-payment has been perceived as illegitimate. In England and Wales, for instance, disconnection of domestic users by the water companies privatized in 1989 faced strong social and political opposition leading to the banning of the practice in 1997 (Herbert and Kempson, 1995; Drakeford, 1998 a, b; Castro *et al.*, 2003: 294).
13. According to recent evaluations, the results have been mixed. While progress has been made in the billing, metering, and improvement of the commercial management of the water utilities, the goals set in 1993 had not been fully achieved. For instance, in the case of reducing leakage, one of the key tasks envisaged in the original contracts, little progress has been made (Libreros, 2003; Torregrosa Armentia *et al.*, 2003).
14. See Appendix (www.staff.ncl.ac.uk/j.e.castro/WPCAppendix.doc), Table II-1 for MCMA data; on international standards see, for instance, Clarke 1991: 19.
15. UNCED, 1992: Section II, Chapter 18 of Agenda 21. The World Health Organization has set up a minimum of 150 per day per household [pdph], while 75 litres pdph are considered adequate for the prevention of waterborne diseases. The World Bank estimates that at least 50 litres per capita per day are necessary to forestall health-related problems.
16. For example, a case study carried out in Chalco and Ecatepec between 1986 and 1992 showed that average water consumption in periods of regular supply was 24 litres per capita per day in Chalco and 19 litres in Ecatepec. However, the amount was sharply reduced to between 4 and 14 litres in Chalco and 7 litres in Ecatepec during the peak of the dry season and again during the rainy season, when it becomes difficult for water trucks to enter the neighborhoods (García Lascuráin, 1995: 132–3). See also the discussion in Chapter 4 and Tables IV-9 a, b and IV-10 in the Appendix (www.staff.ncl.ac.uk/j.e.castro/WPCAppendix.doc).
17. According to the Director of the Federal District Water Commission (CADF), Mr Alfonso Martínez Vaca, 22 cubic metres per second [cmps] out of the 60 cmps consumed in the MCMA are wasted through leakage (*La Jornada*, 20 August 1996).

18. The concept of entitlement refers to 'the set of alternative commodity bundles that a person can command in a society using the totality of rights and opportunities that he or she faces' (Sen, 1981: 497). In turn, these entitlements are bound up with people's endowments, namely the initial ownership that allows them to enter into market exchanges and thus have access to a set of entitlements. A wage labourer, for instance, engages in repeated exchanges with others, starting by selling his labour power for a wage, and then interchanging his or her wage for a collection of commodities. Sen has responded to criticisms by reformulating the original position presented in Poverty and Famines (1981) and offering an extended concept of entitlements (1990).

19. Although it includes soft drinks, fruit juices, and so on (see, for instance, Hewitt de Alcántara and Vera, 1990: 39). For example, in Chalco and Ecatepec in 1990 a *tambo* containing 200 litres represented up to 18 per cent of the minimum wage (García Lascuráin, 1995: 137). See also Appendix (www.staff.ncl.ac.uk/j.e.castro/WPCAppendix.doc), Tables IV-9a, b, and IV-10.

20. The typical cases of market failure discussed in this literature are the existence of 'natural monopolies', 'large economies of scale leading to decreasing costs', 'externalities', 'pure public goods', and 'merit goods'. The 'market failure' arises because in these particular situations private markets are unlikely to provide the most efficient pattern of goods and services preferred by consumers (Roth, 1988: 6–7). See also Lee (1999).

21. Distinctions between the range of positions adopted by pro-market reformers are difficult, but for the sake of clarity it is important to differentiate between extreme free-market positions that aim to reduce state intervention to its minimum expression if not cancelling it altogether (defenders of self-regulating markets), from more moderate arguments proposing the use of market mechanisms (for example, the creation of water markets or the introduction of private-sector management in the running of public utilities) as a public policy tool but recognizing a stronger role for the state (they accept that there are market failures requiring state intervention). For an example of free-market arguments in the water and sanitation sector see, for instance, Brook Cowen and Cowen (1998); and example of moderate pro-market arguments can be found in Roth (1988).

22. See Appendix (www.staff.ncl.ac.uk/j.e.castro/WPCAppendix.doc), Table VI-2 for a more detailed exemplification of the principles and the corresponding references.

23. For perspectives on the concept of governance that are critical of this mainstream approach see, for instance, Kooiman (1993), Hirst (1994), Amin (1997), and Swyngedouw (2000).

24. For instance, Latin America, regardless of the indicators chosen, became the most unequal region in the world during the 1990s (IDB, 1998), which has been confirmed by recent evidence examined by World Bank analysts (Perry *et al.*, 2003). The region was the main experimental field for the neoliberal reforms since the 1980s.

Sources

Archives

Archivo Histórico del Agua (AHA), Mexico City.
Centro de Consulta del Agua (CENCA), Instituto Mexicano de Tecnología del Agua (IMTA), Jiutepec, Morelos, Mexico.
Instituto Mexicano de Tecnología del Agua (IMTA), Subcoordinación de Participación Social (1990–1997), Interviews Archive, Jiutepec, Morelos, Mexico.

Databases

Centro de Consulta del Agua (CENCA) (1991), *Literatura del Agua, Imágenes de México*, Jiutepec, Morelos, Mexico.
Comisión Nacional del Agua (CNA) and Instituto Mexicano de Tecnología del Agua (IMTA) (1990), *Datos Hidrométricos de México 1937–1985)*, Jiutepec, Morelos, Mexico.
Instituto Mexicano de Tecnología del Agua (IMTA) (1996), *Extractor Rápido de Información Climatológica (ERIC) 1940–1990*, Jiutepec, Morelos, Mexico.

Selected interviews

Eng. Ignacio Stamatrio, General Manager, State Managing Board of the Comisión Nacional del Agua in Chiapas, November 1992, Interviews Archive IMTA-SPS (1990–1997) (see above).
Eng. Michael Phillip Jones Taylor, Director General, Industrias del Agua de la Ciudad de México, S.A. de C.V., Mexico City, May 1997.
Ing. Miguel Aguayo y Camargo, Jefe de la Unidad Regional, Comisión Nacional del Agua, Gerencia de Aguas del Valle de México, Unidad Regional de Programas Rurales y Participación Social, Mexico City, May 1997.
Legal Manager, private water company operating in the Federal District [required strict confidentiality], Mexico City, May 1997.
Technical Manager, private water company operating in the Federal District [required strict confidentiality], Mexico City, May 1997.

201

Bibliography

Note: The year indicated between ( ) corresponds to the edition of the work that I have consulted. Where possible, I provide the original date of publication of the first edition between [ ].

Aboites Aguilar., L. (1987) *La Irrigación Revolucionaria. Historia del Sistema Nacional de Riego del Río Conchos, Chihuahua, 1927–1938*, Mexico City: Secretaría de Educación Pública (SEP) and Centro de Investigaciones y Estudios Superiores en Antropología Social (CIESAS).

———— (1998) *El Agua de la Nación. Una Historia Política de México (1888–1946)*, Mexico City: Secretaría de Educación Pública (SEP) and Centro de Investigaciones y Estudios Superiores en Antropología Social (CIESAS).

Aguilar, A.G. (1988) 'Community Participation in Mexico City: A Case Study', *Bulletin of Latin American Research*, #7, pp. 33–46.

Aguilar, A.G., E. Ezcurra, T. García, M. Mazari Hiriart and I. Pisanty (1996), 'The Basin of Mexico', in J. X. Kasperson, R. E. Kasperson and B. L. Turner II (eds), *Regions at Risk. Comparison of Threatened Environments*, Tokyo, New York, Paris: United Nations University Press, pp. 304–66.

Aguilar Camín, H. and L. Meyer (1993) *In the Shadow of the Mexican Revolution: Contemporary Mexican History, 1910–1989*, Austin: University of Texas Press.

Aitken, R., N. Craske, G. Jones, and D. E. Stansfield (1995) *Dismantling the Mexican State?*, Basingstoke Macmillan and New York: St Martin's Press.

Amin, A. (1997) *Beyond Market and Hierarchy: Interactive Governance and Social Complexity*, Cheltenham: Elgar.

Anderson, B. [1983] (1994) *Imagined Communities. Reflections on the Origin and Spread of Nationalism*, rev. and ext., London: Verso.

Aristotle [1946] (1948) 'The Theory of Citizenship and Constitutions. A Citizenship', in E. Barker (translat) *The Politics of Aristotle*, Oxford: Clarendon Press, pp. 92–110.

Asian Development Bank (1995) 'Governance: Sound Development Management', Manila: ADB.

Atherton, C. and D. Windsor (1987) 'Privatization of Urban Public Services', in C. A. Kent (ed.), *Entrepreneurship and the Privatizing of Government*, New York, Westport, Conn., London: Quorum Books, pp. 81–99.

Avineri, S. (ed.) (1969) *Karl Marx on Colonialism and Modernization*, New York: Anchor Books.

Bailey, A. M. and J. R. Llobera (eds) (1981) *The Asiatic Mode of Production. Science and Politics*, London, Boston and Henley: Routledge and Kegan Paul.

Bakewell, P. (1984) 'Mining in Colonial Spanish America', in L. Bethell (ed.) *The Cambridge History of Latin America*, Vol. 2, Cambridge: Cambridge University Press, pp. 105–51.

Ball, Ph. (2000) *H20. A Biography of Water*, London: Phoenix.

Barbalet, J. M. (1993) 'Citizenship, Class Inequality and Resentment', in B. S. Turner (ed.) *Citizenship and Social Theory*, London: Sage.

Bartra, A. (1985) *Los Herederos de Zapata*, Mexico City: Ediciones Era.

Bartra, R. (1978) *Estructura Agraria y Clases Sociales en México*, Mexico City: Ediciones Era.

Basañes, F., E. Uribe and R. Willig (1999) *Can Privatisation Deliver? Infrastructure for Latin America*, Washington, DC: Interamerican Development Bank (IDB).

Bazant, J. [1985] (1994) 'From Independence to the Liberal Republic, 1821–1867' in L. Bethell (ed.) *Mexico since Independence*, 2nd rep., Cambridge: Cambridge University Press, pp. 1–48.

Benavides V., L., J. Olarte, L. Torregrosa and J. M. Torroella (1953) 'Algunas Consideraciones Sobre la Diarrea Infecciosa en México', in *Boletín Médico del Hospital Infantil*, Vol X, pp. 649–72.

Benítez R. and J. B. Morelos (1988) *Grandes Problemas de la Ciudad de México*, Mexico City: Departamento del Distrito Federal (DDF) – Plaza y Valdés.

Bennett, V. (1995) *The Politics of Water: Urban Protest, Gender, and Power in Monterrey, Mexico*, Pittsburgh: University of Pittsburgh Press.

Benton T. (ed.) 1996 *The Greening of Marxism*, New York: Guilford Press.

Birrichaga Gardida, D. (1997) 'El Abasto de Agua en León y San Luis Potosí (1935–1947)', in B. E. Suárez Cortez and D. Birrichaga Gardida, *Dos Estudios sobre Usos del Agua en México (siglos XIX y XX)*, Mexico City: Instituto Mexicano de Tecnología del Agua (IMTA) and Centro de Investigaciones y Estudios Superiores en Antropología Social (CIESAS), pp. 91–149.

Bolos, S. and I. Perdomo (1990) 'Descripción de la Movilización Social por Agua en la Zona Metropolitana de la Ciudad de México 1985–1989', in M. L. Torregrosa Armentia (coord.) (1988–1997) *Programa de Investigación Agua y Sociedad*, Mexico City and Jiutepec, Morelos: Facultad Latinoamericana de Ciencias Sociales (FLACSO) and Instituto Mexicano de Tecnología del Agua (IMTA).

Bond, P. (1997) 'Privatization, Protest and Participation: Citizen Opposition to the World Bank in Haiti and South Africa', Paper presented to the *World Bank/NGO Dialogue on Privatization*, Washington, DC, Friends of the Earth/World Bank.

Borah, W. (1984) 'Trends in Recent Studies of Colonial Latin American Cities' *The Hispanic American Historical Review*, Vol. 64, #3, pp. 535–54.

BorderLines (1995) 'SEMARNAP Quietly Scuttles Key Environmental Regulation', Vol. 3, #11, December.

Boyer, R. E. (1975) *La Gran Inundación. Vida y Sociedad en México (1629–1638)*, Mexico City: SEP.

Brading, D. A. (1980) *Caudillo and Peasant in the Mexican Revolution*, Cambridge: Cambridge University Press.

Bribiesca Castrejón, J. L. [1959] (1975) 'El agua potable en la República Mexicana. Los abastecimientos en el Primer Siglo Independiente (1821–1920)', in Departamento del Distrito Federal, Secretaría de Obras y Servicios (DDF-SOS), 1975, *Memoria de las Obras del Sistema de Drenaje Profundo del Distrito Federal*, Vol. II, Mexico City: DDF, pp. 247–54.

———— [1960] (1975b) 'El Agua Potable en la República Mexicana. El Abastecimiento del Distrito Federal y la Ciudad de México en los Últimos 40 Años (1920–1960)', in Departamento del Distrito Federal, Secretaría de Obras y Servicios (DDF-SOS) (1975) *Memoria de las Obras del Sistema de*

Drenaje Profundo del Distrito Federal, Vol. II, Mexico City: DDF, pp. 303–5, 314, 315.

Brook Cowen, P. J. and T. Cowen (1998) 'Deregulated Private Water Supply: a Policy Option for Developing Countries', *Cato Journal*, Vol. 18, #1, pp. 21–41.

Brubaker, W. R. (1992) *Citizenship and Nationhood in France and Germany*, Cambridge, Mass. and London: Harvard University Press.

Brundage, B. C. (1972) *A Rain of Darts. The Mexica Aztecs*, Austin and London: University of Texas Press.

Burink, F. (1987) 'Privatization in Europe', in C. A Kent (ed.), *Entrepreneurship and the Privatizing of Government*, New York, Westport, Conn., London: Quorum Books, pp. 161–76.

Burkholder, M. A. and L. L. Johnson (1994) *Colonial Latin America*, 2nd edn., Oxford: Oxford University Press.

Buse, K. and G. Walt (2000) 'Global Public-Private Partnerships: Part II – what are the Health Issues for Global Governance?' in *Bulletin of the World Health Organization*, Vol. 78, # 5, pp. 699–709.

Cairncross, S. and V. Kochar (eds) (1994) *Studying Hygiene Behaviour*, New Delhi: Sage.

Calderón, F. R. (1955) *La República Restaurada. La Vida Económica*, Vol. VII-II of D. Cosío Villegas (ed.), Historia de México, Mexico and Buenos Aires: Hermes.

Camdessus, M. (Chair) (2003) 'Financing Water for All', report of the World Panel on Financing Water Infrastructure, World Water Council, Global Water Partnership.

Cano, G. J. (1991) 'Legislación de Aguas: Relación entre Países Americanos y España', in CEHOPU, *Antiguas Obras Hidráulicas en América. Actas del Seminario (México, 1988)*, Madrid: CEHOPU, pp. 371–83.

Carlstein, T. (1982) *Time Resources, Society and Ecology. On the Capacity for Human Interaction in Space and Time*, London: George Allen and Unwin.

Casasús H., C. (1992) 'Una Nueva Estrategia de Agua para la Ciudad de México', in R. Samaniego B. (comp.) *Ensayos sobre la Economía de la Ciudad de México*, Mexico City: Ciudad de México Librería y Editora, pp. 285–96.

Castro, J. E., E. A. Swyngedouw and M. Kaika (2003) 'London: Structural Continuities and Institutional Change in Water Management', in *European Planning Studies*, Vol. 11, #3, pp. 283–98.

Castro, J. E. and N. Laurie (2004) 'Comparative Report on the Socio-political and Cultural Dimension', in J. E. Castro (coord.) *PRINWASS Project*, Oxford: University of Oxford.

Castro, J. E (1992) *El Conflicto por el Agua en México. Los Casos de Tuxtla Gutiérrez, Chiapas y Ciudad Juárez, Chihuahua, 1986–1991* (unpublished thesis, Master in Social Sciences), Mexico City: Latin American Faculty of Social Sciences (FLACSO).

Ceniceros, J. A. (1935) *El Problema Social de la Insalubridad*, Mexico City: Ediciones Botas.

Centro de Estudios Históricos de Obras Públicas y Urbanismo (CEHOPU) (1991) *Antiguas Obras Hidráulicas en América. Actas del Seminario (México, 1988)*, Madrid: CEHOPU.

Chevalier, F. [1952] (1963) *Land and Society in Colonial Mexico: The Great Haciendas*, Berkeley and Los Angeles: University of California Press.

Cifuentes, E., M. Mazari-Hiriart, F. Carneiro, F. Bianchi, and D. González (2002), 'The risk of enteric diseases in young children and environmental indicators in sentinel areas of Mexico City', in *Journal of International of Environmental Health Research*, #12, pp. 53–62.

Cifuentes García E., J. Hernández-Ávila, L. Venczel and M. Hurtado (1999) 'Panorama of Acute Diarrohoeal Diseases in Mexico', in *Health and Place*, #5, pp. 247–55.

Cifuentes, E., U. Blumenthal, G. Ruiz-Palacios, S. Bennett, M. Quigley, A. Peasey and H. Romero-Alvarez (1993) 'Problemas de Salud Asociados al Riego Agrícola con Agua Residual en México', in *Salud Pública de México*, #35, pp. 614–19.

Cifuentes, E., U. Blumenthal and G. Ruiz Palacios (1995) 'Riego Agrícola con Aguas Residuales y sus Efectos Sobre la Salud en México', in I. Restrepo (ed.), *Agua, Salud y Derechos Humanos*, Mexico City: CNDH, pp. 189–201.

Clarke, R. (1991) *Water. The International Crisis*, London: Earthscan Publications Ltd.

Clausewitz, C. von [1832] (1989) *On War*, Indexed and reprinted, Princeton, NJ: Princeton University Press.

Cohen, J. L. and A. Arato (1994) *Civil Society and Political Theory*, Cambridge, Mass., and London: The Massachusetts Institute of Technology (MIT) Press.

Comisión Nacional del Agua (CNA) (1990) *Estrategias 1990–1994*, Colección Desarrollo Institucional Nro 1, Cuernavaca, Mor.: IMTA.

———— (1992) *Desarrollo de la Capacidad del Sector Agua* (DECSAGUA), Mexico City: CNA.

———— (1993b) *Programa de Trabajo 1993*, Mexico City: CNA.

———— (1993c) *Política Hidráulica 1989–1994*, Mexico City: CNA.

———— (1993d) *Informe 1989–1993*, Mexico City: CNA.

———— (1995) *Programa Hidráulico 1995–2000*, Mexico City: CNA.

———— (1997) *Sistema Cutzamala: Agua para Millones de Mexicanos*, Gerencia Regional de Aguas del Valle de México, Mexico City: CNA.

———— (2001) *Programa Nacional Hidráulico 2001–2006*, Mexico City: CNA.

———— (2002) *Compendio Básico del Agua en México*, Mexico City: CNA.

Commander, S. and T. Killick (1988) 'Privatization in Developing Countries: a Survey of the Issues', in P. Cook and C. Kirkpatrick (eds) *Privatization in Less Developed Countries*, Hemel Hempstead: Harvester Wheatsheaf, pp. 91–124.

Connolly, P. (1997) *El Contratista de Don Porfirio. Obras Públicas, Deuda y Desarrollo Desigual*, Zamora, Michoacán and Mexico City: El Colegio de Michoacán, Universidad Autónoma Metropolitana (UAM) and Fondo de Cultura Económica.

———— (1991) 'El Contratista de Don Porfirio. La Construcción del Gran Canal de Desagüe', 3 Vols, Mexico City: UAM-A, División de Ciencias Sociales y Humanidades.

Conrad, G. W. and A. A. Demarest [1984] (1990) *Religion and Empire. The Dynamics of Aztec and Inca Expansionism*, Cambridge: Cambridge University Press.

Cooper, D. B. (1965) *Epidemic Disease in Mexico City 1761–1813. An Administrative, Social, and Medical Study*, Austin, Texas: University of Texas Press.

Córdoba, A. (1973) *La Ideología de la Revolución Mexicana. La Formación del Nuevo Régimen*, Mexico City: Era.

Cornelius, W. A., A. L. Craig and J. Fox (eds) (1994) *Transforming State-Society Relations in Mexico. The National Solidarity Strategy*, San Diego, CA: Center for US-Mexican Studies, University of California, San Diego.

Cortés, H. [15??] (1986) *Letters from Mexico*, New Haven and London: Yale University Press.

Crespo Flores, C., N. Laurie and C. Ledo (2003) 'Cochabamba Case Study', Research Project Report, in J. E. Castro (coord.), *PRINWASS Project*, Oxford, University of Oxford.

Crónica Mexicáyot [1609] (1975), translated by A. León, Mexico City: Universidad Nacional Autónama de México (UNAM), Instituto de Investigaciones Históricas (IIH).

Crosby, A. W. [1986] (1994) *Ecological Imperialism. The Biological Expansion of Europe, 900–1900*, Cambridge: Cambridge University Press.

Dalton, M. (1990) 'El agua y las mil formas de nombrarla: el Centro Mazateco de Investigaciones', *América Indígena*, Vol. L, #2–3, pp. 63–93.

Departamento del Distrito Federal, Secretaría de Obras y Servicios (DDF-SOS) (1975) *Memoria de las Obras del Sistema de Drenaje Profundo del Distrito Federal*, 4 Vols, Mexico City: DDF.

Díaz del Castillo, B. [15??] (1963) *The Conquest of New Spain*, Middlesex: Penguin Books.

Díaz-Marta, M. and J. A. García Diego (1991) 'Obras Hidráulicas Españolas y su Relación con las Americanas', in CEHOPU, *Antiguas Obras Hidráulicas en América. Actas del Seminario (México, 1988)*, Madrid: CEHOPU, pp. 133–52.

Dinavo, J. V. (1995) *Privatization in Developing Countries. Its Impact on Economic Development and Democracy*, Westport, Conn., and London: Praeger.

Dourojeanni, A. (1999) 'Debate Sobre el Código de Aguas de Chile', (LC/R. 1924 – 30 July 1999), Santiago de Chile: UN Economic Commission for Latin America and the Caribbean (ECLAC).

Drakeford, M. (1998a) 'Debt and Disconnection in the Privatized Utilities', in *Contemporary Wales*, #11, pp. 149–66.

_____ (1998b) 'Water Regulation and Pre-Payment Meters', in *Journal of Law and Society*, Vol. 25, #4, pp. 588–602.

Dresser, D. (1994) 'Bringing the Poor back in: National Solidarity as a Strategy of Regime Consolidation', in W. A. Cornelius *et al.* (eds), *Transforming State-Society Relations in Mexico. The National Solidarity Strategy*, San Diego, CA: Center for U.S.-Mexican Studies, University of California, San Diego, pp. 29–45.

Dryzek, J. S. (1997) *The Politics of the Earth: Environmental Discourses*, Oxford: Oxford University Press.

Durán, D. de [15??] [1867] (1967) *Historia de las Indias de Nueva España e Islas de Tierra Firme*, 2 vols, reprint (A. M. Garibay K. [ed.]), Mexico City: Biblioteca Porrúa, No. 36.

Eckstein, S. (1977) *The Poverty of Revolution. The State and the Urban Poor in Mexico*, Princeton, NJ: Princeton University Press.

Ejército Zapatista de Liberación Nacional (EZLN), Comandancia General (1994) 'Declaración de la Selva Lacandona', in A. García de León, E. Poniatowska and C. Monsiváis, *EZLN: Documentos y Comunicados*, Mexico City: Era, pp. 33–5.

Elias, N. [1939] (1994) *The Civilizing Process. The History of Manners, and State Formation and Civilization*, Oxford, UK and Cambridge, Mass.: Basil Blackwell.
_____ (1978) *What is Sociology?*, London: Hutchinson.

Elizondo, C. (1992) *Property Rights in Mexico: Government and Business after the 1982 Bank Nationalization*, D.Phil. Thesis, Oxford: University of Oxford.

Elvin, M. (1994) 'Introduction', in M. Elvin, H. Nishioka, K. Tamura and J. Kwek *Japanese Studies on the History of Water Control in China. A Selected Bibliography*, Canberra and Tokyo: The Institute for Advanced Studies, Australian National University and The Centre for East Asian Cultural Studies for UNESCO, pp. 3–35.

Elvin, M, and S. Ninghu (1995) 'Man against the Sea: Natural and Anthropogenic Factors in the Changing Morphology of Harngzhou Bay, circa 1000–1800', *Environment and History*, Vol. I, #1, pp. 3–54.

Escalante G. F. (1992) *Ciudadanos Imaginarios*, Mexico City: El Colegio de México.

Esman, M. J. (1991) *Management Dimensions of Development: Perspectives and Strategies*, West Hartford: Kumarian Press.

European Commission (2003) *Water for Life. EU Initiative, International Cooperation: from Knowledge to Action*, Luxembourg, European Commission.

_____ (2002a) 'Water Management in Developing Countries: Policy and Priorities for EU Development Cooperation', Communication from the Commission to the Council and the European Parliament.

_____ (2002b) 'EU Water Initiative: Water for Life. Health, Livelihoods, Economic Development, Peace, and Security', Brussels.

_____ (2000) 'The European Community's Development Policy. Communication from the Commission to the Council and the European Parliament', Brussels.

Ezcurra, E. M. Mazari-Hiriart, I. Pisanty and A. G. Aguilar (1999) *The Basin of Mexico. Critical Environmental Issues and Sustainability*, Tokyo, New York, and Paris: University of the United Nations.

Farías Hernández, U. (1993) *Derecho Mexicano de Aguas Nacionales*, Mexico City: Editorial Porrúa.

Farley, P. (1997) 'USAID: setting directions for the next decade of privatization', in *Economic Perspectives. An International Journal of the U.S. Information Agency*, Vol. 2, #1, pp. 10–2.

Feachem, R. G. (1983) 'Infections Related to Water and Excreta: the health dimension of the decade', in B. Dargenfeld (ed.), *Water supply and sanitation in Developing Countries*, London: The Institution of Water Engineers and Scientists, pp. 25–46.

Fernández R., O. (1990) 'La Estructura del Consumo de Agua en el Area Metropolitana de la Ciudad de México (1930–1990): una Perspectiva Descriptiva General', in M. L. Torregrosa Armentia (1988–1997) *Programa de Investigación Agua y Sociedad*, Mexico City: Instituto Mexicano de Tecnología del Agua (IMTA) and Facultad Latinoamericana de Ciencias Sociales (FLACSO).

Finer, S. E. [1952] (1997) *The Life and Times of Sir Edwin Chadwick*, London: Routledge & Thoemmes Press.

Florescano, E. (1984) 'The formation and economic structure of the hacienda in New Spain', in L. Bethell (ed.), *The Cambridge History of Latin America*, Vol. 2, Cambridge: Cambridge University Press, pp. 153–88.

Foster, J. B. (2000) *Marx's Ecology. Materialism and Nature*, New York: Monthly Review Press.

Foucault, M. [1974] (1994a) 'La Vérité et les Formes Juridiques', in D. Defert and F. Ewald (eds) *Dits et Écrits 1954–1988*, Vol. 2, Paris: Gallimard, pp. 538–646.

_____ [1976, 1979] (1994b) 'La Politique de la Santé au XVIIIᵉ Siècle', in D. Defert and F. Ewald (eds) *Dits et Écrits 1954–1988*, Vol. 3, Paris: Gallimard, pp. 13–27, 725–42.

Foweraker, J. (1996) 'Measuring Citizenship in Mexico', in Serrano, M. and V. Bulmer-Thomas (eds), *Rebuilding the State: Mexico after Salinas*, London: University of London, ILAS, pp. 79–98.

Foweraker, J. and A. Craig (eds) (1990) *Popular Movements and Political Change in Mexico*, Boulder, Co.: Lynne Rienner.

Fox, D. (1965) 'Man-Water Relationships in Metropolitan Mexico', *Geographical Review*, Vol. 55, #4, pp. 523–45.

Fox, J. (1990) 'The Difficult Transition from Clientelism to Citizenship. Lessons from Mexico', *World Politics*, Vol. 46, #2, pp. 151–84.

Frankenfeld, Ph. (1992) 'Technological Citizenship: a Normative Framework for Risk Studies', in *Science, Technology and Human Values*, Vol. 17, pp. 459–84.

Fraser, N. and L. Gordon (1994) 'Civil Citizenship against Social Citizenship? On the Ideology of Contract-Versus-Charity', in B. van Steenbergen (ed.), *The Condition of Citizenship*, London: SAGE, pp. 90–107.

Fritz de la Orta, G. (1991) 'La Estructura Operacional de las Obras Hidráulicas en la Nueva España', in CEHOPU, *Antiguas Obras Hidráulicas en América. Actas del Seminario (México, 1988)* Madrid: CEHOPU, pp. 153–64.

Fujigaki L., A. and A. González Galván (1982) 'Epidemias Conocidas en México durante el Siglo XX', in E. Florescano *et al.* (eds), *Ensayos sobre la Historia de las Epidemias en México*, Vol. 2, Mexico City: IMSS, pp. 699–723.

Gaceta de México (1731–38), Vol. I, #43, #58, #90, #123; (1784), Vol. II, #7; (1789), Vol. III, #34, #35, #36; (1790–91), Vol. IV, #1, #5, #26, #39; (1791), Vol. V, #15, Mexico City.

García Lascuráin, M. (1995) 'Calidad de Vida y Consumo de Agua en la Periferia Metropolitana: del Tambo a la Llave de Agua', in I. Restrepo (ed.), *Agua, Salud y Derechos Humanos*, Mexico City: CNDH, pp. 123–62.

García de León, A. (1985) *Resistencia y Utopía. Memorial de agravios y crónica de revueltas y profecías acaecidas en la provincia de Chiapas durante los últimos quinientos años de su historia*, 2 vols, Mexico City: Ediciones Era.

García Quintana, J. and J. R. Romero Galván (1978) *México Tenochtitlan y su Problemática Lacustre*, Mexico City: UNAM-Instituto de Investigaciones Históricas (IIS).

Garibay V., R. M. and L. Aboites Aguilar (1994) *Las Otras Aguas*, Mexico City and Jiutepec, Mor.: CIESAS and Instituto Mexicano de Tecnología del Agua (IMTA).

Garza, G. and A. Damián (1991) 'Ciudad de México. Etapas de Crecimiento, Infraestructura y Equipamiento', in M. Schteingart (ed.), *Espacio y Vivienda en la Ciudad de México*, Mexico City: El Colegio de México and ARDF, pp. 21–49.

Garza, G. and M. Schteingart (1984) 'Ciudad de México: Dinámica Industrial y Estructuración del Espacio en una Metropóli Semiperiférica', in *Demografía y Economía*, Vol. XVIII, #4.

Gayol, R. [1906] (1994) *Dos Problemas de Vital Importancia para México. La Colonización y el Desarrollo de la Irrigación*, Mexico City: IMTA and CIESAS.

Geertz, C. [1973] (1993) *The Interpretation of Cultures*, London: FontanaPress.

_____ (1980) *Negara. The Theatre State in Nineteenth-Century Bali*, Princeton, NJ: Princeton University Press.

Gibson, Ch. (1964) *The Aztecs under Spanish Rule. A History of the Indians of the Valley of Mexico, 1519–1810*, Stanford: Stanford University Press.

Giddens (1982) *Profiles and Critiques in Social Theory*, London: Macmillan.

Gleick, P. H. (1993) 'Water and Conflict: Fresh Water Resources and International Security', *International Security*, Vol. 18, #1, pp. 79–112.

Glick, T. F. (1970) *Irrigation and Society in Medieval Valencia*, Cambridge, Mass.: Harvard University Press.

Global Water Partnership (2003) 'Effective Water Governance. Learning from the Dialogues'.

_____ (2002) 'Dialogue on Effective Water Governance'.

González Casanova., P. (1965a) 'Internal colonialism and national development', *Studies in Comparative International Development*, Vol. I, #4, pp. 27–37.

_____ (1965b) *La Democracia en México*, Mexico City: Era.

Gordillo, G. (1988) *Campesinos al Asalto del Cielo. De la Expropiación Estatal a la Apropiación Campesina*, Mexico City: Siglo XXI.

Goubert, J.-P. (1986) *The Conquest of Water. The Advent of Health in the Industrial Age*, Cambridge and Oxford: Polity Press and Basil Blackwell.

Goudsblom, J. (1977) *Sociology in the Balance. A Critical Essay*, Oxford: Basil Blackwell.

_____ [1992] (1994) *Fire and Civilization*, London: Penguin Books.

Guerra, F. (1985) *Le Mexique de l'Ancien Régime à la Révolution*, Paris: L'Harmattan.

Guha, R. and J. Martínez-Alier (2000) Varieties of Environmentalism. Essays North and South, London: Earthscan.

Gurría Lacroix, J. (1978) *El Desagüe del Valle de México durante la Epoca Novohispana*, Mexico City: UNAM-Instituto de Investigaciones Históricas (IIH).

Hart, J. M. (1987) *Revolutionary Mexico: the Coming and Process of the Mexican Revolution*, Berkeley and London: University of California Press.

Harvey, D. (1996) *Justice, Nature and the Geography of Difference*, New York: Blackwell.

Hassan, J. (1998) *A History of Water in Modern England and Wales*, Manchester: Manchester University Press.

Held, D. (1989) 'Citizenship and autonomy', in D. Held and J. B. Thompson (eds), *Social Theory of Modern Societies: Anthony Giddens and his Critics*, Cambridge: Cambridge University Press, pp. 162–84.

Heller, H. [1934] (1942) *Teoría del Estado*, translation from the German, Mexico City, Fondo de Cultura Económica.

Herbert, A. and E. Kempson (1995) *Water Debt and Disconnection*, London: Policy Studies Institute.

Hernández Rodríguez, R. (1982) 'Epidemias y calamidades en el México prehispánico', in E. Florescano *et al.* (eds), *Ensayos sobre la Historia de las Epidemias en México*, Vol. 1, Mexico City: IMSS, pp. 139–56.

Herrera y Lasso, J. [1919] (1994) *Apuntes sobre Irrigación. Notas sobre su Organización Económica en el Extranjero y en el País*, Mexico City: IMTA and CIESAS.

Herrera Toledo, C. (1997) 'Nacional water master planning in Mexico', in A. K. Biswas, C. Herrera Toledo, H. Garduño Velasco and C. Tortajada Quiroz (eds), *Nacional Water Master Plans for Developing Countries*, pp. 6–53.

Hewitt de Alcántara, C. (1978) *Modernización de la Agricultura Mexicana, 1940–1970*, Mexico City: Siglo XXI.

Hewitt de Alcántara, C. and G. Vera (1990) 'Inside Megalopolis. Exploring Social and Spatial Diversity of Provisioning Structures in Mexico City', *Discussion Paper #4*, Geneva: United Nations Research Institute for Social Development (UNRISD).

Hirst, P. (1994) *Associative Democracy: New Forms of Economic and Social Governance*, Cambridge: Polity Press.

Hoberman, L. S. (1980) 'Technological change in a traditional society: the case of the Desagüe in colonial Mexico', in *Technology and Culture*, Vol. 21, #3, pp. 386–407.

Hobsbawm, E. J. (1997) *On History*, New York: The New Press.

_____ (1994) *Age of Extremes. The Short Twentieth Century (1914–1991)*, London: Penguin Books.

Horn, R. (1997) *Postconquest Coyoacán. Nahua-Spanish Relations in Central Mexico, 1519–1650*, Stanford: Stanford University Press.

Humboldt, A. von (1811) *Voyage de Humboldt et Bonpland, Troisième Partie. Essai Politique sur le Royaume de La Nouvelle-Espagne*, Vol. 1, Paris: F. Schoell.

Hundley, N. (Jr.) (1992) *The Great Thirst. Californians and Water, 1770s–1990s*, Berkeley, Los Angeles, and Oxford: University of California Press.

Icaza Lomelí, L (1991) 'Arquitectura hidráulica en la Nueva España', in CEHOPU, *Antiguas Obras Hidráulicas en América. Actas del Seminario (México, 1988)*, Madrid: CEHOPU, pp. 153–64.

Instituto Nacional de Estadística, Geografía e Informática (INEGI) (1991) *Censo General de Población y Vivienda 1990*, Mexico City: INEGI.

_____ (1990) *Estadísticas Históricas de México*, 2 vols, Mexico City: INEGI.

Inter American Development Bank (IDB) (1998) *Facing up to Inequality in Latin America. Economic and Social Progress in Latin America*, Washington, DC: IDB.

Jones, E. (1981) *The European Miracle*, 2nd ed., Cambridge: Cambridge University Press.

Joseph, G. M. and D. Nugent (eds) (1994) *Everyday Forms of State Formation. Revolution and the Negotiation of Rule in Modern Mexico*, Durham and London: Duke University Press.

Katz, F. (1972) *The Ancient American Civilizations*, London: Weidenfeld and Nicolson.

_____ (1981) *The Secret War in Mexico. Europe, the United States, and the Mexican Revolution*, Chicago and London: The University of Chicago Press.

_____ (ed.) (1988a) *Riot, Rebellion, and Revolution. Rural Social Conflict in Mexico*, Princeton, NJ: Princeton University Press.

_____ (1988b) 'Rural Rebellions after 1810', in F. Katz (ed.) *Riot, Rebellion, and Revolution. Rural Social Conflict in Mexico*, Princeton, NJ: Princeton University Press, pp. 521–60.

_____ [1986] (1994) 'The Liberal Republic and the Porfiriato, 1867–1910', in L. Bethell (ed.), *Mexico since Independence*, 2nd rep., Cambridge: Cambridge University Press, pp. 49–124.

King, D. S. and J. Waldron (1988) 'Citizenship, Social Citizenship and the Defence of Welfare Provision', *British Journal of Political Science*, Vol. 18, #, pp. 415–43.

Klausen, J. (1995) 'Social Rights Advocacy and State Building. T. H. Marshall in the Hands of Social Reformers', *World Politics*, Vol. 47, #2, pp. 244–67.

Knight, A. (1994) 'Solidarity: Historical Continuities and Contemporary implications', in W. A. Cornelius *et al.* (eds) *Transforming State-Society Relations in Mexico. The National Solidarity Strategy*, San Diego, CA: Center for U.S.-Mexican Studies, University of California, San Diego, pp. 29–45.

_____ (1991) 'Land and Society in Revolutionary Mexico: the Destruction of the Great Haciendas', *Mexican Studies* Vol. 7, #1, pp. 73–104.

_____ [1986] (1990) *The Mexican Revolution*, 2 vols, Lincoln and London: University of Nebraska Press and Cambridge University Press.

Knorr Cetina, K. (1999) *Epistemic Cultures. How the Sciences Make Knowledge*, Cambridge, Mass., and London: Harvard University Press.

Kooiman, J. (2000) 'Societal Governance: Levels, Modes, and Orders of Social-Political Interaction', in J. Pierre (ed.), *Debating Governance: Authority, Steering and Democracy*, Oxford University Press, Oxford.

Kooiman, J. (ed.) (1993) *Modern Governance. New Government–Society Interactions*, London: Sage.

Kroeber, C. B. (1994) *El Hombre, la Tierra y el Agua. Las Políticas en Torno a la Irrigación en la Agricultura de México, 1885–1911*, Jiutepec, Mor.: IMTA and CIESAS.

Kumate Rodríguez, J. (1991) Declaration as Federal Health Minister, *La Jornada*, 13 August 1991, p. 44.

Kymlicka, W. and W. Norman (1995) 'Return of the citizen: a survey of recent work on citizenship theory', in R. Beiner (ed.), *Theorizing Citizenship*, Albany: State University of New York Press, pp. 283–315.

Laborit, H. [1983] (1986) *La Paloma Asesinada*, Barcelona: Laia.

Lameiras, B. B. de (1986) *Formación del Estado en el México Prehispánico*, Zamora, Michoacán: El Colegio de Michoacán.

Lameiras, J. (1974) 'Relación en Torno a la Posesión de Tierras y Aguas: un Pleito entre Indios Principales de Teotihuacan y Acolman en el Siglo XVI', in T. Rojas R. *et al.*, *Nuevas Noticias sobre las Obras Hidráulicas Prehispánicas y Coloniales en el Valle de México*, Mexico City: INAH and SEP, pp. 175–228.

Lanning, J. T. (1985) *The Royal Protomedicato. The Regulation of the Medical Professions in the Spanish Empire*, Durham: Duke University Press.

Lanz Cárdenas, J. T. (1982) *Legislación de Aguas en México (Estudio Histórico-Legislativo de 1521 a 1981)*, 4 vols, Tabasco: Consejo Editorial del Gobierno del Estado de Tabasco.

Laski, H. J., W. I. Jennings and W. A. Robson (eds) (1935) *A Century of Municipal Progress 1835–1935*, London: George Allen and Unwin.

Leach, E. R. (1959) 'Hydraulic society in Ceylon', *Past and Present*, pp. 2–26.

Lee, T. R. (1999) *Water Management in the 21st Century. The Allocation Imperative*, Cheltenham: Edward Elgar.

Lee, T. R. and A. Jouravlev (1998) 'Prices, Property and Markets in Water Allocation', (LC/L 1097), Santiago de Chile: UN Economic Commission for Latin America and the Caribbean (ECLAC).

Lemoine Villicaña, E. (1978) *El Desagüe del Valle de México durante la Epoca Independiente*, Mexico City: UNAM-IIH.

León-Portilla, M. (1984) 'The Early Civilizations of Mesoamerica. The Mexicas (Aztecs), in L. Bethell (ed.), *The Cambridge History of Latin America*, Vol. I, Cambridge: Cambridge University Press, pp. 3–36.

Levi Lattes, E. (1991) 'Obras Hidráulicas en México', in CEHOPU, *Antiguas Obras Hidráulicas en América. Actas del Seminario (México, 1988)*, Madrid: CEHOPU, pp. 125–32.

Leys, C. (2001) *Market-Driven Politics. Neoliberal Democracy and the Public Interest*, London: Verso.

_____ (1996) *The Rise and Fall of Development Theory*, London: James Currey.

Libreros, V. (2003) 'Empresa Privada y Servicio de Agua en México, Distrito Federal. Evaluación de una Década', in *Second PRINWASS International Conference*, Mexico City.

Lipsett-Rivera, S. (1993) 'Water and bureaucracy in colonial Puebla de los Angeles', *Journal of Latin American Studies*, #25, pp. 25–44.

Llamas Fernández, R. (1991) 'Abastecimiento de Agua a la Ciudad de México en el Siglo XVI', in CEHOPU, *Antiguas Obras Hidráulicas en América. Actas del Seminario (México, 1988)*, Madrid: CEHOPU, pp. 189–200.

Llerena V., F. A., R. Martínez E. and B. Sánchez B. (1989) 'Aspectos Generales de la Cuenca del Valle de México: Evolución y Perspectivas', in Quadri de la Torre, G. (ed.), *Aguas Residuales de la Zona Metropolitana de la Ciudad de México, Impactos y Perspectivas*, Mexico City: Fundación Friedrich Ebert and DDF, pp. 7–54.

Luckin, B. (1986) *Pollution and Control: a Social History of the Thames in the Nineteenth Century*, London: Adam Hilger.

Lustig, N. (1994) 'Solidarity as a strategy of poverty alleviation', in W. A. Cornelius *et al.* (eds) *Transforming State-Society Relations in Mexico. The National Solidarity Strategy*, San Diego, CA: Center for US-Mexican Studies, University of California, San Diego, pp. 79–96.

Malvido, E. (1982) 'Efectos de las Epidemias y Hambrunas en la Población de México (1519–1810)', in E. Florescano and E. Malvido (eds), *Ensayos sobre la Historia de las Epidemias en México*, Vol. 1, Mexico City: IMSS, pp. 179–99.

Mann, M. (1987) 'Ruling class strategies and citizenship', *Sociology*, Vol. 21, #3, pp. 339–54.

Mansilla, E. (1994) 'De Cómo Porfirio Díaz Dominó las Aguas: Historia de la Construcción de la Obra Hidráulica', Concurso Nacional Sobre Historia y Etnohistoria de los Aprovechamientos Hidráulicos en México, Mexico City: CNA-CIESAS.

Márquez Morfín, L. (1994) *La Desigualdad ante la Muerte en la Ciudad de México. El Tifo y el Cólera*, Mexico City: Siglo XXI.

Marroquín y Rivera, M. (1914) *Memoria Descriptiva de las Obras de Provisión de Aguas Potables para la Ciudad de México*, Mexico City: Müller Hermanos-Indianilla.

Marshall, T.H. [1950] (1992) 'Citizenship and Social Class', in T.H. Marshall and T. Bottomore, *Citizenship and Social Class*, London and Concord, Mass.: Pluto Perspectives, pp. 3–51.

_____ (1981) *The Right to Welfare and Other Essays*, London: Heinemann Educational Books.

Martin, B. (1994) *In the Public Interest? Privatisation and Public Sector Reform*, London: Zed Books Ltd.

Martínez Alier, J. (2002) *The Environmentalism of the Poor: A Study of Ecological Conflicts and Valuation*, Cheltenham, UK and Northampton, MA.: Edward Elgar.

214 *Bibliography*

Martínez Omaña, M. C. (2002) *La Gestión Privada de un Servicio Público. El Caso del Agua en el Distrito Federal, 1988–1995*, Mexico City: Instituto Mora and Plaza y Valdez.

Martínez Saldaña, T., and J. Palerm Viqueira (eds) (1997) *Antología Sobre Pequeño Riego*, Mexico City: Colegio de Posgraduados.

Martins, H. (1998) 'Risco, Incerteza e Escatologia – Reflexões Sobre o Experimentum Mundi Tecnológico em Curso', en *Episteme*, Vol. 1, #1, pp. 99–121 y Episteme, Vol. 1, #2, pp. 41–75.

Marx, K. [1867] (1946) *Capital. A Critical Analysis of Capitalist Production*, Vol. 1, London: Allen and Unwin.

_____ [1843] (1975) 'On the Jewish Question', in K. Marx and F. Engels, *Collected Works*, Vol. 3, London: Lawrence and Wishart, pp. 146–74.

_____ [1857–58] (1978) *Pre-capitalist Economic Formations*, ed. by E. Hobsbawm, London: Lawrence and Wishart.

McGranahan, G., P. Jacobi, J. Songsore, Ch. Surjadi and M. Kjellén (2001) *The Citizens at Risk. From Urban Sanitation to Sustainable Cities*, London: Earthscan.

McNeill, W. H. (1977) *Plagues and Peoples*, Oxford: Basil and Blackwell.

Mead, L. (1986) *Beyond Entitlement: The Social Obligations of Citizenship*, Free Press: New York.

Mehta, M. (1998) 'Risk and Decision Making: a Theoretical Approach to Public Participation in Techno-Scientific Conflict Situations', *Technology and Society* Vol. 20, #1, pp. 87–98.

Mennell, S. [1989] (1992) *Norbert Elias. An Introduction*, Oxford and Cambridge, Mass.: Blackwell.

Meyer, J. A. (1994) 'Revolution and reconstruction in the 1920s', in L. Bethell (ed.), *Mexico since Independence*, Cambridge: Cambridge University Press, pp. 201–40.

_____ (1973) *La Revolution Mexicaine, 1910–1940*, Paris: Calmann-Lévy.

Meyer, M. C. (1984) *Water in the Hispanic Southwest. A Social and Legal History, 1550–1850*, Tucson, Arizona: The University of Arizona Press.

Meyers, W. K. (1977) 'Politics, Vested Rights, and Economic Growth in Porfirian Mexico: the Company Tlahualilo in the Comarca Lagunera, 1885–1911', *Hispanic American Historical Review*, Vol. 57, #3, pp. 425–54.

Millward, B. (1991) 'Emergence of Gas and Water Monopolies in Nineteenth Century Britain: Contested Markets and Public Control', in James Foreman-Peck (ed.), *New Perspectives in Late Victorian Economy: Essays in Quantitative Economic History 1860–1914*, London: Cambridge University Press.

Moguel, J. (1994) 'The Mexican left and the social program of salinismo', in W. A. Cornelius, A. L. Craig and J. Fox (eds), *Transforming State-Society Relations in Mexico. The National Solidarity Strategy*, San Diego, CA: Center for U.S.-Mexican Studies, University of California, San Diego, pp. 167–76.

Molina Enríquez, A. [1908] (1964) *Los Grandes Problemas Nacionales*, Mexico City: Instituto Nacional de la Juventud Mexicana (INJM).

Moncada Maya, J.O. (1991) 'Intervención de los Ingenieros Militares Españoles en las Obras Hidráulicas de la Nueva España (Siglos XVII y XVIII)', in CEHOPU, *Antiguas Obras Hidráulicas en América. Actas del Seminario (México, 1988)*, Madrid: CEHOPU, pp. 337–49.

Montemayor, C. (1997) *Chiapas. La Rebelión Indígena de México*, Mexico City: Joaquín Mortiz.

Mora R., J. (1989) 'Agua e Hidrología en la Cuenca del Valle de México: Antecedentes, Diagnóstico, Perspectivas y Alternativas', in L. M. Guerra *et al.* (eds) *Agua e Hidrología en la Cuenca del Valle de México: Antecedentes, Diagnóstico, Perspectivas y Alternativas*, Mexico City: Fundación Friedrich Ebert and INAINE, pp. 9–74.

Morse, R. M. (1984) 'The Urban Development of Colonial Spanish America', in L. Bethell (ed.) *The Cambridge History of Latin America*, Vol. 2, Cambridge: Cambridge University Press, pp. 67–104.

―――― (1972) 'A Prolegomenon to Latin American Urban History', Hispanic American Historical Review, Vol. 52, #3, pp. 359–94.

Mumford, L. (1940) *The Culture of Cities*, London: Secker and Warburg.

Musset, A. (1991) *De l'Eau Vive à l'Eau Morte. Enjeux Techniques et Culturels dans la Vallée de Mexico (XVIe-XIXe Siècles)*, Paris: Éditions Recherche sur les Civilisations (ERC).

National Academy of Sciences (NAS) (1995) *Mexico City's Water Supply. Improving the Outlook for Sustainability*, Washington, DC: National Academy Press.

National Research Council (2002) *Privatization of Water Services in the United States. An Assessment of Issues and Experience*, Washington, DC: National Academy Press.

Nellis, J. R., and S. Kikeri (1989) 'Public enterprise reform: privatization and the World Bank', in *World Development*, Vol. 17, #5, pp. 659–72.

Newbery, D. M. (1999) *Privatization, Restructuring, and Regulation of Network Utilities. The Walras-Pareto Lectures*, Cambridge, Mass. and London: The MIT Press.

Newby, H. (1996) 'Citizenship in a green world: global commons and human stewardship', in M. Bulmer and A. Rees (eds), *Citizenship Today. The Contemporary relevance of T. H. Marshall*, Londres, UCL Press, pp. 209–21.

Ogle, M. (1999) 'Water Supply, Waste Disposal, and the Culture of Privatism in the Mid-Nineteenth-Century American City', in *Journal of Urban History*, Vol. 25, No. 3, pp. 321–47.

Ohlsson, L. (ed.) (1992) *Regional Case Studies of Water Conflicts*, Göteborg: University of Göteborg, Peace and Development Research Institute (PADRIGU).

O'Leary, B. (1989) *The Asiatic Mode of Production. Oriental Despotism, Historical Materialism, and Indian History*, Oxford and Cambridge Ma.: Basil Blakwell.

Orive Alba, A. (1970) *La Irrigación en México*, Mexico City: Grijalbo.

Oswald, U., R. Rodríguez and A. Flores (1986) *Campesinos Protagonistas de su Historia: (la Coalición de los Ejidos Colectivos de los Valles del Yaqui y Mayo: una Salida a la Cultura de la Pobreza)*, Mexico City: Universidad Autónoma Metropolitana (Xochimilco) (UAM-X).

Palacios, L. [1909] (1994) *El Problema de la Irrigación*, Mexico City: IMTA and CIESAS.

Palerm, A. (1990) *México Prehispánico. Ensayos sobre Evolución y Ecología*, Mexico City: CONACULTA.

Pani, A. J. (1916) *La Higiene en México*, Mexico City: Imprenta de J. Ballesca.

Partido Revolucionario Institucional (PRI) – Instituto de Estudios Políticos, Económicos y Sociales (IEPES) (1987) 'El Agua: Recurso Vital', *Diálogo Nacional. Revista de la Consulta Popular*, Mexico City: (IEPES).

―――― (1982) *Consulta Popular. Agua y Desarrollo*, Mexico City: IEPES.

Payno, M. [1891] (1983) *Los Bandidos de Río Frío*, Mexico City: Porrúa.

Peet, R. (1985) 'Introduction to the Life and Thought of Karl Wittfogel (with an appendix on the Asiatic Mode of production)', *Antipode*, Vol. 17, #1, pp. 3–20.

Pérez Picazo, M. T. and G. Lemeunier (1990) 'Introducción', in M. T. Pérez Picazo and G. Lemeunier (eds), *Agua y Modo de Producción*, Barcelona: Crítica, pp. 21–53.

Perló Cohen, M. (1989) 'Problemas Sociopolíticos para la Utilización de las Aguas Residuales', in G. Quadri (ed.), *Aguas Residuales de la Zona Metropolitana de la Ciudad de México, Impactos y Perspectivas*, Mexico City: Fundación Friedrich Ebert and DDF, pp. 89–102.

Perry, G. E., Francisco H.G. Ferreira and M. Walton (2003) 'Inequality in Latin America and the Caribbean: Breaking with History?', Washington: World Bank.

Pfaffenberger, B. (1992) 'Social anthropology of technology', in *Annual review of Anthropology*, Vol. 21, pp. 491–516.

Piaget, J. (1971) *Structuralism*, London: Routledge and Kegan Paul.

―――― (1977) *The Grasp of Conciousness*, London: Routledge and Kegan Paul.

―――― (1978) *The Development of Thought. Equilibration of Cognitive Structures*, Oxford: Basil Blackwell.

Picciotto, R. (1997) 'Putting institutional economics to work: from participation to governance' in Ch. K. Clague (ed.), *Institutions and Economic Development: Growth and Governance in Less-developed and Post-socialist Countries*, Baltimore and London: John Hopkins University Press, pp. 343–67.

Polanyi, K. [1944] (1957) *The Great Transformation: the Political and Economic Origins of Our Time*, Boston: Beacon Press.

Presidencia de la República Mexicana (1992a) *Iniciativa de Ley de Aguas Nacionales*, Mexico City: IMTA.

―――― (1992b) *Ley de Aguas Nacionales*, Mexico City: IMTA.

―――― (1997) *Ley Federal de Derechos en Materia de Agua*, Mexico City: CNA.

Public Services International Research Unit (PSIRU) (2003) *Reports on Water Privatization*, Greenwich, UK, University of Greenwich (http://www.psiru.org).

Redclift, M. and T. Benton (1994) *Social Theory and the Global Environment*, New York: Routledge.

Roberts, B. R. (1995) *The Making of Citizens. Cities of Peasants Revisited*, London: Arnold.

Rodríguez Kuri, A. (1996) *La Experiencia Olvidada. El Ayuntamiento de México: Política y Gobierno, 1876–1912*, Mexico City: UAM-A and El Colegio de México.

Roemer, A. (1997) *Derecho y Economía: Políticas Públicas del Agua*, Mexico City: Centro de Investigación y Docencia Económicas (CIDE), Sociedad Mexicana de Geografía y Estadística (SMGE), and Miguel Angel Porrúa.

Roemer, S. and S. Radelet (1991) 'Macroeconomic reform in developing countries', in D. Perkins and M. Roemer, *Reforming Economic Systems in Developing Countries*, Cambridge, MA: Harvard University Press, pp. 55–80.

Rogozinski, J. (1993) *La Privatización de Empresas Paraestatales. Una Visión de la Modernización de México*, Mexico City: Fondo de Cultura Económica.

―――― (1998) *High Price for Change: Privatization in Mexico*, Washington, DC: Inter-American Development Bank.

Rojas R., T. (1974) 'Aspectos tecnológicos de las obras hidráulicas coloniales', in T. Rojas R. *et al.*, *Nuevas Noticias sobre las Obras Hidráulicas Prehispánicas y Coloniales en el Valle de México*, Mexico City: INAH and SEP, pp. 19–133.

Rowland, A. and P. Gordon (1996) 'Mexico City: no longer a leviathan?', in A. Gilbert (ed.) *The Mega-City in Latin America*, Tokyo and New York: United Nations University Press, pp. 173–202.

Roth, G. (1988) *The Private Provision of Public Services in Developing Countries*, Washington, DC: The World Bank and Oxford University Press.

Roxborough, I. (1994) 'Clausewitz and the Sociology of War', *British Journal of Sociology*, Vol. 45, #4, pp. 619–36.

Ruiz, S. L. de (1973) *Desarrollo Urbano de México-Tenochtitlan según las Fuentes Históricas*, Mexico City: SEP-INAH.

Saavedra Shumidzu, J. C., G. Lugo García and M. G. Macay Lim (1991) 'Tarifas de Agua Potable y Alcantarillado en México en 1990', in *Ingeniería Hidráulica en México*, May-August, pp. 28–40.

Sáez, C. (1980) 'Ideology and Politics in México 1878–1904. Aspects of Científico Theory and Practice' (D.Phil. Thesis), Oxford: University of Oxford.

Sahab Haddad, E. (1991) 'La lucha por el agua y contra el agua en el Valle de México', in CEHOPU, *Antiguas Obras Hidráulicas en América. Actas del Seminario (México, 1988)*, Madrid: CEHOPU, pp. 153–64.

Samson, P. and B. Charrier (1997) 'International freshwater conflict. Issues and prevention strategies', Geneva, Green Cross International.

Sanders, W. T. and B. J. Price (1968) *Mesoamerica: the Evolution of a Civilization*, New York: Random House.

Saunders, P. (1993) 'Citizenship in a liberal society', in B. S. Turner (ed.), *Citizenship and Social Theory*, London: Sage, pp. 57–90.

Savedoff, W. and P. Spiller (1999) *Spilled Water. Institutional Commitment in the Provision of Water Services*, Washington, DC: Interamerican Development Bank (IDB).

Schmidt, C. (1993) 'On economization and ecologization as civilizing processes', in *Environmental Values*, #2, pp. 33–46.

Schteingart, M. (ed.) (1989) *Los Productores del Espacio Habitable. Estado, Empresas y Sociedad en la Ciudad de México*, México: El Colegio de México.

Schteingart, M., I. Plaza, L. Cadena, M. de Lourdes G. and C. Romero (no date [circa 1989]) 'El sector informal de vivienda urbana en México', Mexico City: El Colegio de México – Centro de Estudios Demográficos y de Desarrollo Urbano (CEDDU).

Schultz, S. K. and C. McShane (1978) 'To Engineer the Metropolis: Sewers, Sanitation, and City Planning in Late-Nineteenth Century America', in *The Journal of American History*, Vol. 65, # 2, pp. 389–411.

Secretaría de Agricultura y Recursos Hidráulicos (SARH), Comisión del Plan Nacional Hidráulico (1981) *Plan Nacional Hidráulico*, Mexico City: SARH.

Secretaría de Agricultura y Recursos Hidráulicos (SARH) (1988) *Agua y Sociedad: una Historia de las Obras Hidráulicas en México*, Mexico City: SARH.

Sen, A. (1981) *Poverty and Famines. An Essay on Entitlement and Deprivation*, Oxford: Clarendon Press.

―――― (1990) 'Food, economics, and entitlements', in J. Drèze and A. Sen (eds), *The Political Economy of Hunger*, Oxford: Clarendon Press, pp. 34–52.

Shaw, R. and C. Stewart (1994) 'Introduction: problematizing syncretism', in C. Stewart *et al.* (eds), *Syncretism/Anti-Syncretism. The Politics of Religious Synthesis*, London and New York: Routledge, pp. 1–26.

Siemens, A. H. (1998) *A Favored Place. San Juan River Wetlands, Central Veracruz, A.D. 500 to the Present*, Austin: University of Texas Press.

Simpson, L. B. [1941] (1963) *Many Mexicos*, 3rd edn, Berkeley and Los Angeles: University of California Press.

Sims, J. and M. E. Butter (2000) 'Gender, Equity and Environmental Health', Working Paper Series, Harvard Center for Population and Development Studies, Harvard University.

Solanes, M. (1999) 'Servicios públicos y regulación' (LC/L 1203 – 10 May 1999), Santiago de Chile: UN Economic Commission for Latin America and the Caribbean (ECLAC).

Steenbergen, B. van (1994) *The Condition of Citizenship*, London: SAGE.

Stiglitz, J. E. (2002) *Globalization and its Discontents*, London, Penguin.

Streeck, W. and Ph. Schmitter (1985) *Private Interest Government*, London: Sage.

Strauss K., R. A. (1974) 'El ´Área Septentrional del Valle de México: Problemas Agrohidráulicos Prehispánicos y Coloniales', in T. Rojas R. *et al.*, *Nuevas Noticias sobre las Obras Hidráulicas Prehispánicas y Coloniales en el Valle de México*, Mexico City: INAH and SEP, pp. 135–74.

Streeck, W. and Ph. Schmitter (1985) *Private Interest Government*, London: Sage.

Suárez Cortez, B. E. (Coord). (1998) *Historia de los Usos del Agua en México. Oligarquías, Empresas, y Ayuntamientos (1840–1940)*, Mexico City: Comisión Nacional del Agua (CNA), Centro de Investigaciones y Estudios Superiores en Antropología Social (CIESAS), and Instituto Mexicano de Tecnología del Agua (IMTA).

Swyngedouw, E. A. (2000) 'Authoritarian Governance, Power, and the Politics of Rescaling', *Environment and Planning D; Society and Space*, Vol. 18, pp. 63–76.

——— (1999) *Flows of Power: Nature, Society and the City*, Oxford: Oxford University Press.

——— (1997) 'Power, Nature and the City. The Conquest of Water and the Political Ecology of Urbanization in Guayaquil, Ecuador, 1880–1980', *Environment and Planning A*, Vol. 29, #2, pp. 311–32.

——— (1995) *La Crisis del Abastecimiento de Agua en Guayaquil*, Quito: Ed. ILDIS.

——— (1995b) 'The contradictions of urban water provision', *Third World P Review*, Vol. 17, #4, pp. 387–405.

Swyngedouw, E. A., M. Kaika and J. E. Castro (2002) 'Urban water: a Political-Ecology Perspective', in *Built Environment*, Special Issue on Water Management in Urban Areas, Vol. 28, #2, pp. 124–37.

Talavera Ibarra, O. U. (1997) 'Entre la Escasez y el Desperdicio: El Agua en la Ciudad de México en el Siglo XIX (1821–1880)', Thesis in History, Universidad Autónoma Metropolitana – Azcapotzalco (UAM-A) (consulted in the library of the Archivo del Agua), Mexico City.

Tannenbaum, F. [1950] (1965) *Mexico. The Struggle for Peace and Bread*, London: Jonathan Cape.

Taylor, G. (1999) *State Regulation & the Politics of Public Service: The Case of the Water Industry*, London and New York: Mansell.

Thompson, J. E. S. (ed.) (1958) *Thomas Gage's Travels in the New World [1648]*, Norman: University of Oklahoma Press.

Tilly, Ch. (1975) 'Reflections on the History of European State-Making', in Ch. Tilly (ed.), *The Formation of National States in Western Europe*, Princeton, NJ: Princeton University Press, pp. 3–83.

Torquemada, J. de [1615] (1964) *Los Veinte i un Libros Rituales i Monarchia Indiana ...*, 3rd edn, Vol. 1, Mexico City: UNAM-IIH.

Torregrosa Armentia, M. L. (coord.) (1988–1997) *Programa de Investigación Agua y Sociedad*, Mexico City and Jiutepec, Morelos: Facultad Latinoamericana de Ciencias Sociales (FLACSO) and Instituto Mexicano de Tecnología del Agua (IMTA).

—— (1990) 'Dimensiones Macroestructurales', Research Report, in M. L. Torregrosa Armentia (coord.) (1988–1997) *Programa de Investigación Agua y Sociedad*, Mexico City and Jiutepec, Morelos: Facultad Latinoamericana de Ciencias Sociales (FLACSO) and Instituto Mexicano de Tecnología del Agua (IMTA).

Torregrosa Armentia, M. L., F. Saavedra, E. Padilla, A. Quiñones, K. Kloster, G. Cosío and Ch. Lenin (2003) 'Aguascalientes (Mexico) case study', in J. E. Castro (Coord.), *PRINWASS Project*, Oxford, University of Oxford.

Tortolero V., A. (1996) 'Tierra, Agua y Bosques en la Cuenca de México: la Innovación Tecnológica y sus Repercusiones en un Medio Rural, Chalco (1890–1925)', Mexico City: Universidad Autónoma Metropolitana-Iztapalapa (UAM-I).

—— (1994) 'Haciendas, Pueblos y Gobierno Porfirista: los Conflictos por el Agua en la Región de Chalco', in C. Viqueira L. *et al.* (eds), *Sistemas Hidráulicos, Modernización de la Agricultura y Migración*, Mexico City: El Colegio Mexiquense and Universidad Iberoamericana, pp. 385–425.

Triche, Th. A. (1990) 'Private participation in the delivery of Guinea's water supply services', Working Papers #47, Infrastructure and Urban development Programme, World Bank, Washington, DC: World Bank.

Turner, B. S. (1986) *Citizenship and Capitalism: The Debate over Reformism*, London: Allen and Unwin.

Tutino, J. (1986) *From Insurrection to Revolution in Mexico: Social Bases of Agrarian Violence 1750–1940*, Princeton, NJ: Princeton University Press.

—— (1988) 'Agrarian Social Change and Peasant Rebellion in Nineteenth-Century Mexico: the Example of Chalco', in F. Katz (ed.), *Riot, Rebellion, and Revolution. Rural Social Conflict in Mexico*, Princeton, NJ: Princeton University Press, pp. 95–140.

United Nations (2002) 'The right to water (articles 11 and 12 of the International Covenant on Economic, Social, and Cultural Rights', New York: UN.

—— (2002b) 'Key Commitments, Targets and Timetables from the Johannesburg Plan of Implementation', World Summit on Sustainable Development, Johannesburg.

—— (2000) United Nations Millennium Declaration, New York: UN.

—— (1980) *International Drinking Water Supply and Sanitation Decade: Report of the Secretary General*, New York: United Nations.

United Nations (1992) *Conference on Environment and Development (The Earth Summit)*, Rio de Janeiro: UNCED.

—— (1992b) 'The Dublin Statement on Water and Sustainable Development', International Conference on Water and the Environment (ICWE), Dublin: UN.

United Nations Development Programme (1997) *Governance for Sustainable Growth and Equity*, New York: UNDP.

United Nations Economic Commission for Europe (UNECE) and World Health Organization – Regional Office for Europe (WHO-Europe) (2002) *The Protocol on Water and Health. What it is. Why it Matters*, Geneva: UNECE-WHO-Europe.

Varley, A. (1993) 'Clientelism or Technocracy? The Politics of Urban Land Regularisation', in N. Harvey (ed.), *Mexico: Dilemmas of Transition*, London: Institute of Latin American Studies (ILAS) and British Academic Press, pp. 249–76.

_____ (1996) 'Delivering the Goods: Solidarity, Land Regularisation and Urban Services', in R. Aitken *et al.* (eds), *Dismantling the Mexican State?*, Basingstoke: Macmillan and New York: St. Martin's Press, pp. 204–23.

Ward, C. (1997) *Reflected in Water. A Crisis of Social Responsibility*, London and Washington: Cassell.

Ward, P. (1986) *Welfare Politics in Mexico: Papering over the Cracks*, Boston: Allen and Unwin.

Warner, B. (1987) *The Private City: Philadelphia in Three Periods of its Growth*, (2nd ed.) Philadelphia: University of Pennsylvania Press.

Weber, M. [1918-] (1995) *From Max Weber: Essays in Sociology*, (ed.) B. S. Turner, 2nd ed., 2nd rep., London: Routledge.

_____ [1922] (1978) *Economy and Society*, Berkeley, Los Angeles and London: University of California Press.

Webre, S. (1990) 'Water and society in a Spanish American city: Santiago de Guatemala, 1555–1773', *The Hispanic American Historical Review*, Vol. 70, #1, pp. 57–84.

Whitehead, L. (1995) 'An elusive transition: the slow motion demise of authoritarian dominant party rule in Mexico', in *Democratization*, Vol. 2, #3, pp. 246–69.

_____ (1994a) 'Prospects for a "transition" from authoritarian rule in Mexico', in M. L. Cook, K. J. Middlebrook, and J. Molinar H. (eds), *The Politics of Economic Restructuring. State-Society Relations and Regime Change in Mexico*, San Diego: Center for U.S.-Mexican Relations, University of California, pp. 327–46.

_____ (1994b) 'The peculiarities of "transition" a la mexicana', in N. Harvey and M. Serrano (eds), *Party Politics in an 'Uncommon Democracy': Political Parties and Elections in Mexico*, University of London, Institute of Latin American Studies.

_____ (1992) 'The alternatives to liberal democracy: a Latin American perspective', *Political Studies*, Vol. XL, Special Issue on 'Prospects for Democracy', pp. 146–59.

Whitmore, Th. M. (1992) *Disease and Death in Early Colonial Mexico. Simulating Amerindian Depopulation*, Boulder, San Francisco, and Oxford: Westview Press.

Wilkie, J. W. (1967) *The Mexican Revolution: Federal Expenditure and Social Change since 1910*, Berkeley and Los Angeles: University of California Press.

Wittfogel, K. A. (1956) 'The hydraulic civilizations', in W. L. Thomas (ed.), *Man's Role in Changing the Face of the Earth*, Chicago: The University of Chicago Press, pp. 152–64.

_____ [1957] (1959) *Oriental Despotism. A Comparative Study of Total Power*, 3rd rep., New Haven: Yale University Press.

Womack Jr., J. (1969) *Zapata and the Mexican Revolution*, New York: Alfred A. Knopf.

_____ (1991) 'The Mexican Revolution, 1910–1920', in L. Bethell (ed.), *Mexico since Independence*, 2nd rep., Cambridge: Cambridge University Press, pp. 125–200.

World Bank (1998) *Facilitating Private Involvement in Infrastructure: an Action Programme*, Washington, DC: World Bank.

World Health Organization (2003a) 'Domestic Water Quantity, Service, Level, and Health', Geneva: WHO.

_____ (2003b) 'Water Supply, Sanitation and Hygiene Development', Geneva: WHO).

_____ (2003c) 'Health in Water Resources Development', Geneva: WHO.

World Health Organization – Regional Office for Europe (WHO-Europe) (2003) 'Dealing with uncertainty: how can the precautionary approach help protect the future of our children?', in Fourth Ministerial Conference on Environment and Health, Stockholm, 26–27 June 2003.

Worster, D. (1985) *Rivers of Empire. Water, Aridity, and the Growth of the American West*, New York-Oxford: Oxford University Press.

Zerbe Jr., R. O. and H. McCurdy (2000) 'The end of market failure', *Regulation*, Vol. 23, #2, pp. 10–14.

Glossary

Aguador/es	Water vendors (seventeenth to nineteenth century)
Aljibe/s	Cisterns used for the storage of waters from different sources, mainly for domestic use
Amparo	Special provision of the Mexican Legal system for the protection of the citizens against state actions perceived as harmful for their rights
Audiencia	Court and governing body under the viceroy; area of jurisdiction
Ayuntamiento	Municipality
Burreros/as	Water sellers who use donkeys to carry water loads (literally 'donkey owners')
Chinampa/s	Artificial cultivation islands made of a structure of reed covered with fertile mud and anchored to the bed of the lakes with wooden posts
Científicos	Intellectual and scientific elite during the Porfiriato deeply influenced by nineteenth-century Positivism
Ciudadanía	Citizenship (also citizenry)
Ciudadano/s	Citizen/s
Ciudad/es perdida/s	Shanty town/s
Coatequitl	Mexican labour system for the construction of public works
Colonia/s	Urban quarter/s
Colono/s	Dweller/s of a colonia (twentieth century)
Conquistador/es	The Spanish conquerors
Delegación/es (política/s)	Departmental jurisdictions in the Federal District
Demandante/s	Claimants, in the jargon of the Mexican water authorities. The people who present petitions, demands, and denunciations about water services
Desagüe, El	The Valley's master drain built between the seventeenth and nineteenth centuries
Ejido/s	Community land
Ejidal	Character of land owned under the ejido system
Ejidatario/s	Tenants of ejidal land
Encomendero/s	The holder of an encomienda
Encomienda	Early colonial system of exploitation of Indian labour, and extraction of tributes by royal grant
Gente de bien/ decente	Respectable families
Gracia	See Merced
Hacendado	The owner of a hacienda
Hacienda	Large estate specializing in livestock and foodstuffs

Jagüey/es	Device for the storage of rainwater, though also was occasionally used to collect spring water
Leyes de Indias	Special body of law issued by the Spanish crown to rule its American possessions
Merced	Royal grant for the usufruct of Crown property
Merced de aguas	Royal grant for the usufruct of water. Early colonial form of water rights
Mestizo	Of white and Indian ancestor
Noria/s	Waterwheel, normally animal-driven, used to elevate water from a lower level to a higher level
Panista/s	Members of the PAN (National Action Party)
Pipa/s	Water tankers
Pipero/s	Water-tanker driver/s. Used to refer either to private water vendors or municipal, state or other official water distributors (e.g. PRONASOL)
Porfiriato	The regime of General Porfirio Díaz (1884–1911)
Priísta/s	Members of the PRI
Pueblo	Town
Rancho	Farm, small hacienda
Repartimiento	The allocation of an Indian chieftain and his people to Spaniards for providing forced (paid) labour. It was based on the old indigenous institution of coatequitl
Sexenio	The six-year presidential period in the Mexican political system
Sobrante/s	
sobras	Water rights over water in excess of the amount needed or wanted by the owner of a primary right in Spanish water law
Tambo	Water container of about 200 litres
Telpochcalli	Institution in charge of providing training to the youth in the duties owed to the state
Tolvanera/s	Dust storm/s resulting from the action of surface winds on the dusty soils of the dry beds of former lakes Texcoco, Chalco, Xochimilco, among other areas. February and March are the peak periods
Usuario/s	User/s. The people connected to networked water services
Zócalo	The main plaza in the city, and a favourite meeting point

Index

Lightning Source UK Ltd.
Milton Keynes UK
UKHW011147170622
404578UK00003B/878